ORIGAMI
FOR KIDS

Learning
THROUGH ACTIVITIES

SPECIAL BONUS!

Want The Video Tutorials For FREE?

Get FREE access to every video tutorial from 3 of the Origami Books by joining our community!

Scan W/ Your Camera To Get The Videos!

Table of Contents

Introduction 1

Origami for kids

Dog 4

Fox 5

Cat 6

Mouse 7

Boat 8

Rabbit 10

Pig 11

Plane 12

Crab 14

Heart 16

Penguin 17

Ladybug 18

Turtle 20

Fish 22

Star 24

Car 26

Rocket 28

Shirt 30

Snake 32

Ice Cream 34

Butterfly 36

Bat 38

Bookmark 40

Whale 41

Dolphin 42

Bird 44

Seal 46

Crane 48

Seahorse 50

Hummingbird 52

Lotus Flower 54

Brachiosaurus 56

Elephant 60

Dragon 64

Pop-it Toy 68

Fish 70

Peacock 72

Frog 78

Tulip 80

Koala 82

Table of Contents

Carrot 84

Box 86

Ninja Star I 88

Triceratops 90

Ninja Star II 96

Magic Circle 98

Water Lily 100

Christmas Tree 102

Pop-it Triangle 106

Origami for kids 2

Tall Hat 111

Cup 112

Envelope 113

Ship 114

House 115

Dress 116

Chick 117

Cupcake 119

Cicada 121

Bee 123

Samurai Helmet 125

Dracula 127

Mushroom 129

Lantern 131

Strawberry 133

Jack-O'-Lantern 135

Sunglasses 137

Ring 139

Big House 141

Little Bird 143

Lotus Flower 54

Pinwheel 145

Tie 147

Whale 149

Chair 151

Table 153

Water Bomb 155

Nodding Dog 157

Crown 159

Hen 161

Dove 163

Rocket 165

Table of Contents

Rabbit 167

Ghost 170

Heart Envelope 173

Pecking Crow 176

Moving Lips 179

Chinese Boat 182

Dinosaur 185

Hat 189

Chatterbox 193

Chatterbox Games 195

Origami Animals

Owl 201

Bear 202

Polar Bear 203

Monkey 204

Pig 205

Woodpecker 206

Bat 207

Sheep 208

Ladybug 210

Duck 212

Penguin 214

Rabbit 216

Gorilla 218

Puppy 220

Cow 222

Pigeon 224

Elephant 226

Swan 228

Fox 230

Koala 232

Tiger 234

Dog 236

Crab 238

Bull 240

Chameleon 242

Fish 245

Wild Duck 247

Horse 249

Whale 253

Origami Boxes

Box 257

Table of Contents

Triangle Box 259

Pencil Case 261

Cat Box 263

Cube 265

Dice 267

Star Box 269

Candy Box 272

Chinese Dish 275

Table Box 278

Container 281

Gift Box 284

Bowl 287

Pyramid Box 290

Vase 293

Basket 297

Diamond Box 301

Hinged Box 305

Rectangular Box 310

Tall Box 317

Dollar Bill Origami

Heart 324

Swan 326

Pigeon 328

Rocket 330

Car 332

Shirt 334

Pants 336

Diamond 338

Fish 340

Santa's Hat 344

Bottle 346

Home 348

Bell 350

Gown 352

Bow Tie 354

Tree 356

Wallet 358

Butterfly 361

Dog 364

Conclusion 367

Introduction

Origami is the art of transforming a sheet of paper, usually square but also rectangular, into a sculpture without using other instruments, such as scissors or glue.

This technique helps improve your concentration, abstract thinking, fine motor skills, and your hand-eye-coordination. In addition, it is a great activity to relax, improve patience and boost your creativity!

We have combined all 5 of our books in this book as 1. You will find precisely 160 designs to create and immerse yourself in.

What Books Are Included?

Book 1: Origami For Kids
Book 2: Origami For Kids 2
Book 3: Origami Animals
Book 4: Origami Boxes
Book 5: Dollar Bill Origami

With all these books, you can create your own little Origami world!

Introduction

In each book, we have started the designs as easy as possible for you. On top of this, we have video tutorials included in the following books:

Book 1: Origami For Kids
Book 3: Origami Animals
Book 4: Origami Boxes

If you are stuck on any designs in these books, you can watch video tutorials showing every step in creating the Origami designs.

Are you ready to discover this new world? Let the fun begin!

Origami
for kids

Learning
THROUGH ACTIVITIES

Dog

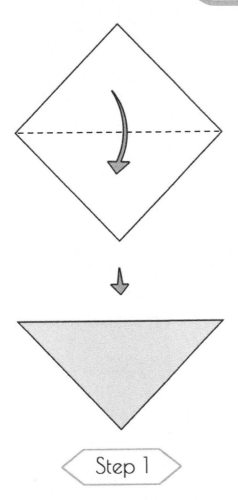

Step 1

Fold the sheet down along one of its diagonals.

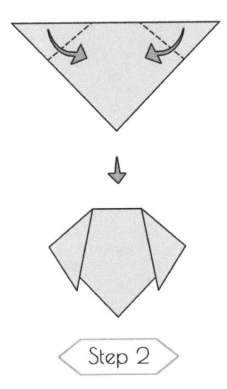

Step 2

Fold the side corners at an angle so that they stick out at the bottom.

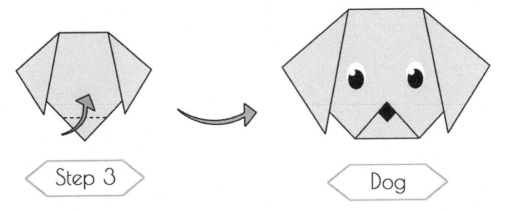

Step 3

Fold the bottom corner up both sides of the paper at the same time.

Dog

Fox

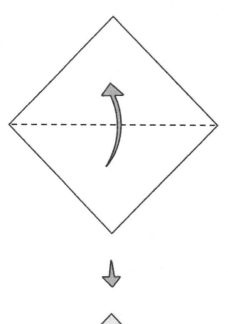

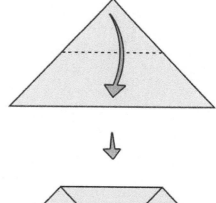

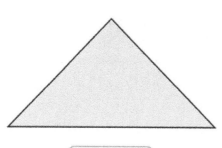

Step 1

Fold the sheet up along one of its diagonals.

Step 2

Fold the top corner down all the way to the bottom edge.

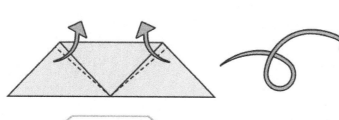

Step 3

Fold the side corners so that their vertices end up pointing up.

Fox

Cat

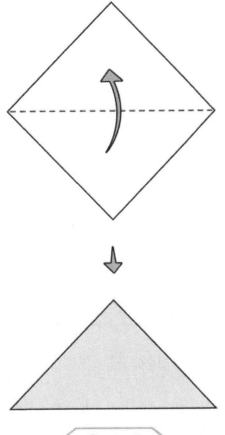

Step 1

Fold the sheet up along one of its diagonals.

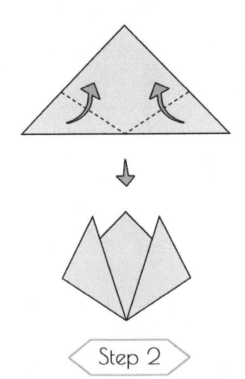

Step 2

Fold the side corners so that their vertices end up pointing up, and there is some space left between them.

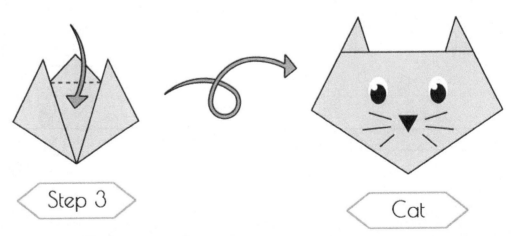

Step 3

Fold the top corner all the way down to the flaps you made in the previous step.

Cat

Mouse

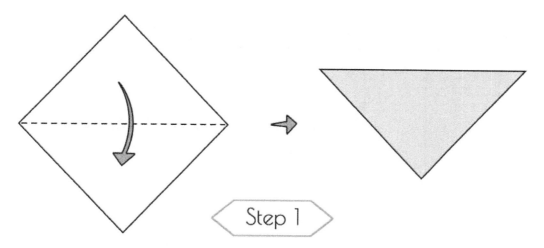

Fold the sheet down along one of its diagonals.

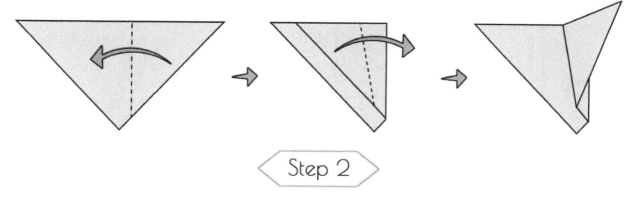

Step 2

Fold a little less than the right half of the triangle inward. Then fold a part of that flap out again, but this time at a slight angle.

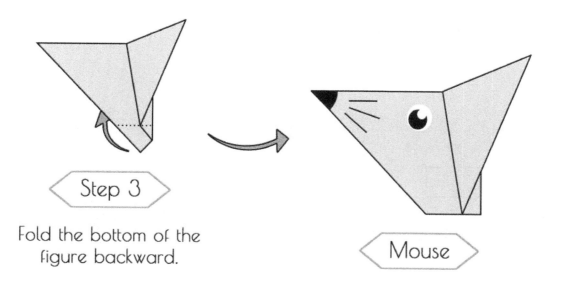

Step 3

Fold the bottom of the figure backward.

Mouse

7

Boat

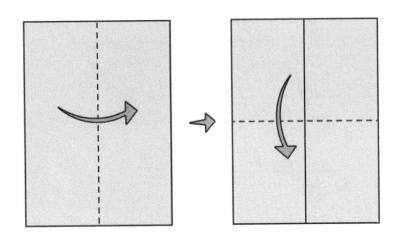

Step 1

Fold in half lengthwise
and unfold. Then
fold in half crosswise.

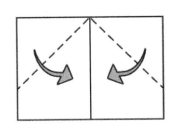
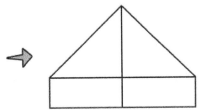

Step 2

Fold both corners forward.

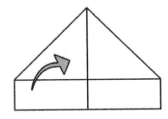
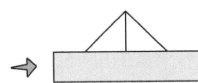

Step 3

Fold up the bottom edges
of both sides of the sheet.

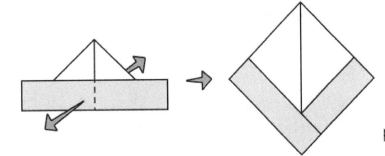

Step 4

From the midline, pull out
in opposite directions and
press to get a diamond shape.

8

Boat

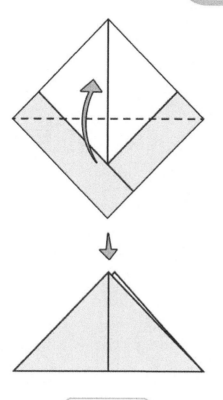

Fold up the bottom halves of both faces to get a triangle.

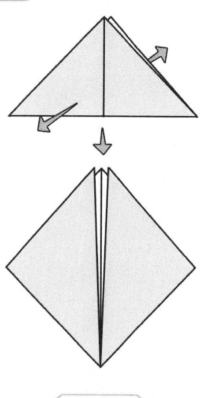

Step 6

Again, pull out from the midline and flatten to get a diamond shape with two flaps.

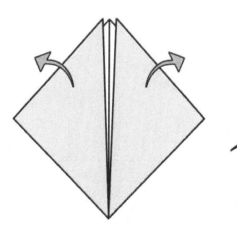

Step 7

Pull the flaps to the sides and press.

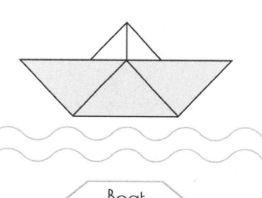

Boat

Rabbit

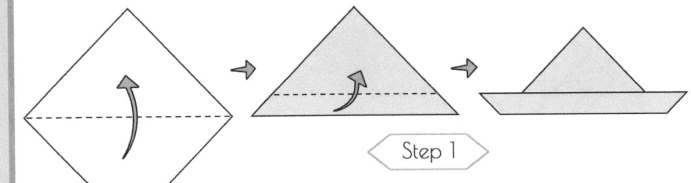

Step 1

Fold the sheet up along one of its diagonals, then fold the bottom edge up.

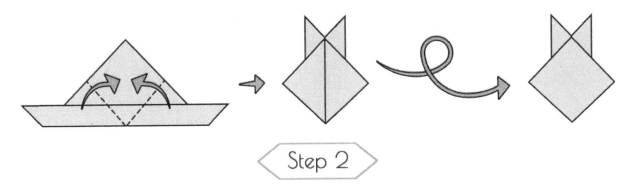

Step 2

Bring both side corners in toward the midline, and turn the figure over.

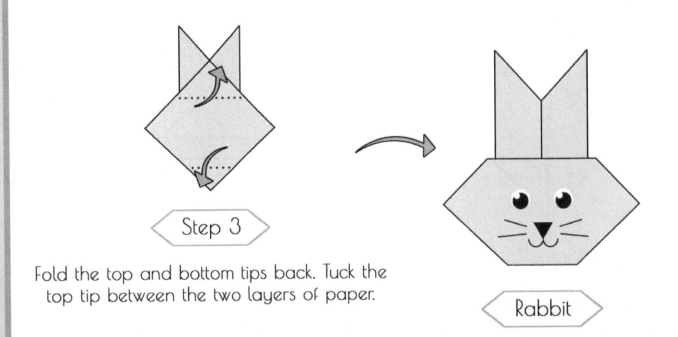

Step 3

Fold the top and bottom tips back. Tuck the top tip between the two layers of paper.

Rabbit

Pig

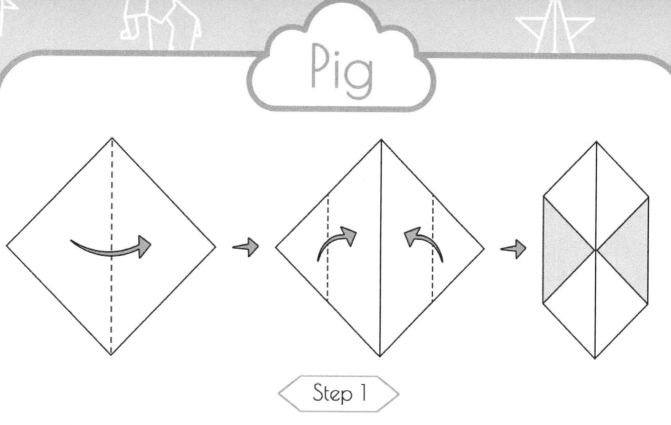

Fold along a diagonal and unfold. Then bring the side corners to the midline.

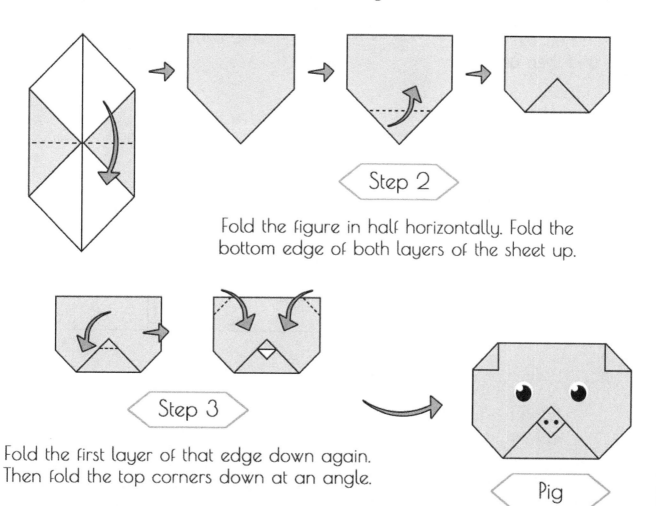

Step 2

Fold the figure in half horizontally. Fold the bottom edge of both layers of the sheet up.

Step 3

Fold the first layer of that edge down again. Then fold the top corners down at an angle.

Pig

11

Plane

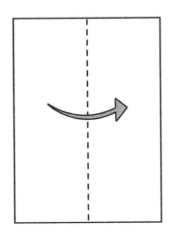

Fold the paper sheet
in half lengthwise
and then unfold it.

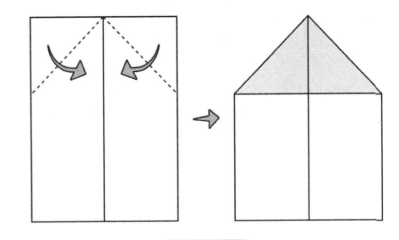

Step 2

Bring the top corners down
to the center line.

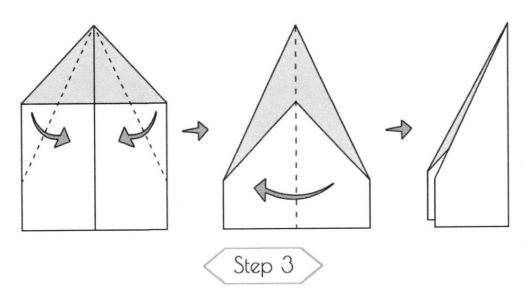

Step 3

Bring the top corners down to the center line. Then fold the
plane in half along the crease you made in the first step.

Plane

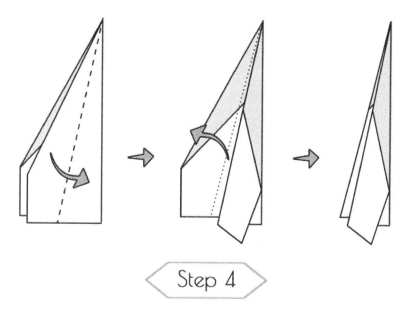

Step 4

Fold one wing down along its center line,
repeat with the other wing, and press.

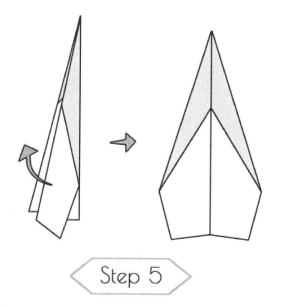

Step 5

Unfold both wings halfway up so
they are perpendicular to the plane.

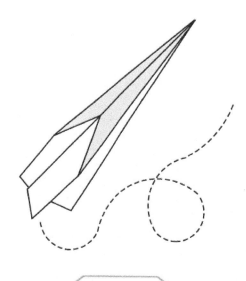

Plane

Crab

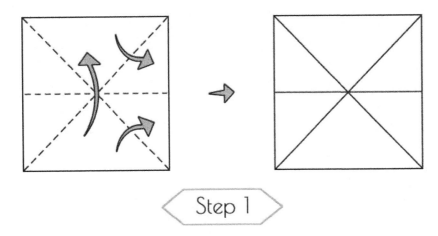

Step 1

Fold in half crosswise and along the two diagonals, then unfold.

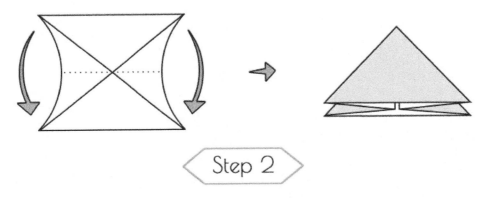

Step 2

Fold the sides to the center and flatten to get a triangle.

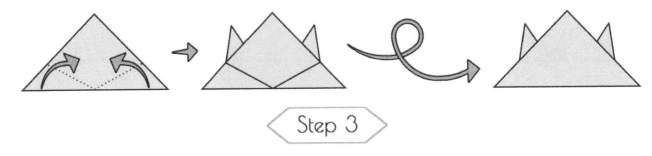

Step 3

Fold the side corners of the top layer inward
at a slight angle and turn the figure over.

Crab

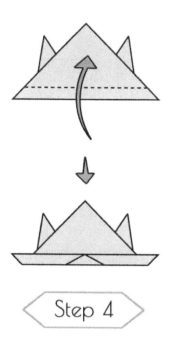

Step 4

Fold the bottom edge up.

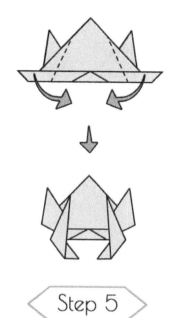

Step 5

Fold the side corners of the top layer inward at a slight angle.

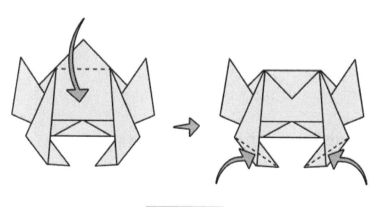

Step 6

Fold the top corner down, then fold the bottom legs in half and flip the figure over.

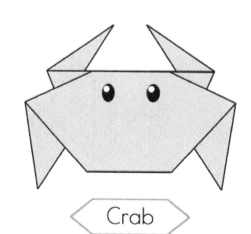

Crab

Heart

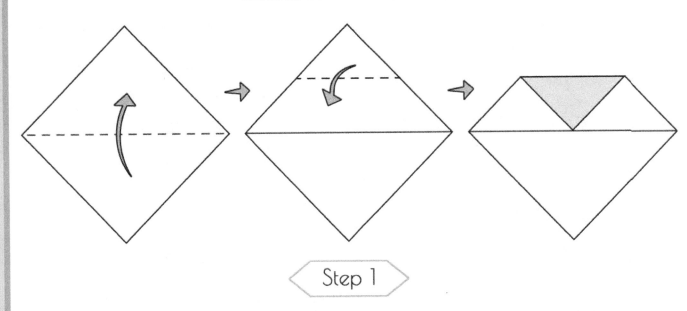

Step 1

Fold along a diagonal and unfold. Then fold the top corner toward the midline.

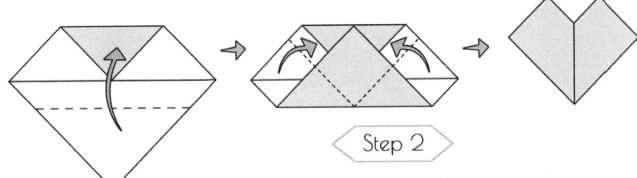

Step 2

Fold the bottom corner to the top edge. Then fold both sides at an angle toward the midline.

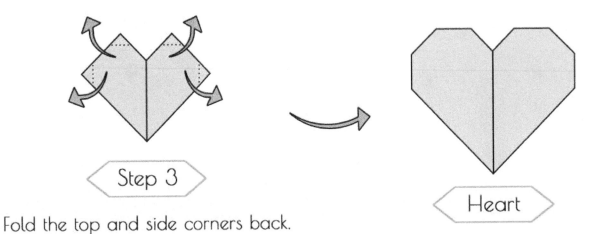

Step 3

Fold the top and side corners back.

Heart

Penguin

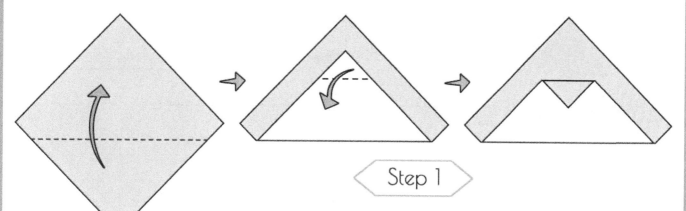

Step 1

Fold the bottom part up to just below the midline, then fold the tip of that same corner down.

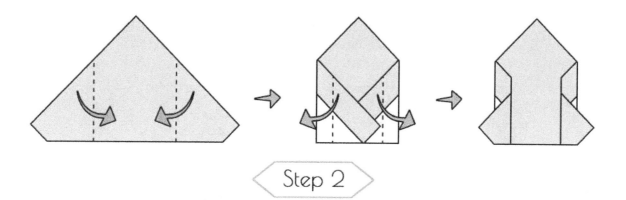

Step 2

Flip the sheet over and fold the side corners in so they overlap, then fold half of those flaps out again.

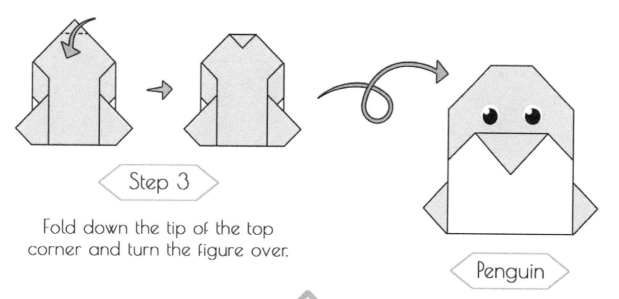

Step 3

Fold down the tip of the top corner and turn the figure over.

Penguin

17

Ladybug

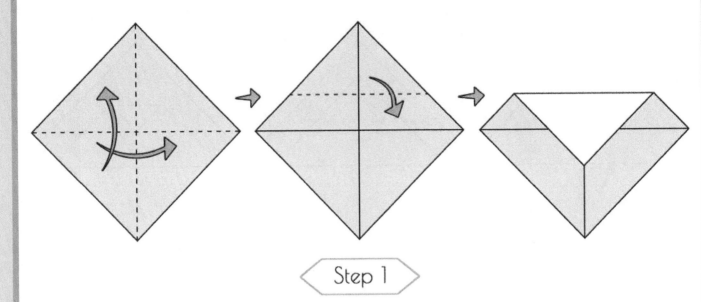

Step 1

Fold along both diagonals and unfold. Then fold the top corner down to just below the midline.

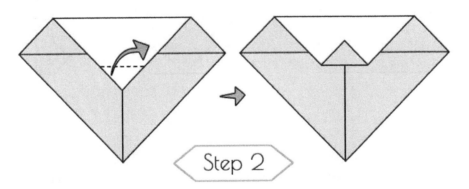

Step 2

Fold the tip of that same corner up and forward.

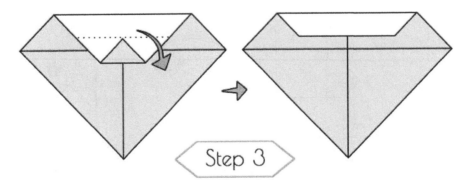

Step 3

Fold that section again, up and backward this time.

Ladybug

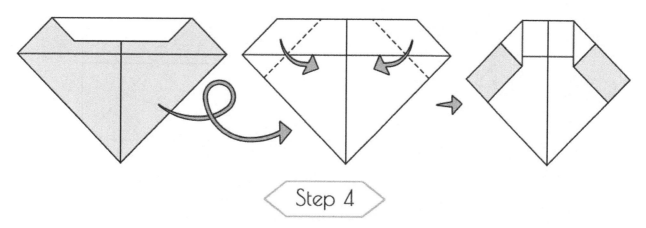

Step 4

Turn the figure over and fold the side corners at an angle so that the top edge ends up parallel to the midline.

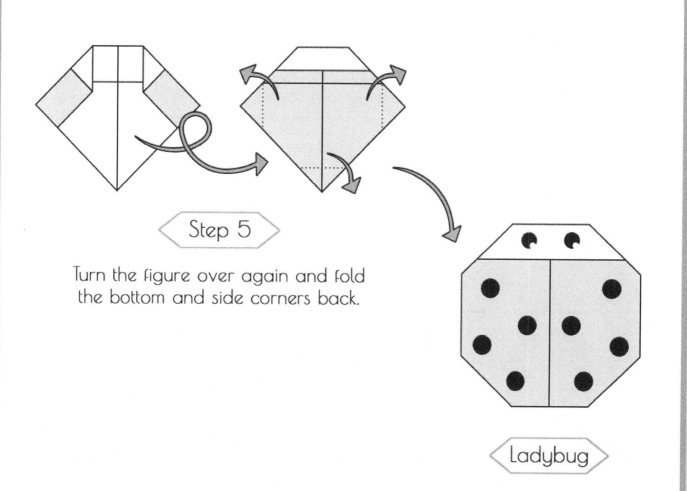

Step 5

Turn the figure over again and fold the bottom and side corners back.

Ladybug

Turtle

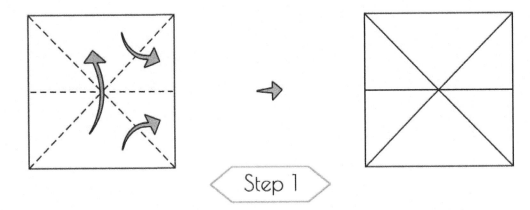

Step 1

Fold in half crosswise and along the two diagonals, then unfold.

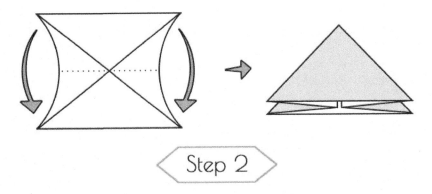

Step 2

Fold both sides in towards the center and press the edges to make a triangle.

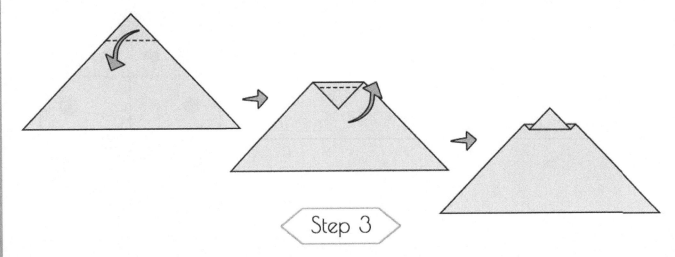

Step 3

Fold the top corner down, then fold it up again to make the head.

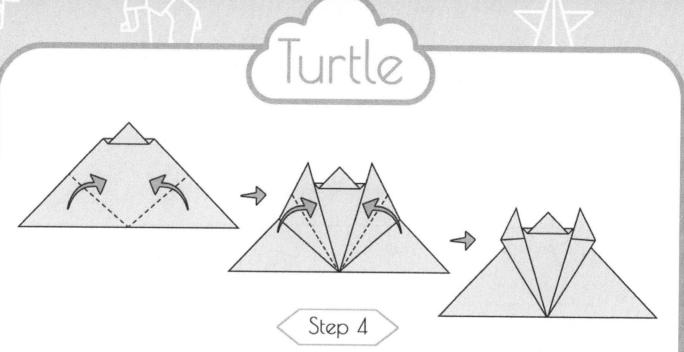

Step 4

Fold the sides of the top layer of the triangle towards the head. Fold these flaps you just made in half again towards the head. These are the front legs.

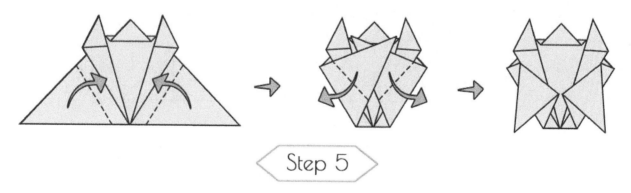

Step 5

Fold the sides of the triangle up, parallel to the front legs you just made. Then fold the tip down at an angle so that the tips stick out the sides.

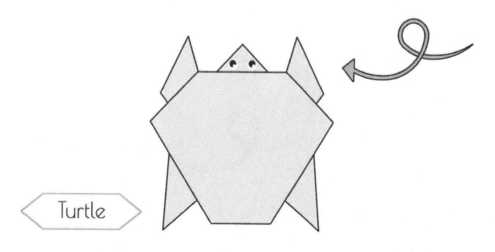

Turtle

Fish

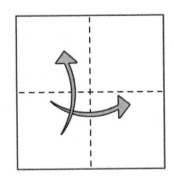

Fold in half lengthwise
and crosswise, and unfold.

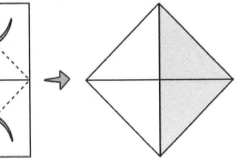

Step 2

Fold the two left corners backward
and the two right corners forward,
and press the edges.

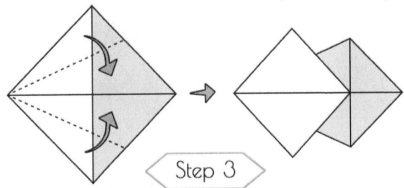

Step 3

Bring the top and bottom corners to the midline and press the edges.
You will see the corners that we folded backward sticking out from the sides.

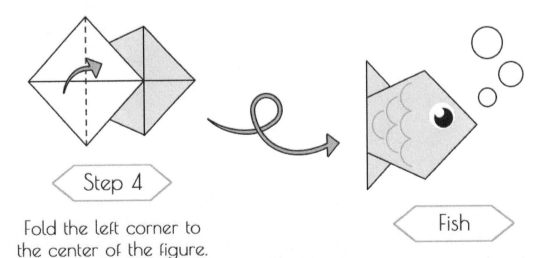

Step 4

Fold the left corner to
the center of the figure.

Fish

Fish

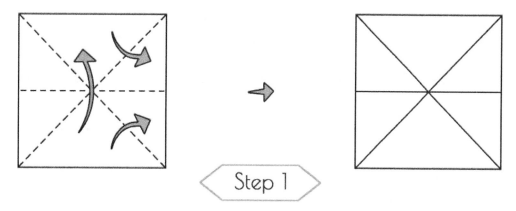

Fold in half crosswise and along the two diagonals, then unfold.

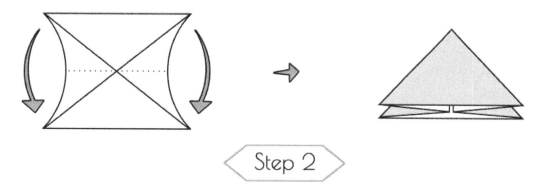

Step 2

Fold the sides to the center and flatten to get a triangle.

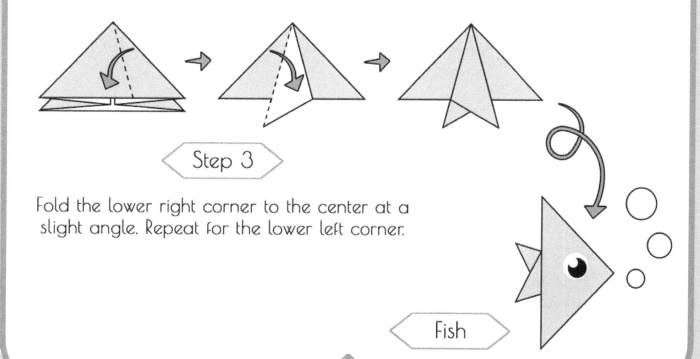

Step 3

Fold the lower right corner to the center at a slight angle. Repeat for the lower left corner.

Fish

Star

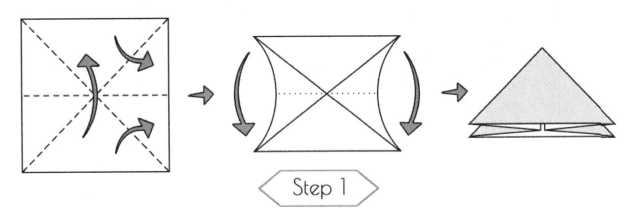

Step 1

Fold in half crosswise and along the two diagonals, and unfold. Then fold both sides in toward the center and press the edges to make a triangle.

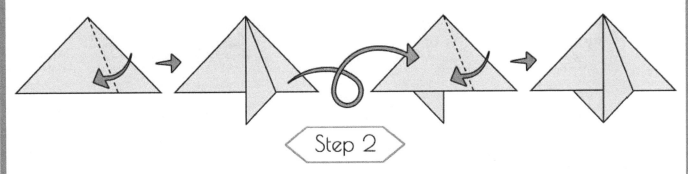

Step 2

Fold the right corner of the top layer toward the midline and press. Turn the figure over and repeat the same step with the back right corner.

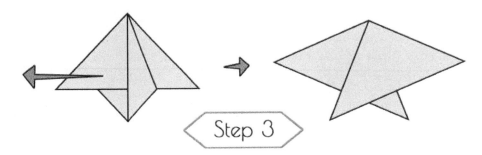

Step 3

Pull the left corner to expand the figure until the two flaps you made in the previous step swap their positions.

Star

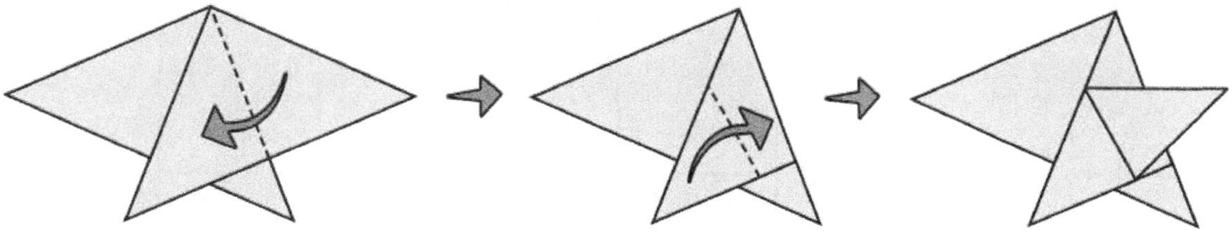

Step 4

Fold the top layer (right corner) in half so that the two bottom tips overlap. Then fold it up again at an angle so that the top edge ends up horizontal.

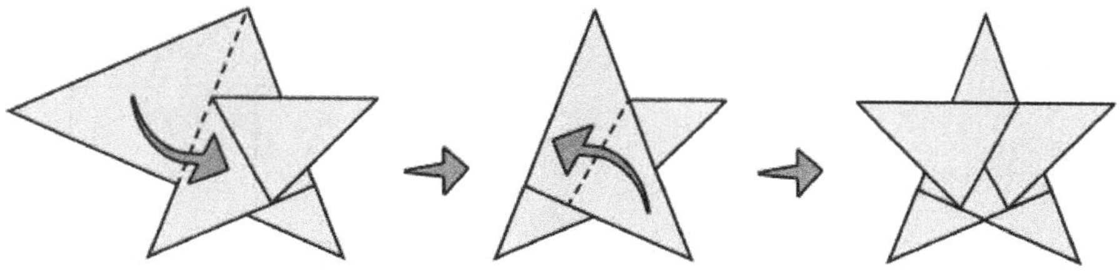

Step 5

Repeat the previous step with the bottom layer (left corner), and turn the figure over.

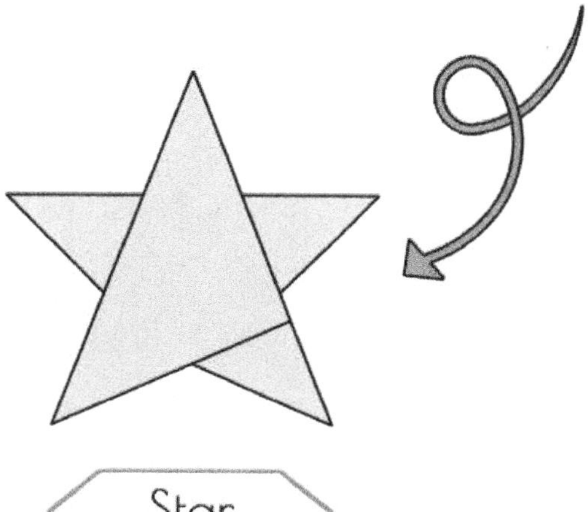

Star

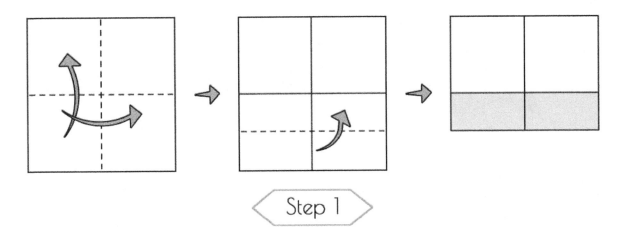

Fold in half lengthwise and crosswise and unfold.
Then fold the bottom edge toward the midline.

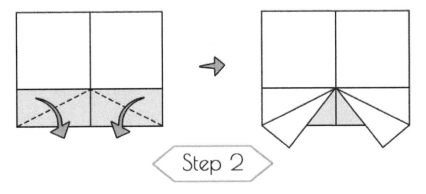

Fold down the top corners of the flap you just made.

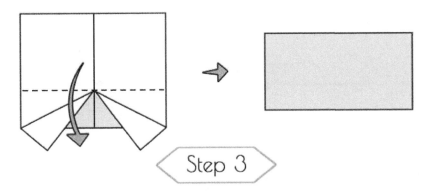

Fold the top half of the sheet forward down, covering the lower half.

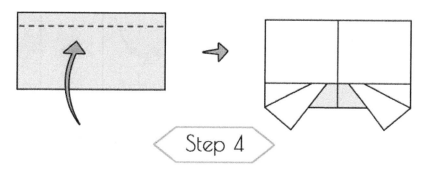

Step 4

Now fold about 3/4 of that same flap back up.

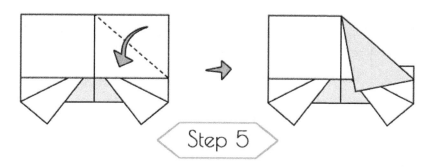

Step 5

Fold the upper right corner down and turn the figure over.

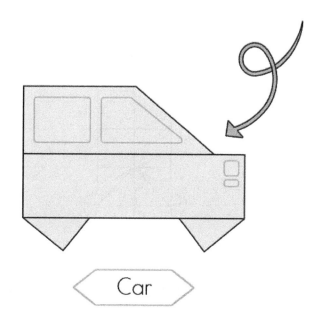

Car

Rocket

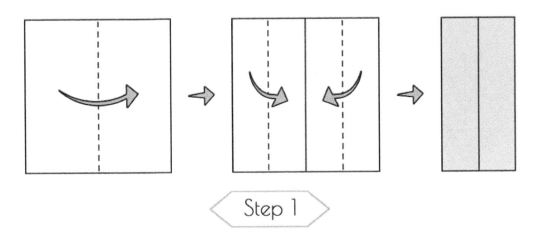

Fold in half lengthwise and unfold. Then fold each side again in half inward.

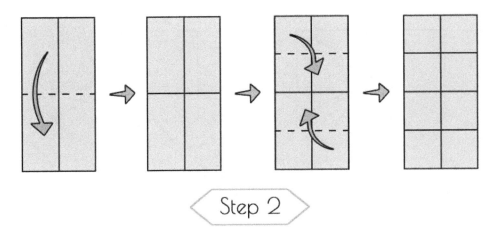

Step 2

Fold in half crosswise and unfold. Then bring the upper and lower edges forward toward the midline and unfold again.

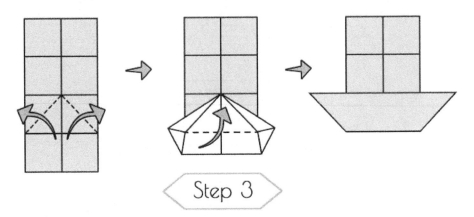

Step 3

From the bottom, fold the second section diagonally outward. As you fold it, the back layer also folds up. Press so that the top edges are horizontal.

28

Rocket

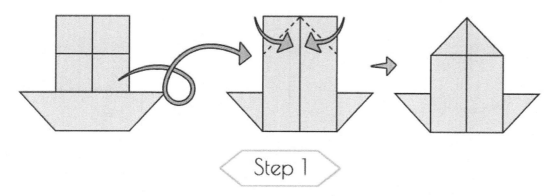

Step 1

Turn the figure over and fold the top corners toward the midline.

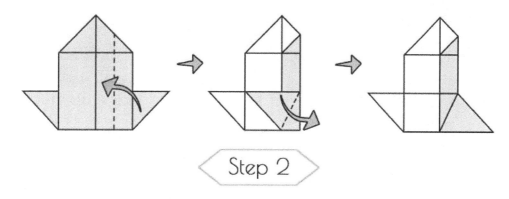

Step 2

Bring the right side to the midline and fold its corner outward at an angle, so that the bottom edge ends up horizontal.

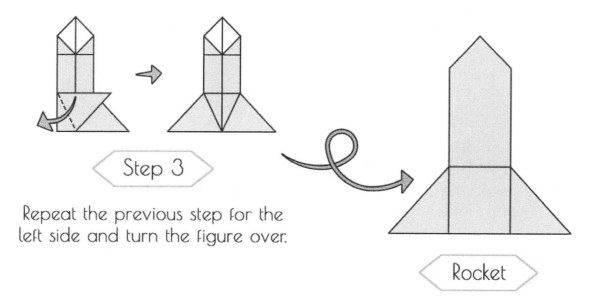

Step 3

Repeat the previous step for the left side and turn the figure over.

Rocket

29

Shirt

Step 1

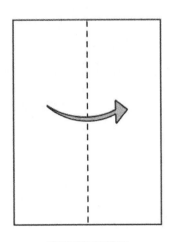

Fold the paper sheet
in half lengthwise
and then unfold it.

Step 2

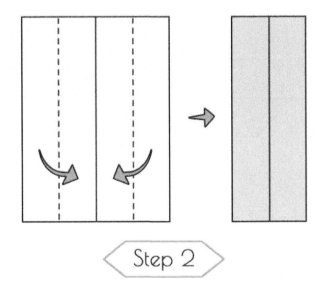

Fold each of these halves
again in half lengthwise to get
two flaps and leave them folded.

Step 3

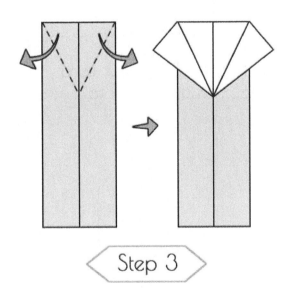

Fold the top third of those
flaps outward, at an angle that
forms a V between both flaps.
These are the sleeves of the shirt.

Step 4

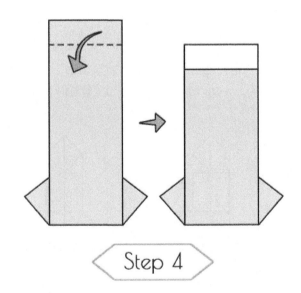

Turn the sheet over so that
the V is facing the table. On
the edge opposite the V, fold a 1"
piece of paper down toward you.

Shirt

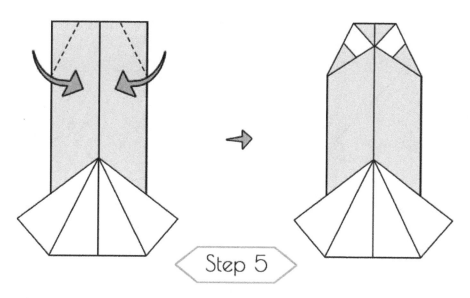

Step 5

Turn the sheet over again, so that the V is back in its original position. Fold the corners of the edge that you folded in the previous step toward the center of the sheet at an angle, so that the two corners touch at the midline. This is the collar of the shirt.

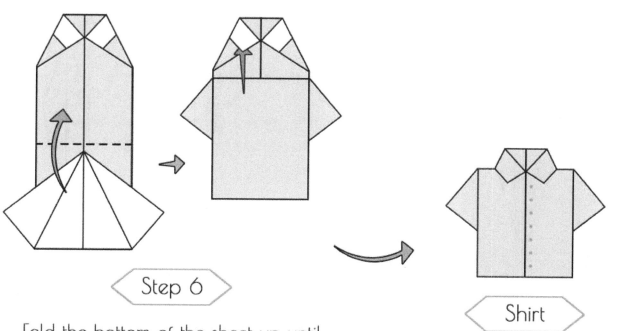

Step 6

Shirt

Fold the bottom of the sheet up until the edge with the V fits under the collar of the shirt and press the bottom edge.

Snake

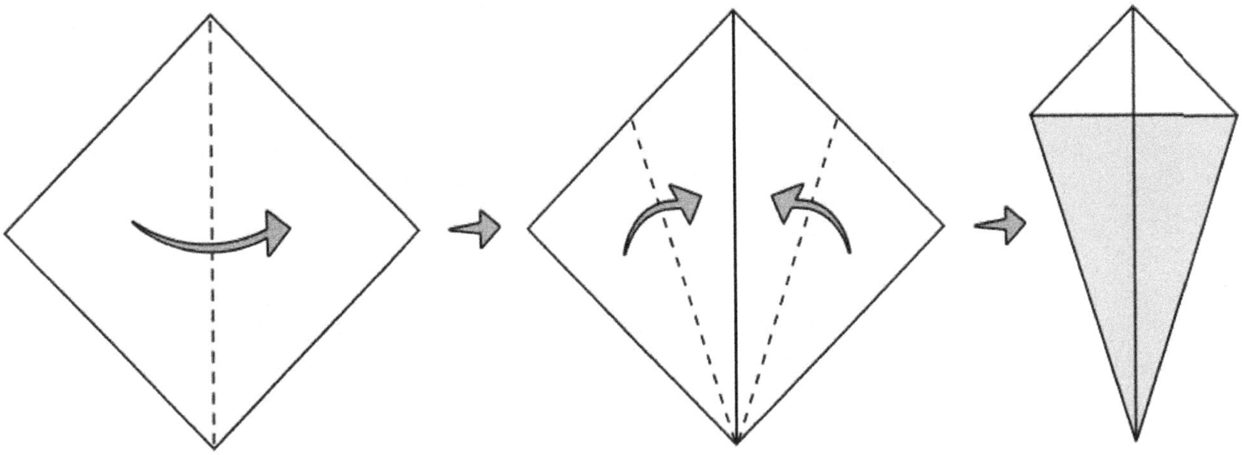

Step 1

Fold vertically along a diagonal and unfold, then bring the bottom of the side corners toward the midline.

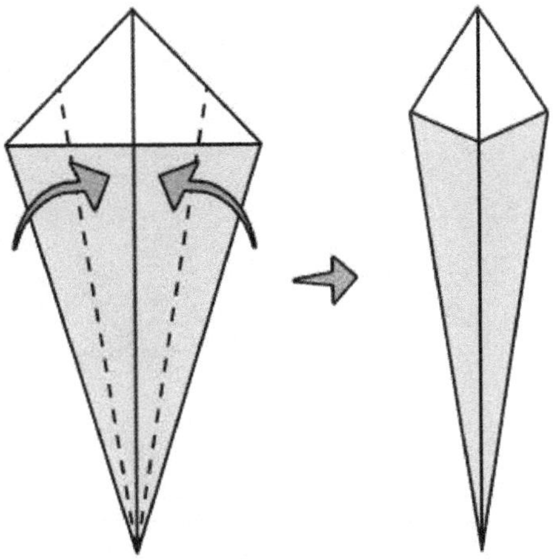

Step 2

Bring the bottom of the side corners toward the midline again.

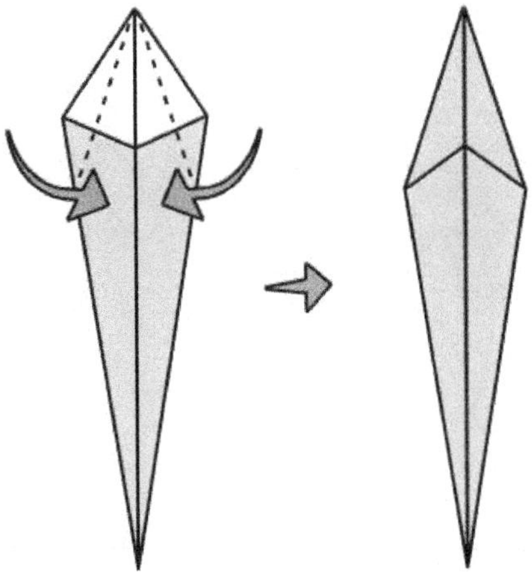

Step 3

Now bring the top of the side corners toward the midline.

Snake

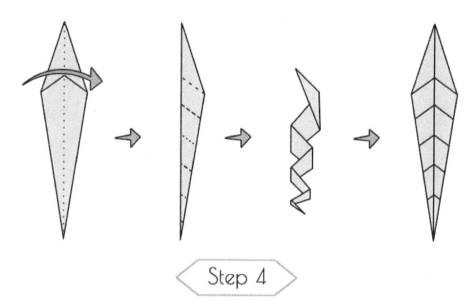

Step 4

Fold back in half and then alternate valley and mountain folds starting at the head and working up to the tail. When you're done, unfold.

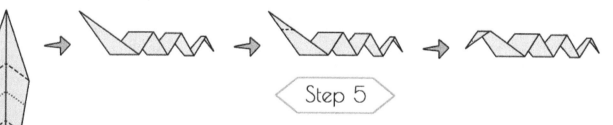

Step 5

Follow the creases you just made, and alternate valley and mountain folds as shown. Then fold the head down with a valley fold and the tip in with a mountain fold.

Snake

Ice Cream

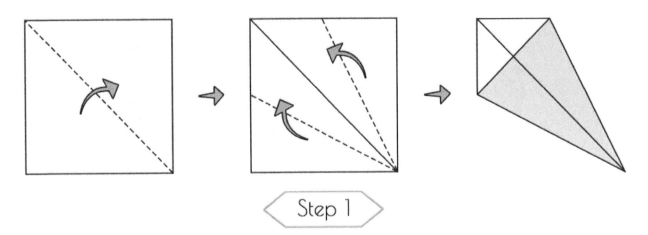

Fold along a diagonal and unfold, then bring the upper
right and lower left corners forward to that diagonal.

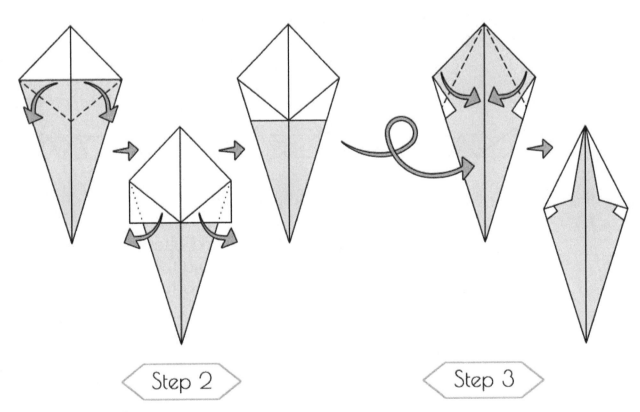

Step 2

Fold both flaps outward at an
angle so their bottom edges end
up horizontal. Then fold back the
tips that stick out from the sides.

Step 3

Turn the figure over and fold
the side corners forward
toward the midline (without
touching it) at an angle.

Ice Cream

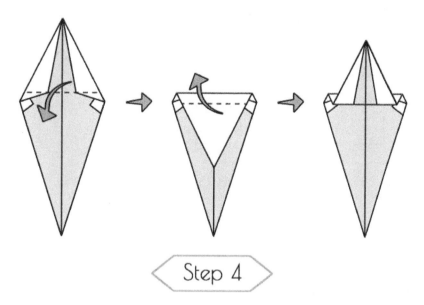

Step 4

Fold the top of the figure down, and then fold it up again.

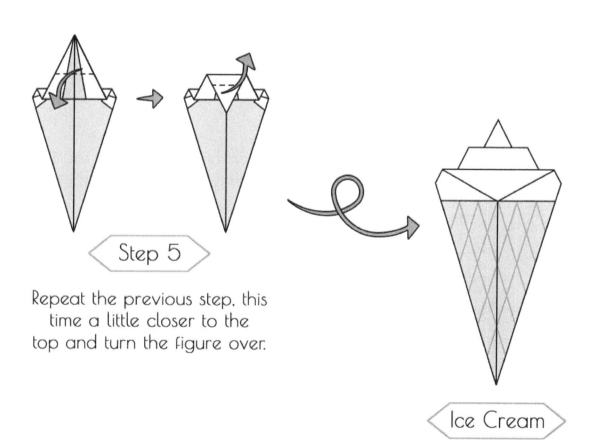

Step 5

Repeat the previous step, this time a little closer to the top and turn the figure over.

Ice Cream

Butterfly

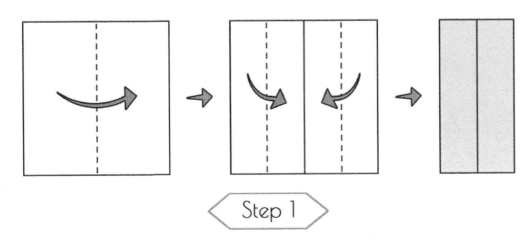

Fold in half lengthwise and unfold. Then fold each side again in half inward.

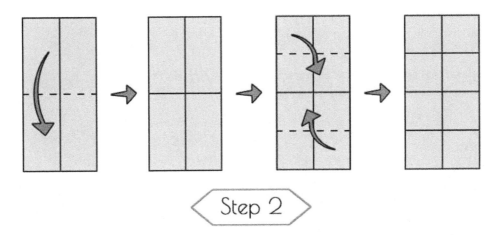

Step 2

Fold in half crosswise and unfold. Then bring the upper and lower edges forward toward the midline and unfold again.

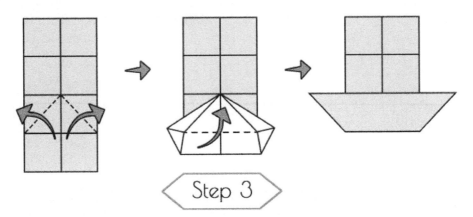

Step 3

From the bottom, fold the second section diagonally outward. As you fold it, the back layer also folds up. Press so that the top edges are horizontal.

36

Butterfly

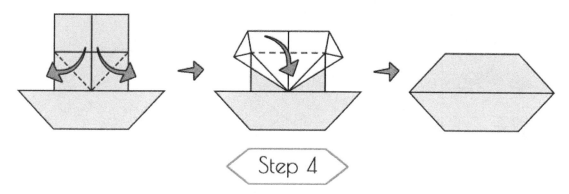

Step 4

Repeat the previous step on the top edge.

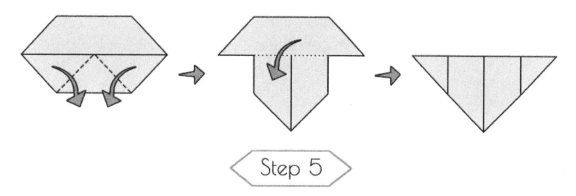

Step 5

Fold the sides of the lower half down toward the midline.
Then fold the top half down towards the back.

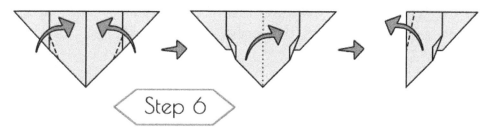

Step 6

Fold the sides of the top layer inward
at a slight angle. Then fold the figure in
half and make a crease in the top half.
Unfold and turn the figure over.

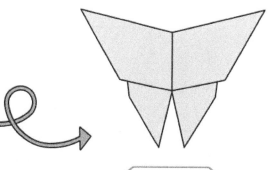

Butterfly

37

Bat

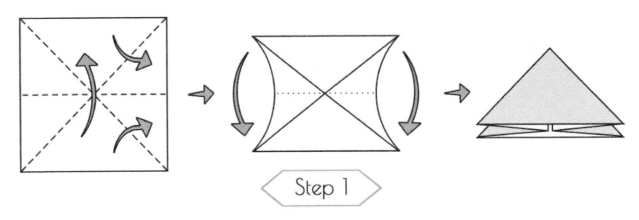

Step 1

Fold in half crosswise and along the two diagonals, and unfold.
Then fold the sides to the center and flatten to get a triangle.

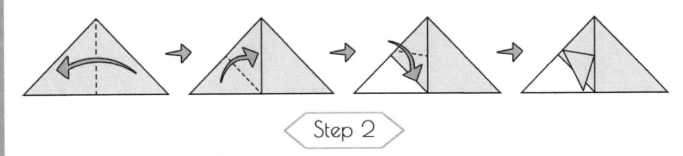

Step 2

Fold the right side of the top layer to the left and fold it again in half up.
Then fold it down at an angle so that only the tip sticks out.

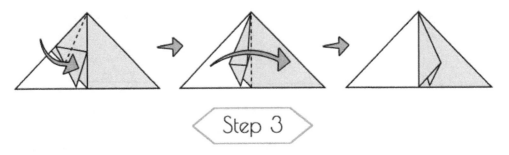

Step 3

Bring the left side to the midline and then fold it all the way to the
right so that the top right layer returns to its starting position.

Bat

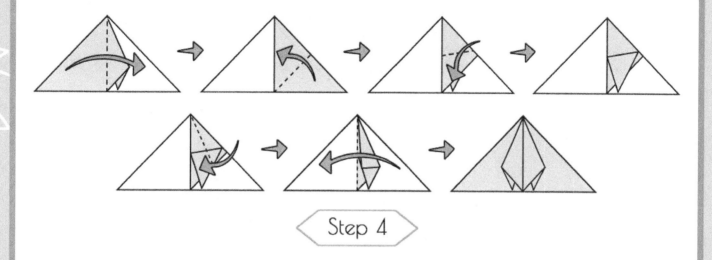

Step 4

Repeat steps 2 and 3 on the left side.

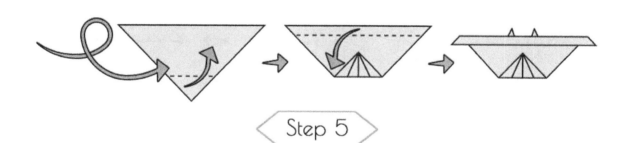

Step 5

Turn the figure over and fold the bottom corner up. Then fold the top edge down (except for the two small tips).

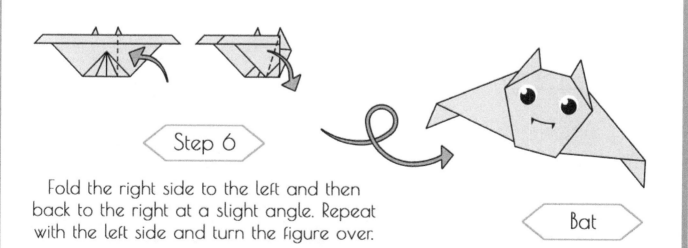

Step 6

Fold the right side to the left and then back to the right at a slight angle. Repeat with the left side and turn the figure over.

Bat

Bookmark

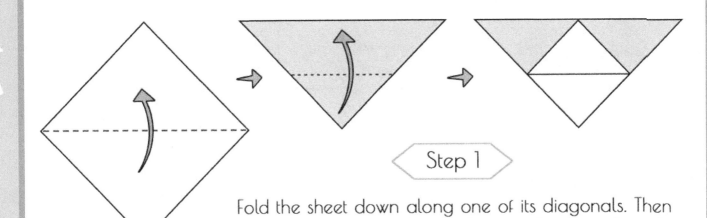

Step 1

Fold the sheet down along one of its diagonals. Then fold the bottom tip of the top layer only up to the edge.

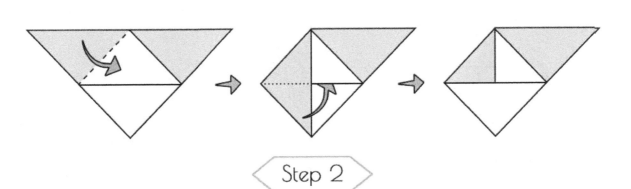

Step 2

Fold the left corner down to the midline. Then fold it up and insert it behind the flap from the previous step.

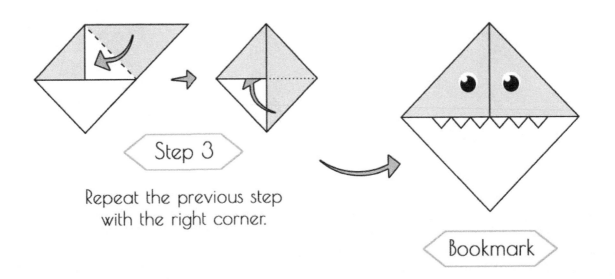

Step 3

Repeat the previous step with the right corner.

Bookmark

Whale

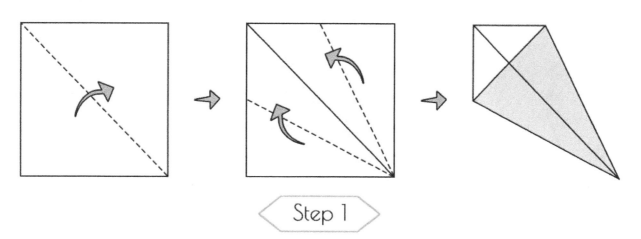

Step 1

Fold along a diagonal and unfold, then bring the upper right and lower left corners forward to that diagonal.

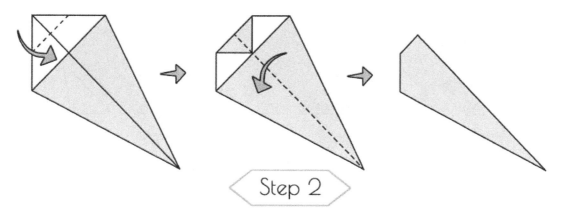

Step 2

Fold the upper left corner forward to the edge of the flaps from the previous step, then fold the figure in half.

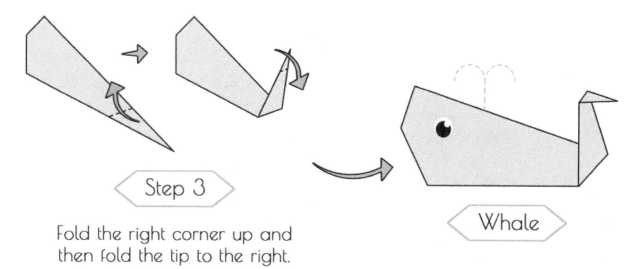

Step 3

Fold the right corner up and then fold the tip to the right.

Whale

41

Dolphin

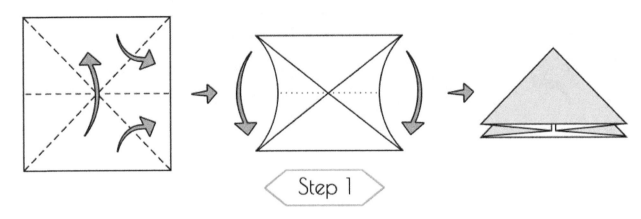

Step 1

Fold in half crosswise and along the two diagonals, and unfold.
Then fold the sides to the center and flatten to get a triangle.

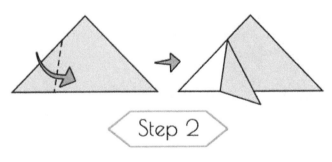

Step 2

Fold the left corner inward
at an angle, so that the tip
sticks out at the bottom edge.

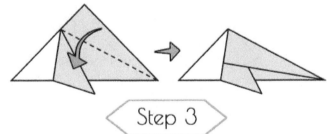

Step 3

Fold the upper right
part down to the
flap you just made.

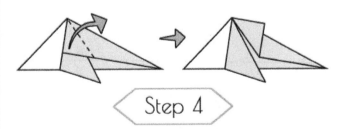

Step 4

Fold up the left side of the
flap from the previous step
so that the tip sticks out.

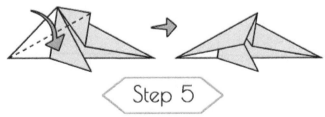

Step 5

Fold the top left part down
to join the left corner and the
tip of the flap you just folded.

Dolphin

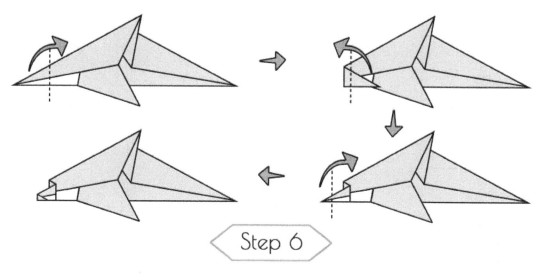

Step 6

Fold the left corner in, then out, and back in to make the dolphin's nose.

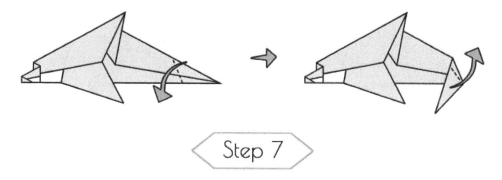

Step 7

Fold the right corner down at an angle so that the tip sticks out at the bottom edge. Now the tricky part: in that tip there are two overlapping layers of paper, leave the inner layer in that position and fold only the top layer up at an angle, then turn the figure over.

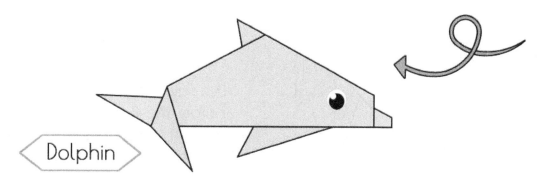

Dolphin

Bird

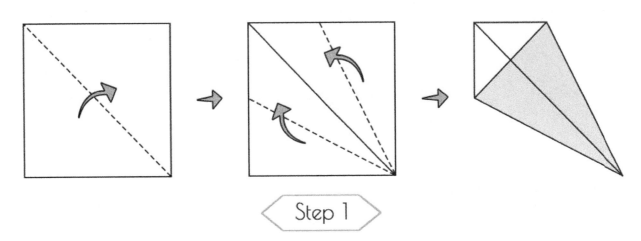

Fold along a diagonal and unfold, then bring the upper right and lower left corners forward to that diagonal.

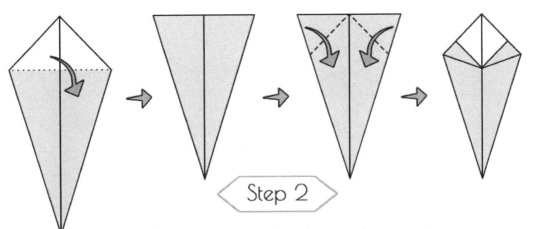

Step 2

Fold the top corner back and then both side corners forward toward the midline.

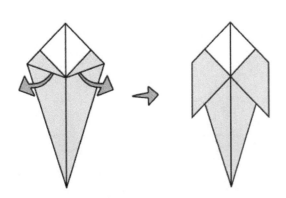

Step 3

The folds from step 1 are just below the flaps from step 2. Unfold them diagonally so that they stick out and point down.

Bird

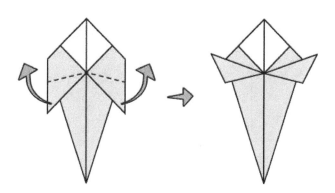

Fold the bottom tips of the sides up.

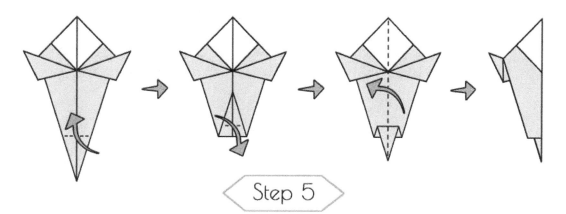

Step 5

Fold the bottom corner up and down again. Then fold the whole figure in half.

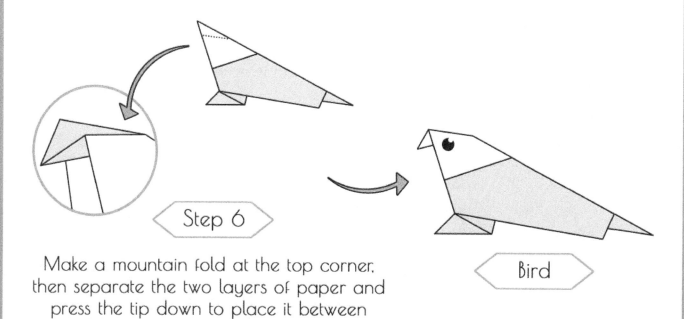

Step 6

Make a mountain fold at the top corner, then separate the two layers of paper and press the tip down to place it between them. This is called an inside reverse fold.

Bird

Seal

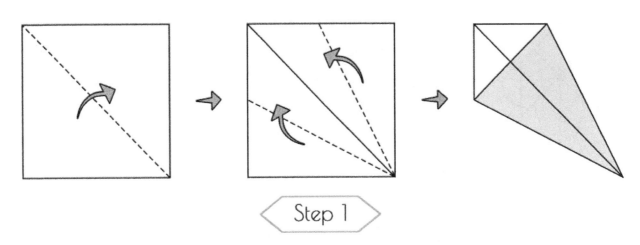

Step 1

Fold along a diagonal and unfold, then bring the upper right and lower left corners forward to that diagonal.

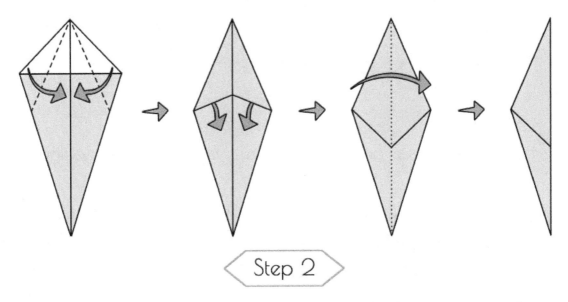

Step 2

Fold the sides down toward the midline. Then unfold the flaps from the previous step that are underneath them, so that they also end up parallel to the midline. Lastly, fold the entire figure in half.

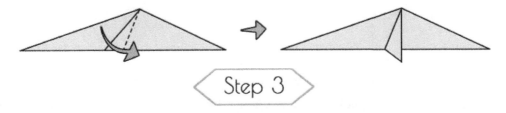

Step 3

Fold the flaps on both sides of the sheet until their edge is vertical.

Seal

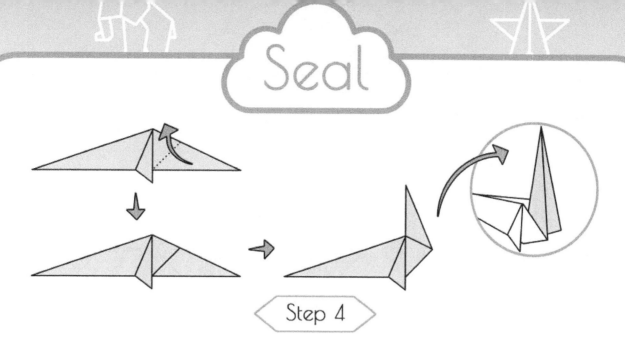

Fold the right side up, unfold, and follow that crease to make an inside reverse fold (the fold ends up between both sides of the sheet).

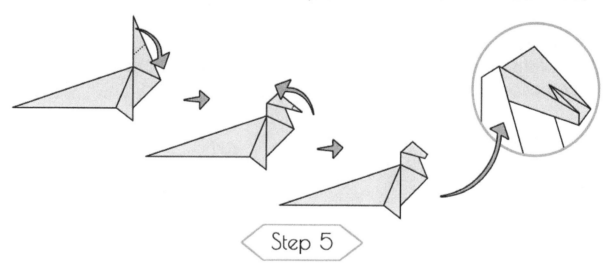

Step 5

Fold that same end down and unfold, then make another inside reverse fold along that crease. Repeat the same step right at the tip.

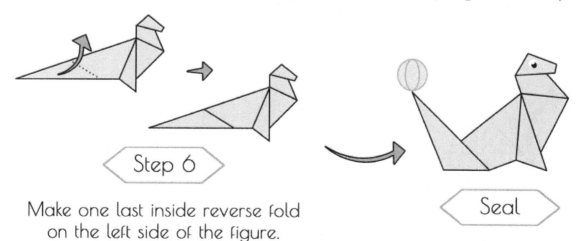

Step 6

Make one last inside reverse fold on the left side of the figure.

Seal

47

Crane

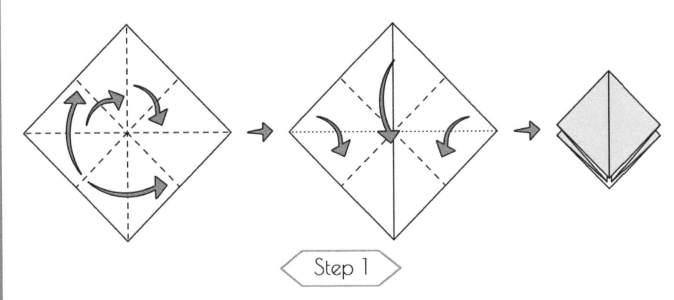

Step 1

Fold the sheet lengthwise, crosswise and along both diagonals, and unfold. Then fold the top and side corners down and in toward the bottom corner so that the figure collapses into a smaller square.

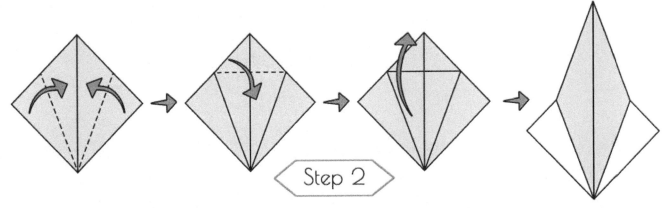

Step 2

Fold the sides toward the midline, the top corner down, and unfold. Then pull the bottom corner all the way up following those creases.

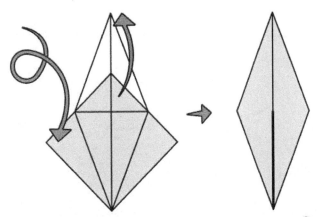

Step 3

Turn the figure over and repeat the previous step on the other side following the same creases. Note that there is an opening in the lower half of the midline.

Crane

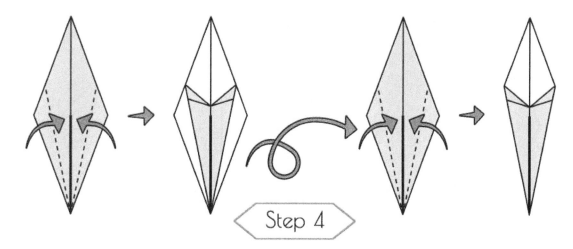

Step 4

Fold the bottom of the sides toward the midline, then turn the figure over and repeat on the other side.

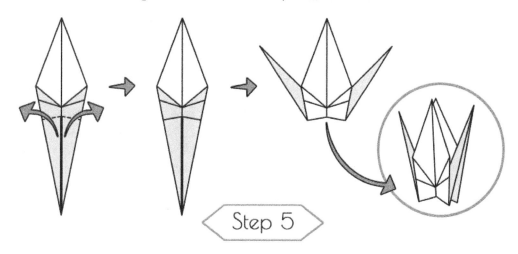

Step 5

Fold the sections on both sides of the opening at a small angle and unfold. Then make an inside reverse fold on them, so that they end up pointing up.

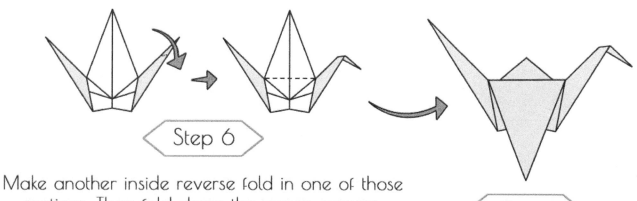

Step 6

Make another inside reverse fold in one of those sections. Then fold down the upper corners.

Crane

Seahorse

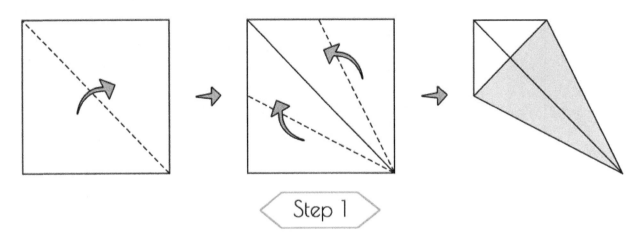

Step 1

Fold along a diagonal and unfold, then bring the upper right and lower left corners forward to that diagonal.

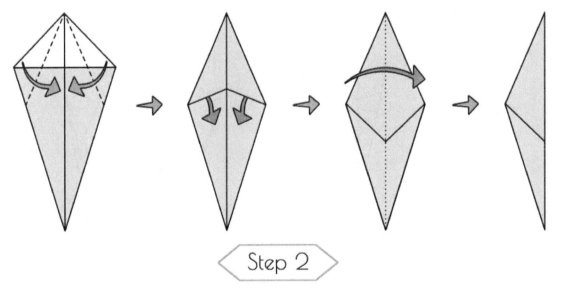

Step 2

Fold the sides down toward the midline. Then unfold the flaps from the previous step that are underneath them, so that they also end up parallel to the midline. Lastly, fold the entire figure in half.

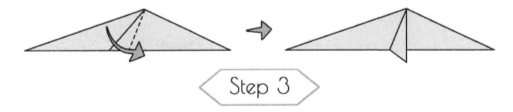

Step 3

Fold the flaps on both sides of the sheet until their edge is vertical.

Seahorse

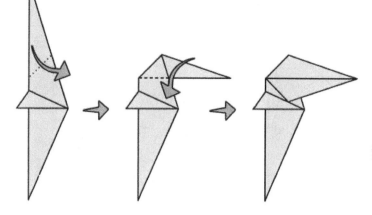

Make an inside reverse fold halfway up the figure, then fold the top layer down to open it.

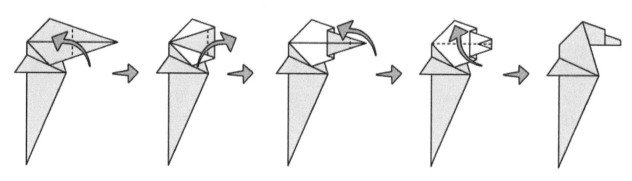

Step 5

Fold the flap you opened in the previous step to the left in half. Now leave a small gap before folding it back to the right and another one to fold it again to the left. Close the reverse fold by folding it up.

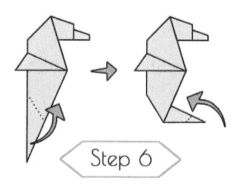

Step 6

Make an inside reverse fold halfway down the figure. Then make a valley fold at the tip and unfold to make a crease, slightly separate the layers of paper and fold them up backward following that crease. This is called an outside reverse fold.

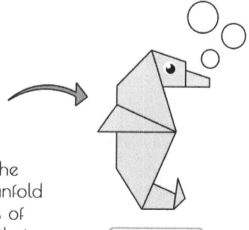

Seahorse

51

Hummingbird

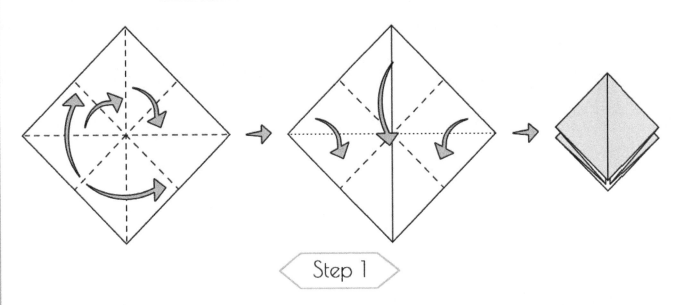

Step 1

Fold the sheet lengthwise, crosswise and along both diagonals, and unfold. Then fold the top and side corners down and in toward the bottom corner so that the figure collapses into a smaller square.

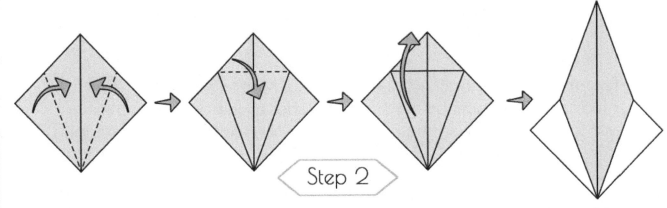

Step 2

Fold the sides toward the midline, the top corner down, and unfold. Then pull the bottom corner all the way up following those creases.

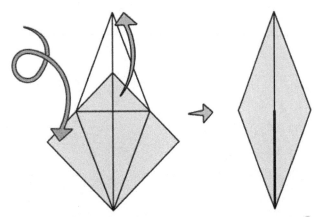

Step 3

Turn the figure over and repeat the previous step on the other side following the same creases. Note that there is an opening in the lower half of the midline.

Hummingbird

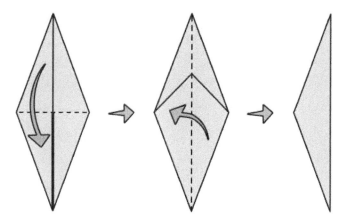

Fold the top layer down in half. Then fold the entire figure in half lengthwise.

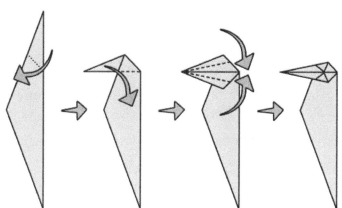

Step 5

Make an inside reverse fold halfway up the figure, and fold the top layer down to open it. Then fold each side in half.

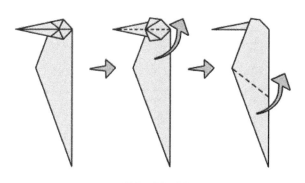

Step 6

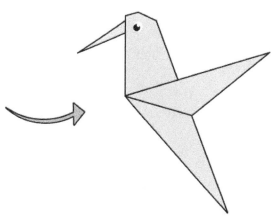

Hummingbird

When you fold in half in the previous step, you will see that two pockets form on the right side. Pull them out so that they stick out a bit both at the top and the bottom. Then close the inside reverse fold again, and fold the flaps on either side of the lower half of the figure up to the right.

Lotus Flower

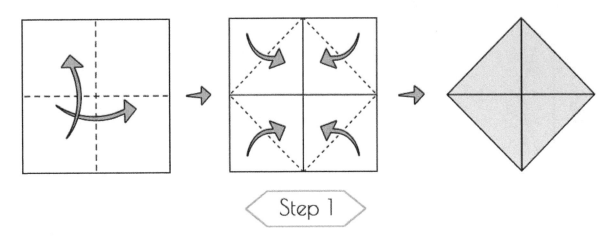

Fold in half lengthwise and crosswise, and unfold.
Then fold all corners toward the center of the sheet.

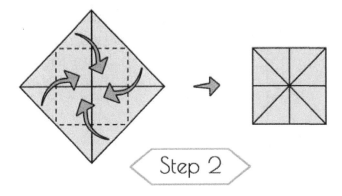

Step 2

Fold all corners toward the center of the sheet again.

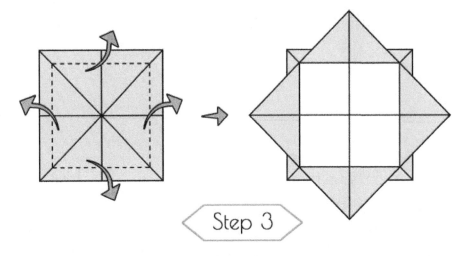

Step 3

Fold the corner tips outward so that they stick out a little from the sides.

54

Lotus Flower

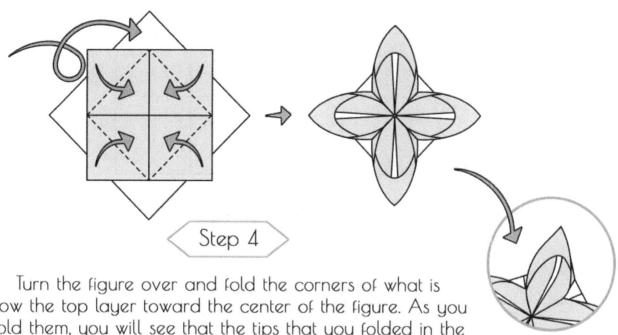

Step 4

Turn the figure over and fold the corners of what is now the top layer toward the center of the figure. As you fold them, you will see that the tips that you folded in the previous step lift up, so once they are vertical give them a rounded shape so that they look like petals.

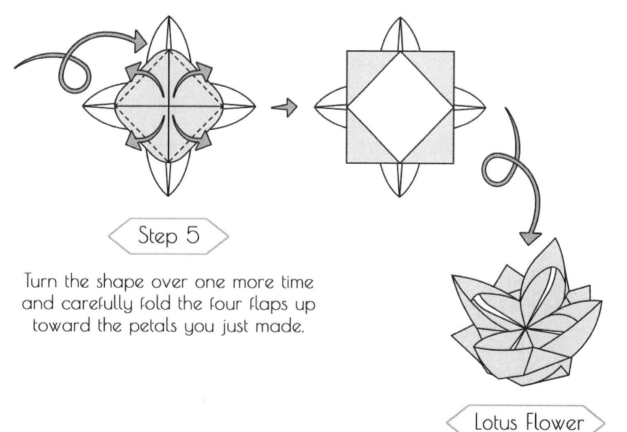

Step 5

Turn the shape over one more time and carefully fold the four flaps up toward the petals you just made.

Lotus Flower

Brachiosaurus

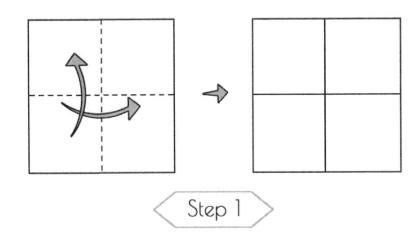

Step 1

Fold in half lengthwise and crosswise, and unfold.

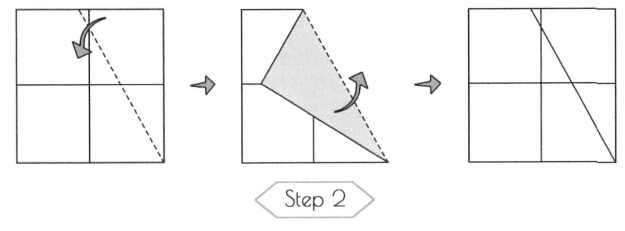

Step 2

Bring the upper right corner to the left side of the horizontal crease and unfold.

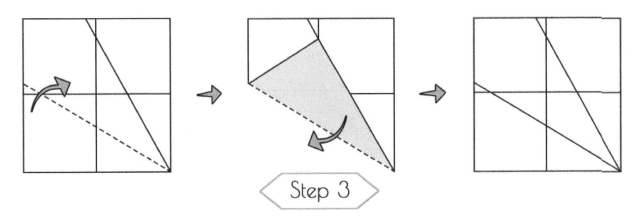

Step 3

Bring the lower left corner to the upper side of the vertical crease and unfold.

Brachiosaurus

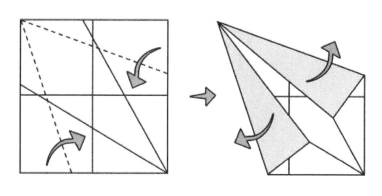

Starting now from the upper left corner, bring the upper right and lower left corners toward the creases from steps 2 and 3, and unfold.

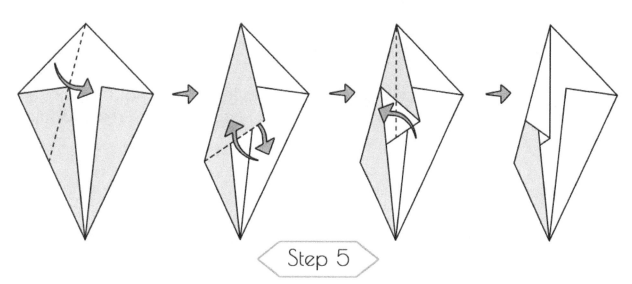

Step 5

Turn the figure a little and fold the upper left side inward along the crease from step 2. Then unfold the layer that is immediately below and fold it up following the same edge that you just made. Lastly, fold that entire section in half outward.

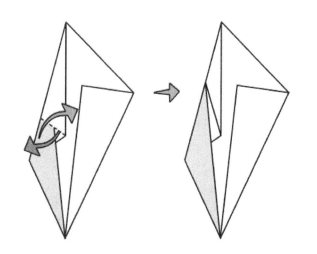

Step 6

Unfold the layer immediately below again and fold it up the edge of the top layer, so the tip is now on top but still in the same position.

Brachiosaurus

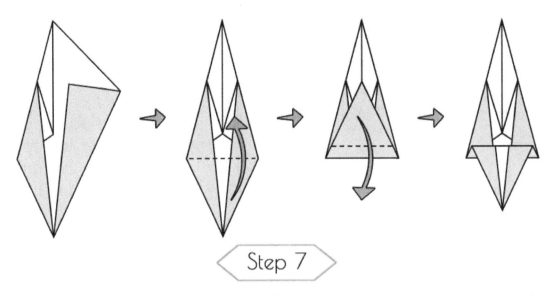

Repeat steps 5 and 6 on the right side of the figure. Then fold the bottom corner up and down again, leaving a small space between the two folds.

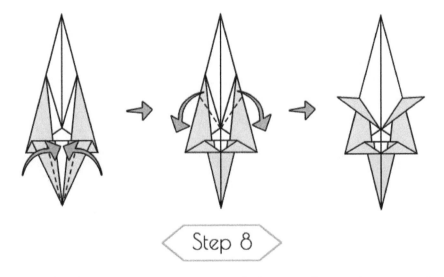

Step 8

Fold the sides of the lower section toward the midline. As you do so, you will see that the corners separate from the bottom layer; flatten them into a triangle shape. Then fold the side flaps outward so they stick out the sides.

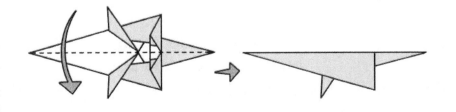

Step 9

Rotate the figure to the left and fold it in half.

Brachiosaurus

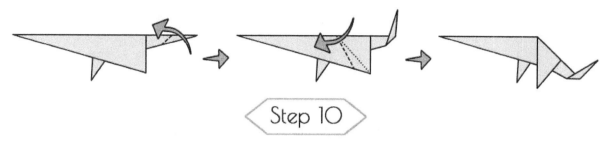

Step 10

Make an outside reverse fold at the right end. Then bring both lower tips to the left with a valley and a mountain fold so that they overlap with the rest of the figure and their edge ends up vertical.

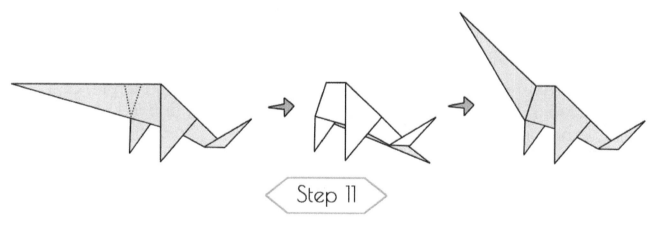

Step 11

Make two inside reverse folds in a row: the first (right dotted line) will make the left end of the figure face down between the two layers of paper, the second (left dotted line, can't be seen in the middle step) will make that end point up and left at an angle.

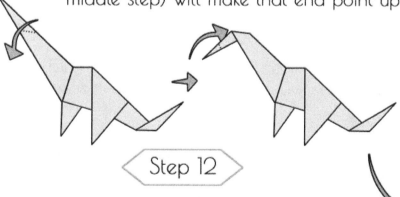

Step 12

Make two inside reverse folds at the tip of the upper left corner, the first downward and the second upward.

Brachiosaurus

Elephant

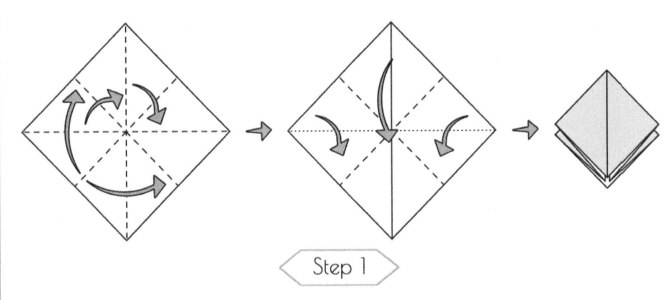

Step 1

Fold the sheet lengthwise, crosswise and along both diagonals, and unfold. Then fold the top and side corners down and in toward the bottom corner so that the figure collapses into a smaller square.

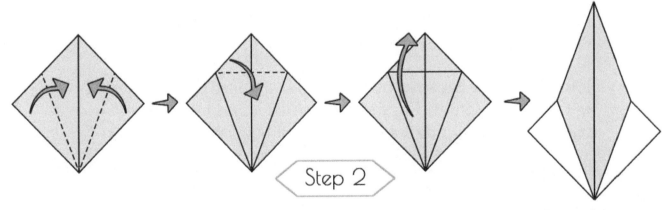

Step 2

Fold the sides toward the midline, the top corner down, and unfold. Then pull the bottom corner all the way up following those creases.

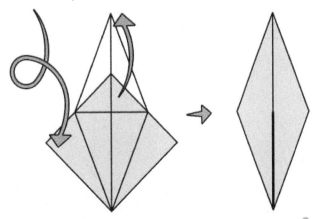

Step 3

Turn the figure over and repeat the previous step on the other side following the same creases. Note that there is an opening in the lower half of the midline.

Elephant

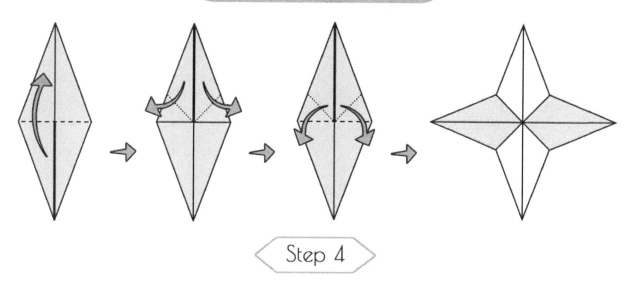

Step 4

Fold the bottom section with the opening up, then fold each side diagonally outward and unfold. Each side piece has two layers of paper, use those creases you just made to unfold them down and press.

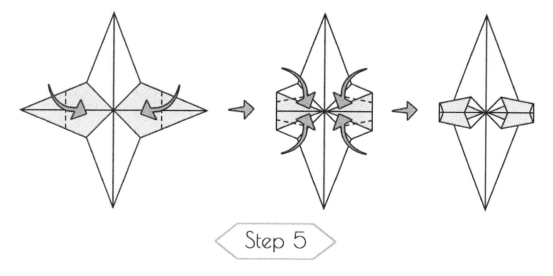

Step 5

Fold the sides in half toward the center. Then bring their edges to the midline.

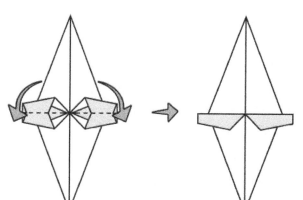

Step 6

Fold both side pieces down in half. These are the front legs.

Elephant

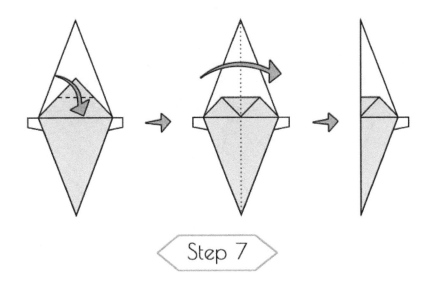

Step 7

Turn the figure over and fold the tip in its center down in half. Then fold the entire figure in half.

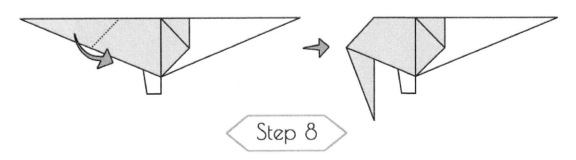

Step 8

Rotate the figure to the right. Make an inside reverse fold at the left end so that its right edge ends up vertical.

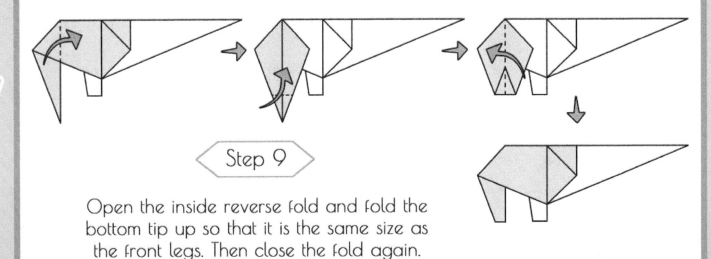

Step 9

Open the inside reverse fold and fold the bottom tip up so that it is the same size as the front legs. Then close the fold again.

Elephant

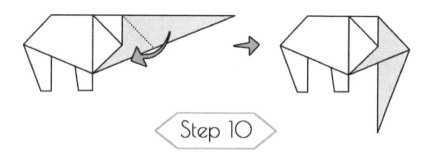

Step 10

Make an inside reverse fold at the right end so that its left edge ends up vertical.

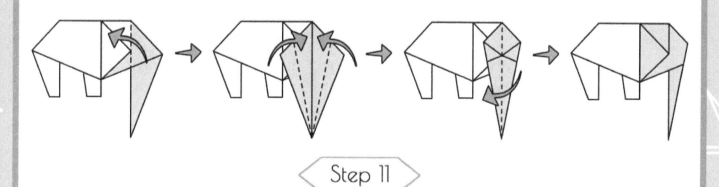

Step 11

Open the inside reverse fold and fold its side edges toward the midline. Then close the fold again. This is the elephant's trunk.

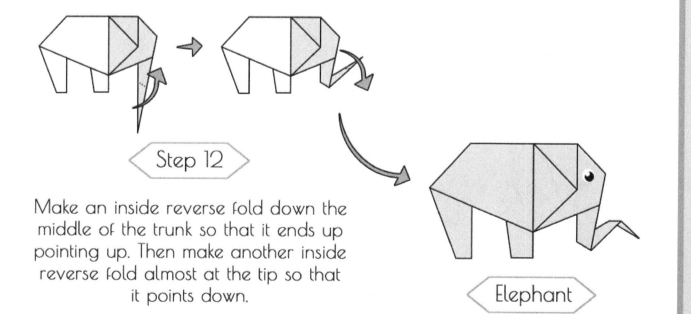

Step 12

Make an inside reverse fold down the middle of the trunk so that it ends up pointing up. Then make another inside reverse fold almost at the tip so that it points down.

Elephant

Dragon

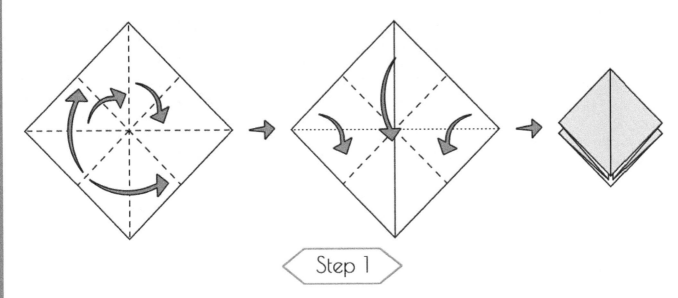

Step 1

Fold the sheet lengthwise, crosswise and along both diagonals, and unfold. Then fold the top and side corners down and in toward the bottom corner so that the figure collapses into a smaller square.

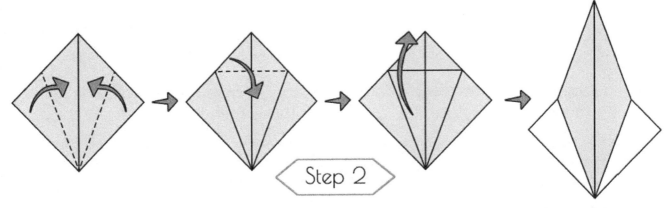

Step 2

Fold the sides toward the midline, the top corner down, and unfold. Then pull the bottom corner all the way up following those creases.

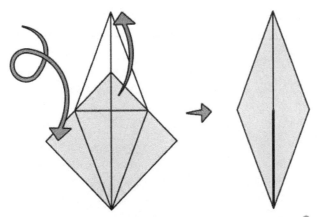

Step 3

Turn the figure over and repeat the previous step on the other side following the same creases. Note that there is an opening in the lower half of the midline.

64

Dragon

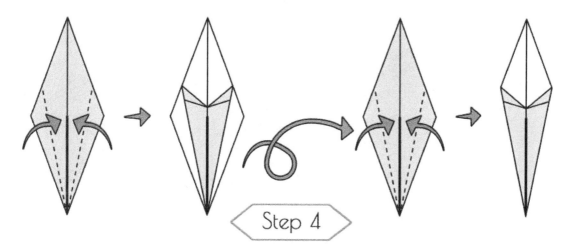

Step 4

Fold the bottom of the sides toward the midline, then turn the figure over and repeat on the other side.

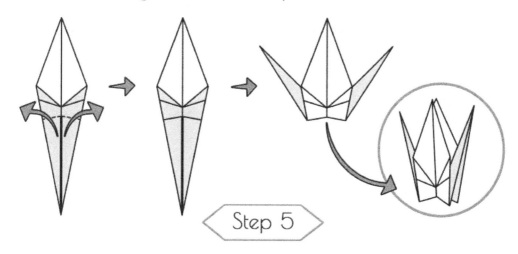

Step 5

Fold the sections on both sides of the opening at a small angle and unfold. Then make an inside reverse fold on them, so that they end up pointing up.

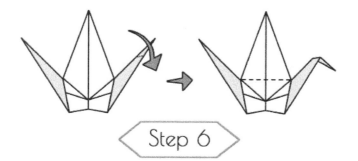

Step 6

Make an inside reverse fold toward the tip of one of those sections.

Dragon

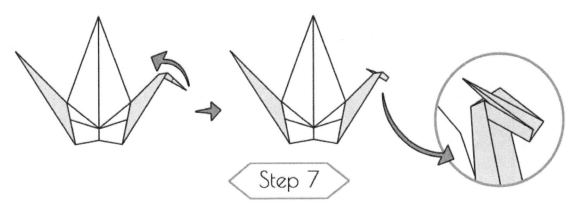

Step 7

Make another inside reverse fold at that end, so that it sticks out at the top.

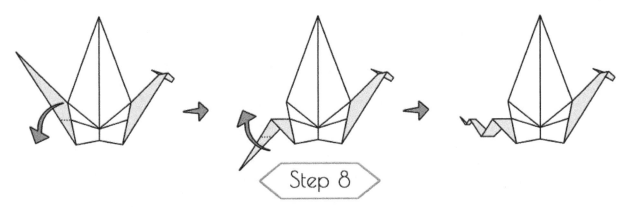

Step 8

Make an inside reverse fold on the opposite section so that it points down. Then make another inside reverse fold so that it points up and keep repeating this movement until the entire section is folded.

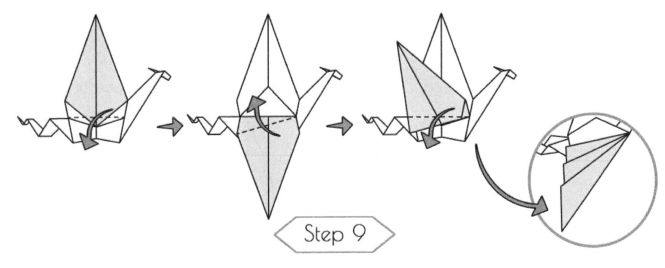

Step 9

Fold the top corner horizontally down, then up at an angle and back down horizontally. Keep folding up and down like this until the entire section is folded.

Dragon

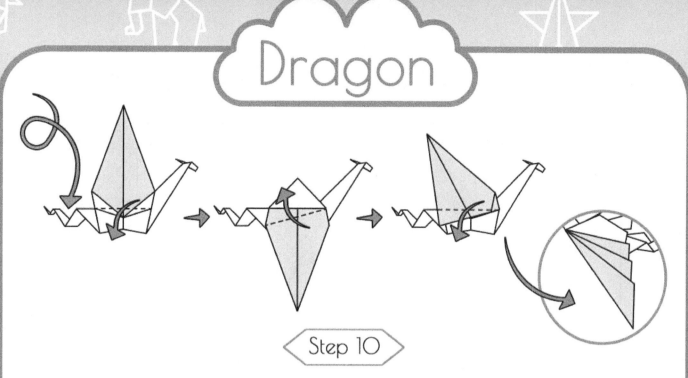

Step 10

Turn the figure over and repeat step 9 with the top corner on the other side.

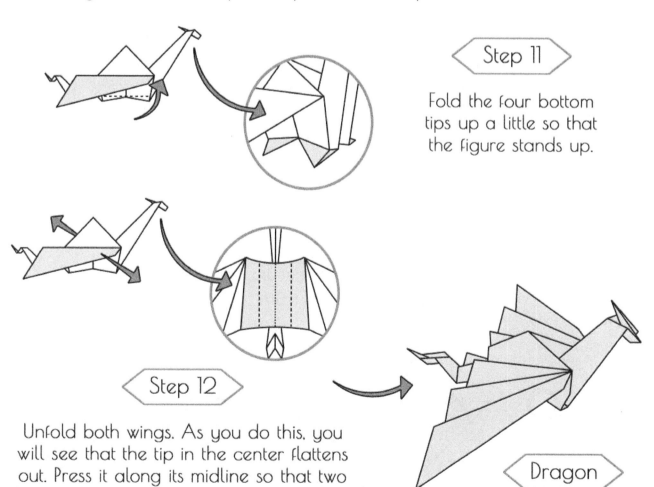

Step 11

Fold the four bottom tips up a little so that the figure stands up.

Step 12

Unfold both wings. As you do this, you will see that the tip in the center flattens out. Press it along its midline so that two valley folds form on both sides and it doesn't stick out as much (see top view zoom).

Dragon

Pop-it Toy

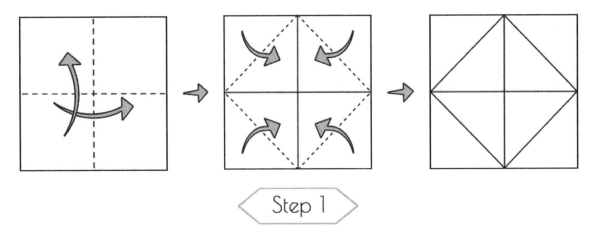

Fold in half lengthwise and crosswise, and unfold. Then fold all corners toward the center of the sheet and unfold again.

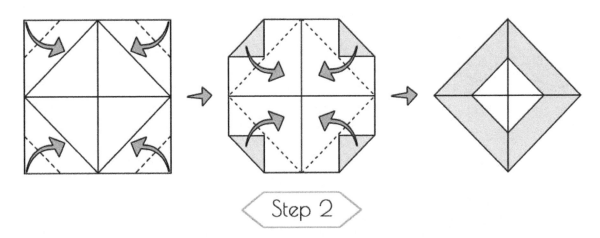

Step 2

Fold the corners inward toward the diagonal creases from the previous step. Then fold inward again along those creases.

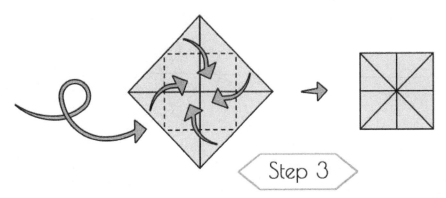

Step 3

Turn the figure over and fold all corners toward the center of the sheet.

Pop-it Toy

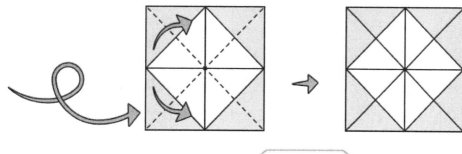

Step 4

Turn the figure over and fold along both diagonals, then unfold.

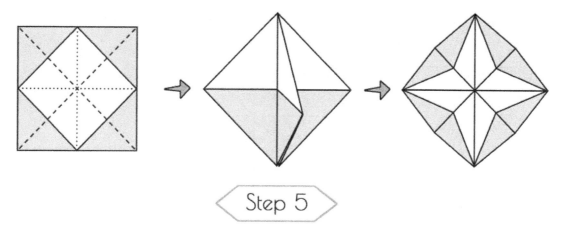

Step 5

Make mountain folds along the vertical and horizontal creases, and valley folds along the diagonals to collapse the figure. Then open those folds a bit, but without returning to its flat position to make it look three-dimensional.

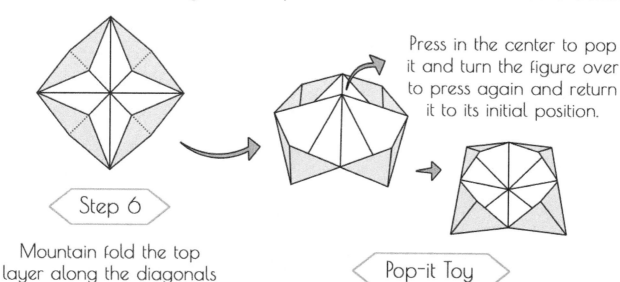

Press in the center to pop it and turn the figure over to press again and return it to its initial position.

Step 6

Mountain fold the top layer along the diagonals to form a pocket.

Pop-it Toy

Fish

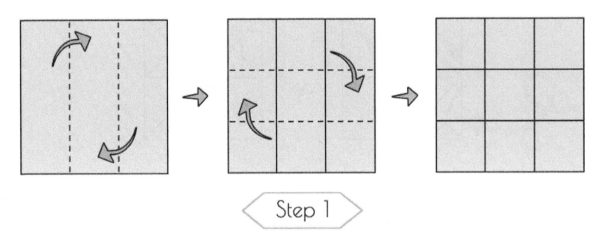

Fold the sheet in three equal parts lengthwise and crosswise, then unfold.

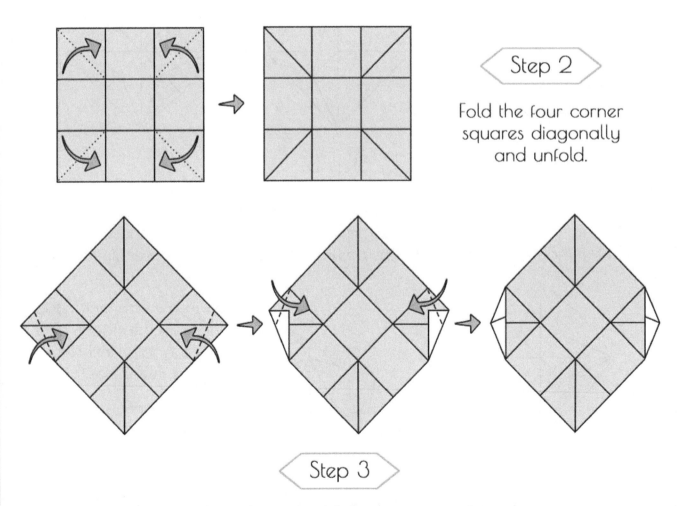

Step 2

Fold the four corner squares diagonally and unfold.

Step 3

Turn the sheet to the side and fold the bottom of the side corners up until their edge is vertical. Repeat with the top of both side corners.

Fish

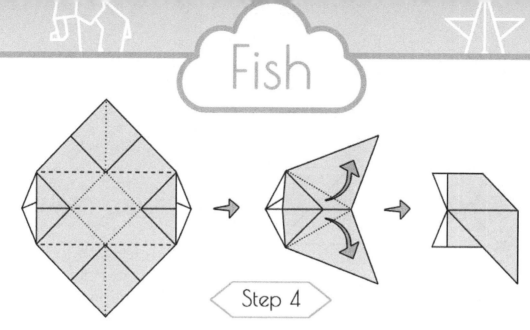

Step 4

Make mountain and valley folds carefully as shown in the figure (there are no arrows to show all lines more clearly). Then fold the flaps that form at the top and bottom, turn vertically and flatten the figure.

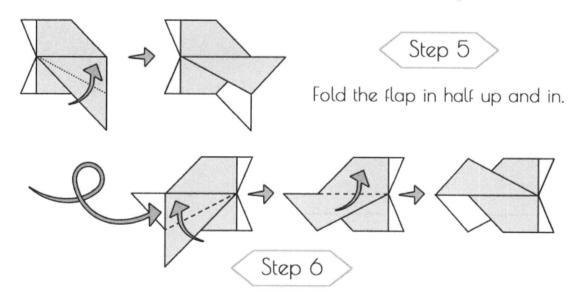

Step 5

Fold the flap in half up and in.

Step 6

Turn the shape over. Fold the flap up in half and then again all the way up.

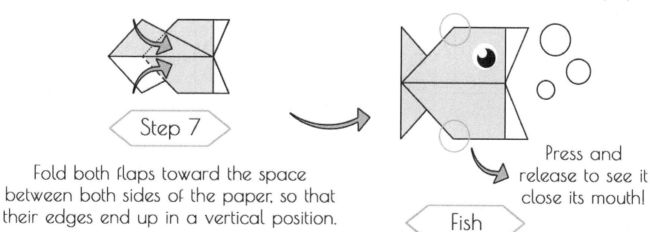

Step 7

Fold both flaps toward the space between both sides of the paper, so that their edges end up in a vertical position.

Press and release to see it close its mouth!

Fish

Peacock

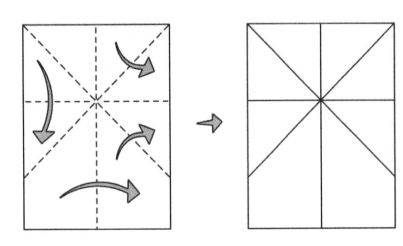

Step 1

Fold both top corners diagonally, then fold vertically and horizontally at the point where those creases meet, and unfold.

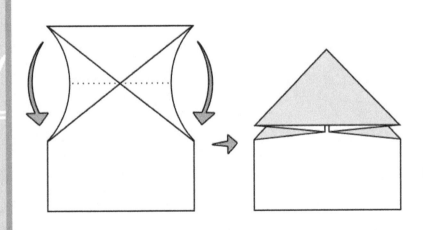

Step 2

Fold the sides to the center and flatten to get a triangle with a piece of paper left unfolded (the longer this piece, the bigger the tail will be).

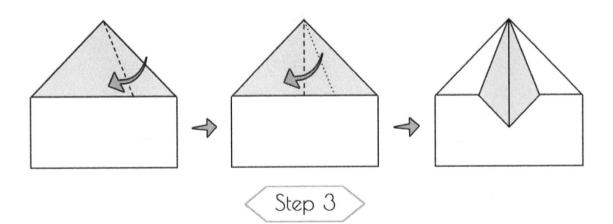

Step 3

Fold the top right side toward the midline and unfold. Then unfold the two layers of that section following that crease and flatten.

Peacock

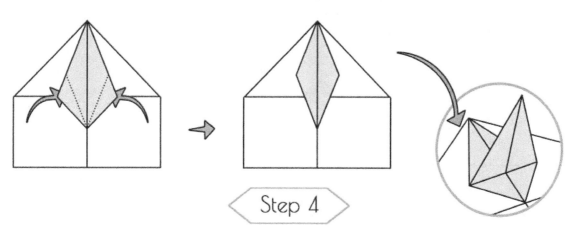

Fold the sides in toward the midline, so that the upper edge ends up being horizontal. Check the 3D view to see how it should look if you fold the bottom tip up (not part of the process though).

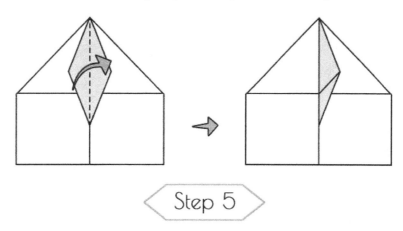

Step 5

Fold that section in half to the right.

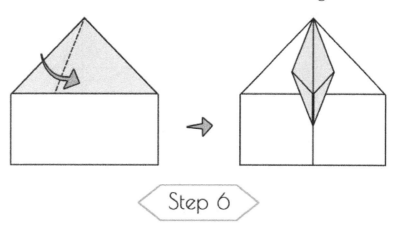

Step 6

Repeat steps 3 through 5 on the top left side. Note that there is an opening between the lower sections.

Peacock

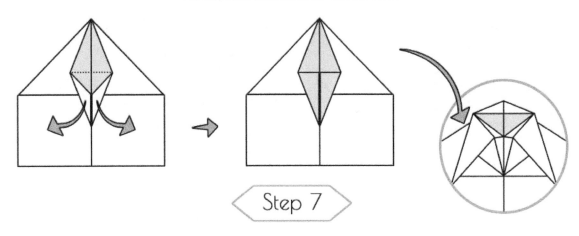

Step 7

Pull the bottom sections to the sides to open a gap between them
and insert the tip that is above them inward and upward.

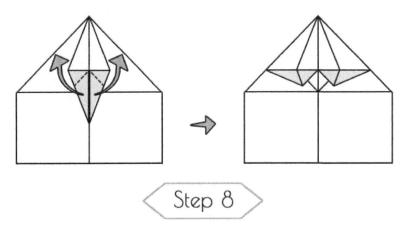

Step 8

Make an inside reverse fold on the bottom sections
so that the top edge ends up horizontal.

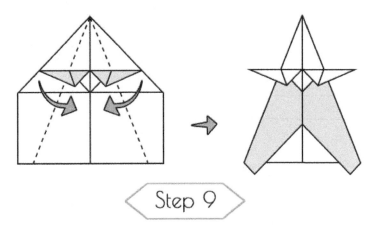

Step 9

Bring the top of the bottom layer toward the midline,
but behind the section you've been folding so far.

Peacock

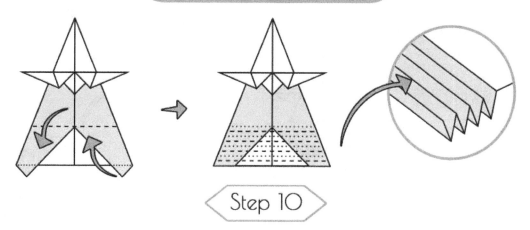

Step 10

Fold back the tips that stick out the bottom edge, then fold the figure horizontally where the two flaps touch, and unfold. With that crease as the limit, fold the lower part in an accordion shape, alternating valley and mountain folds.

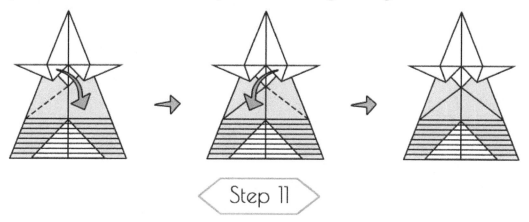

Step 11

Fold the top corner diagonally to the right toward the crease from the previous step and unfold. Then repeat to the left and unfold again.

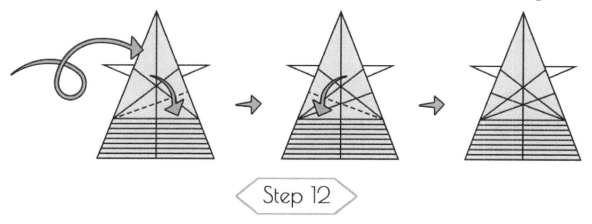

Step 12

Turn the figure over and fold in the same way as in the previous step, but at a slightly smaller angle.

Peacock

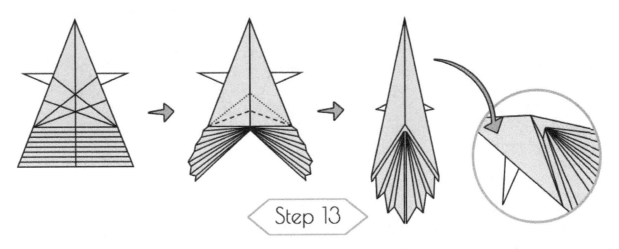

This is the trickiest step: fold the entire accordion section in half, as you form a triangle between the creases from steps 11 and 12. You will see that the figure folds in half lengthwise as you make that triangle. This way, the base of the tail ends up hidden between the two sides of the sheet.

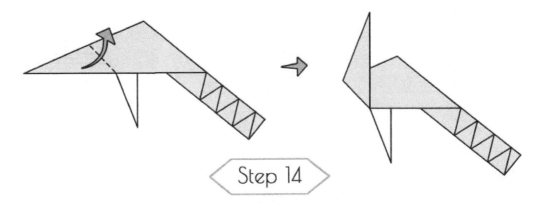

Step 14

Turn the figure to the side and flatten. Then make an outside reverse fold on the opposite end of the tail, so that it ends up vertical.

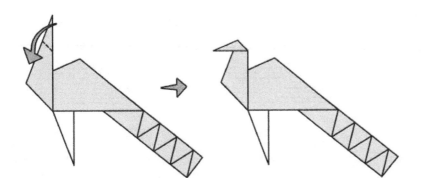

Step 15

Make another outside reverse fold at the tip of that section.

Peacock

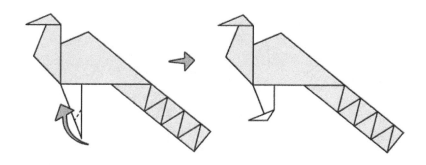

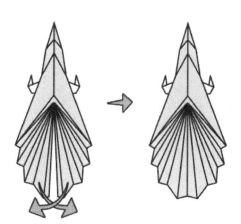

Step 16

Make outside reverse folds on the two sections that are pointing down.

Step 17

To be sure that the tail won't open along its center opening, place the first fold on one side over the first one on the other side and fold them in half all along their back.

Press carefully here to see the peacock's tail lift up and open.

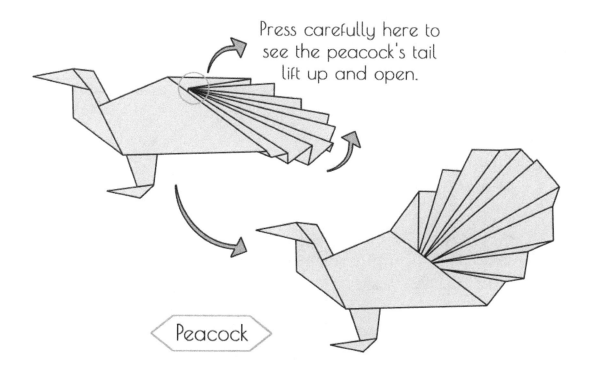

Peacock

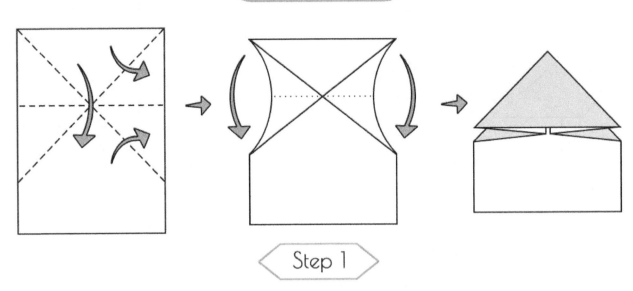

Step 1

Fold both top corners diagonally until they reach the opposite edge of the sheet, then fold horizontally at the point where those diagonals meet, and unfold. Then fold the sides to the center and flatten to get a triangle with a piece of paper left unfolded.

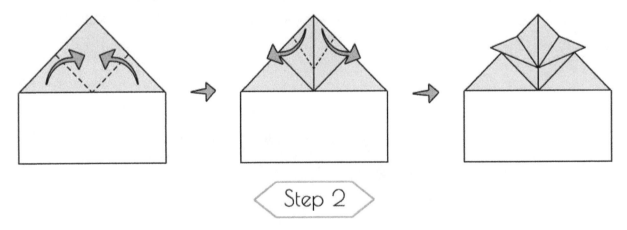

Step 2

Fold the sides of the top layer up in half. Then fold them back down at an angle so that the tips stick out of the sides of the figure.

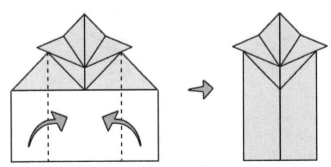

Step 3

Fold the sides of the bottom layer in toward the midline.

Frog

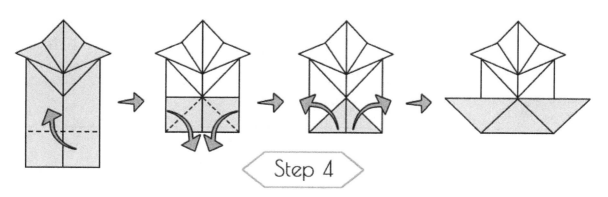

Step 4

Fold the bottom of the figure up in half and its corners back down diagonally. Then pull those flaps sideways to unfold them and press.

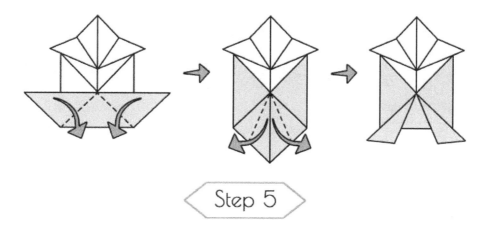

Step 5

Fold the sides down along the creases from the previous step. Then fold them up slightly so that the tips stick out from both sides of the figure.

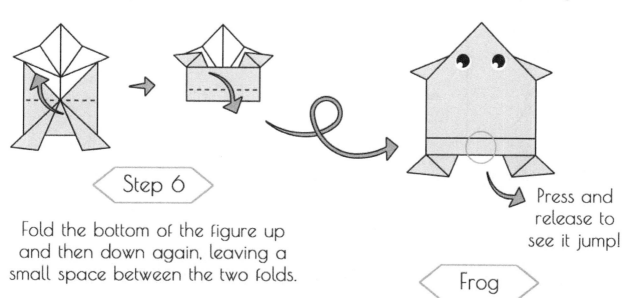

Step 6

Fold the bottom of the figure up and then down again, leaving a small space between the two folds.

Press and release to see it jump!

Frog

79

Tulip

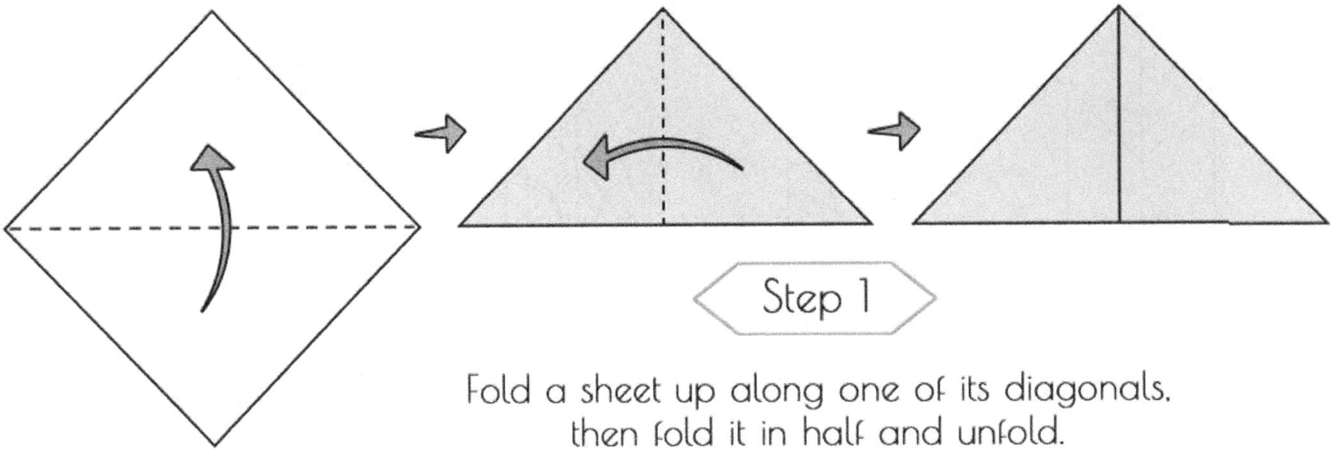

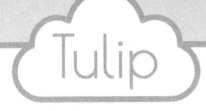

Step 1

Fold a sheet up along one of its diagonals, then fold it in half and unfold.

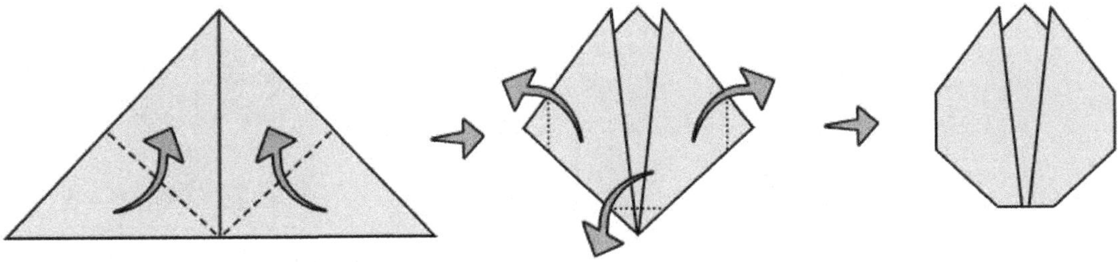

Step 2

Fold both side corners up so they stick out on both sides of the top tip. Then fold the side and bottom tips back and the flower is ready.

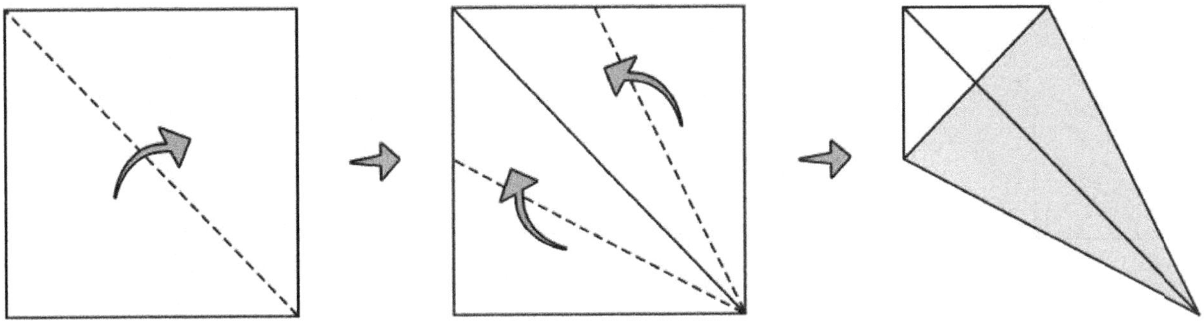

Step 3

Take another sheet, fold along a diagonal, and unfold. Then bring the upper right and lower left corners forward to that diagonal.

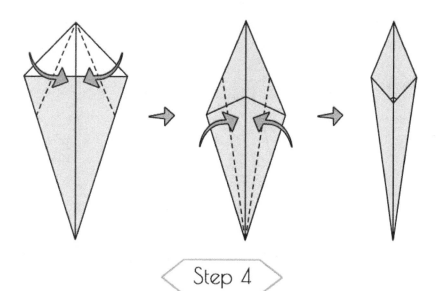

Step 4

Fold the sides down towards the midline and then back up again in the same way.

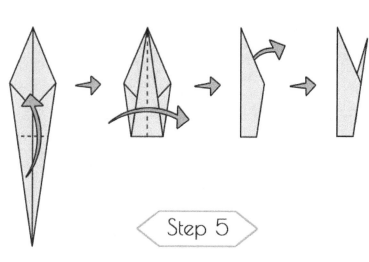

Step 5

Fold the figure in half lengthwise and then widthwise. Angle the tip that remains on the inside of the fold outward and the stem is done.

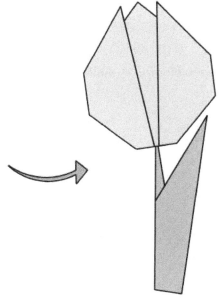

Tulip

Koala

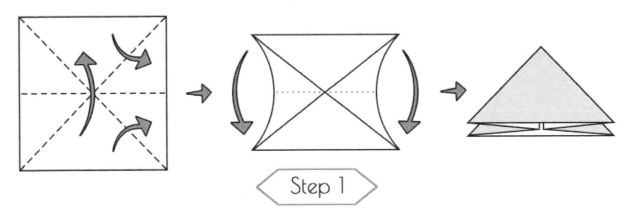

Step 1

Fold in half crosswise and along the two diagonals, and unfold. Then fold both sides in toward the center and press the edges to make a triangle.

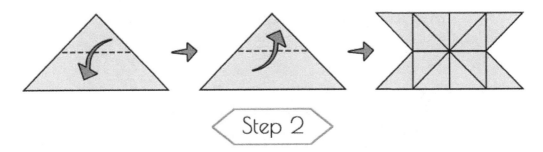

Step 2

Fold the figure in half and unfold. Then fold the top layer up along that crease and the flaps that are between the two layers will also move up. Flatten the entire figure, including those inside flaps.

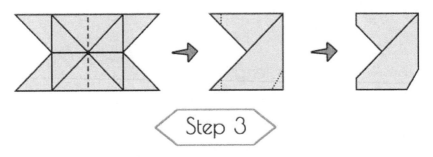

Step 3

Fold the figure in half to the left. Then make inside reverse folds in all the left corners and in the lower right corner.

Koala

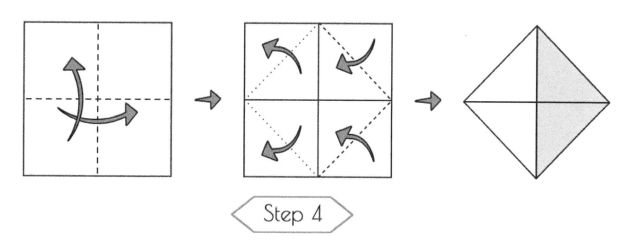

Step 4

Fold another sheet in half lengthwise and crosswise, and unfold. Then fold the two left corners backward and the two right corners forward.

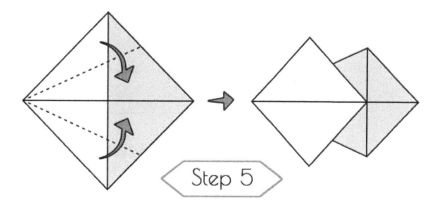

Step 5

Bring the top and bottom corners to the midline and press the edges. You will see the corners that we folded backward sticking out from the sides.

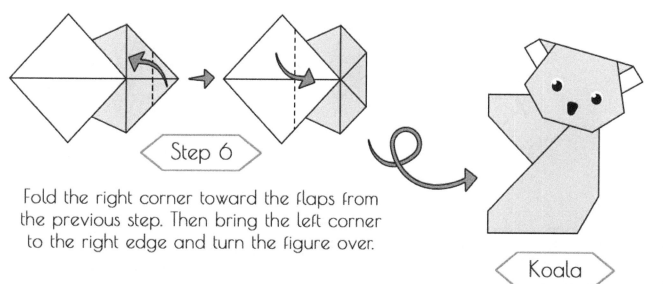

Step 6

Fold the right corner toward the flaps from the previous step. Then bring the left corner to the right edge and turn the figure over.

Koala

83

Carrot

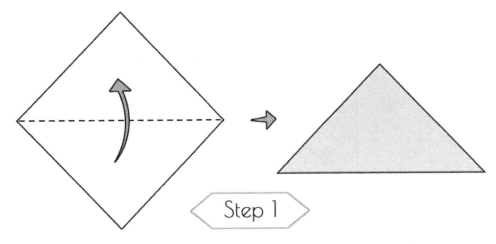

Step 1

Fold a sheet up along one of its diagonals.

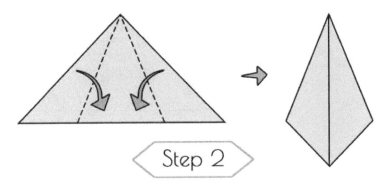

Step 2

Fold both side corners down towards the midline.

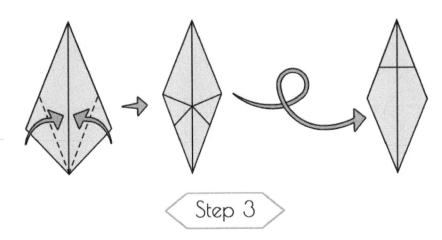

Step 3

Fold both side corners up towards the midline, then turn the figure over.
This is the body of the carrot.

Carrot

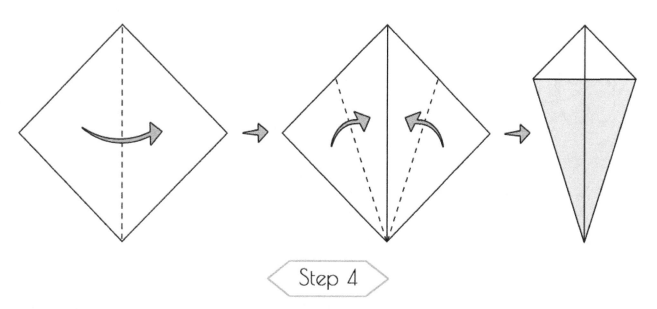

Step 4

Take a sheet smaller than the previous one. Fold vertically along a diagonal and unfold, then bring the bottom of the side corners toward the midline.

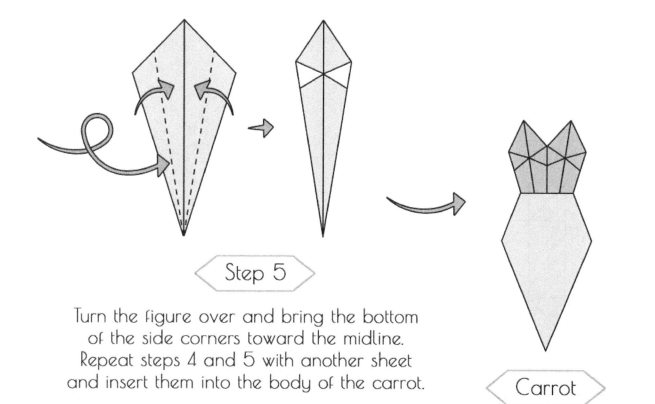

Step 5

Turn the figure over and bring the bottom of the side corners toward the midline. Repeat steps 4 and 5 with another sheet and insert them into the body of the carrot.

Carrot

Box

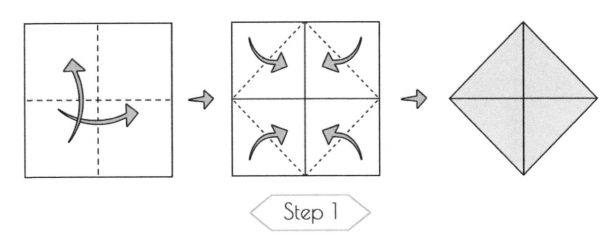

Step 1

Fold in half lengthwise and crosswise, and unfold. Then fold all corners toward the center of the sheet. Repeat with a slightly larger sheet.

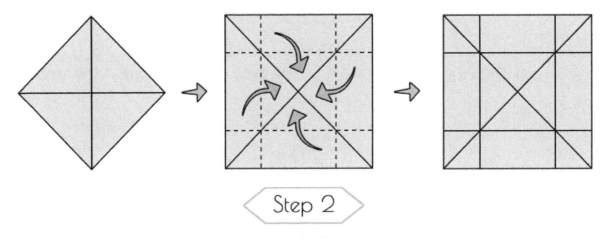

Step 2

Rotate the figure a little to the side. Then fold all the edges forward toward the center of the sheet and unfold. Repeat on the other sheet.

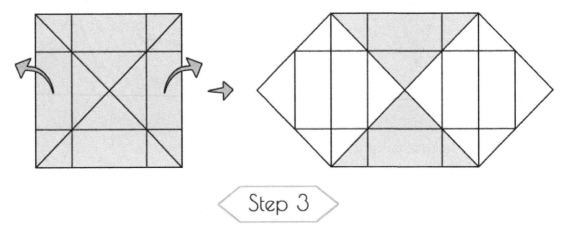

Step 3

Unfold the side corners. Repeat on the other sheet.

Box

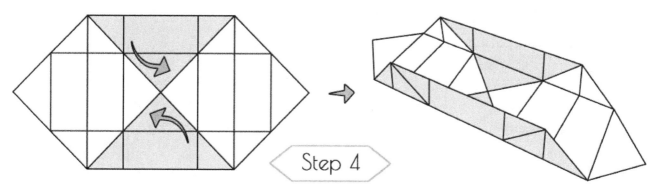

Step 4

Fold the top and bottom edges up so they end up vertical to the center of the figure. Repeat on the other sheet.

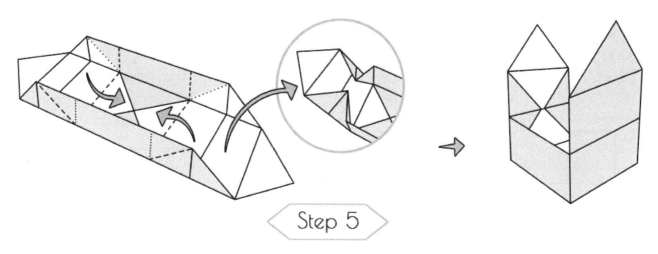

Step 5

Fold both side corners up so they end up vertical as well. As you do this, you will see a flap form between those sections and the ones from step 4: fold them inward with a diagonal valley fold and a vertical mountain fold. Repeat on the other sheet.

Step 6

Fold those sections back down just above the flaps that you folded in, then fold the tips up so that they end parallel to the bottom. Repeat on the other sheet and turn it over to use it as a lid.

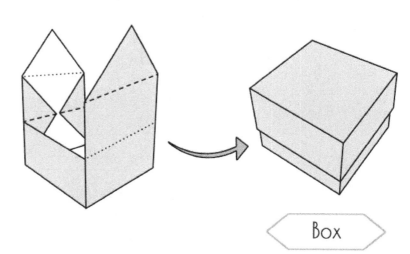

Box

Ninja Star 1

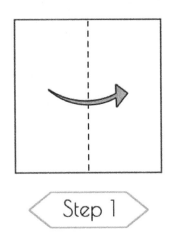

Step 1

Fold one paper sheet in half lengthwise, then unfold. Repeat with another sheet.

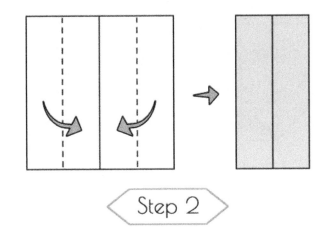

Step 2

Fold each of these halves again in half lengthwise to get two flaps. Repeat with the other sheet.

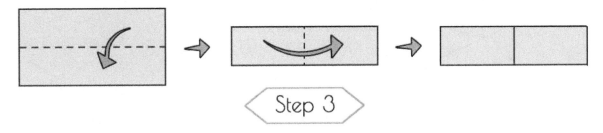

Step 3

Fold both sheets in half lengthwise. Then fold them in half crosswise and unfold.

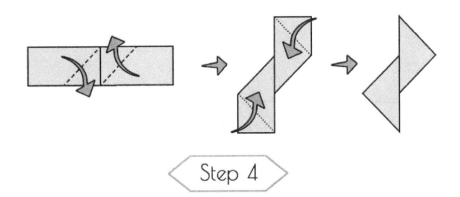

Step 4

Fold the left half of the first sheet down and the right half up. Then fold the top right and bottom left corners back.

Ninja Star I

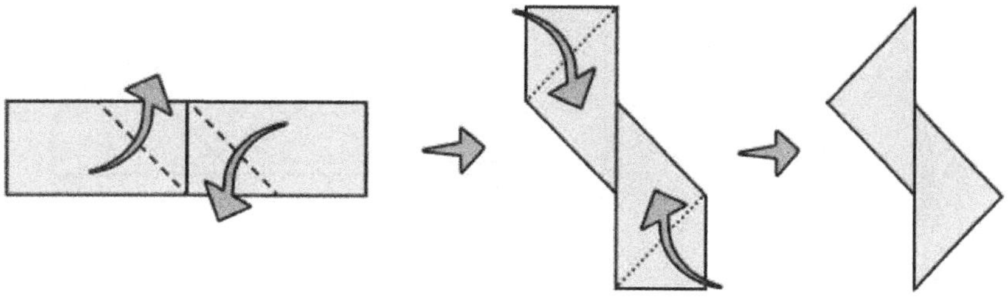

Step 5

Fold the left half of the other sheet up and the right half down. Then fold the top left and bottom right corners back.

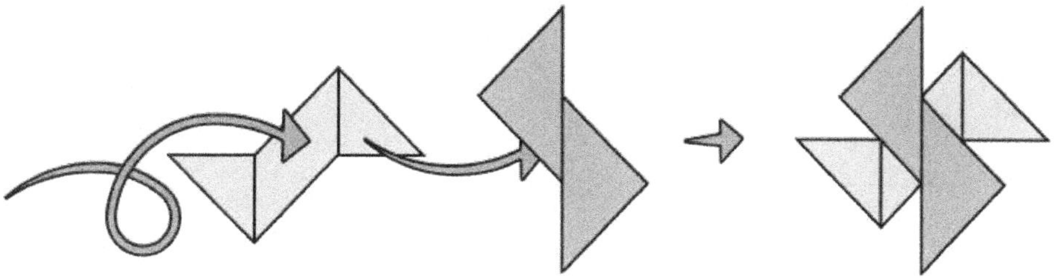

Step 6

Turn one of the figures over and place it on top of the other in an X shape. From now on the two sheets wil be of different shades for clarity.

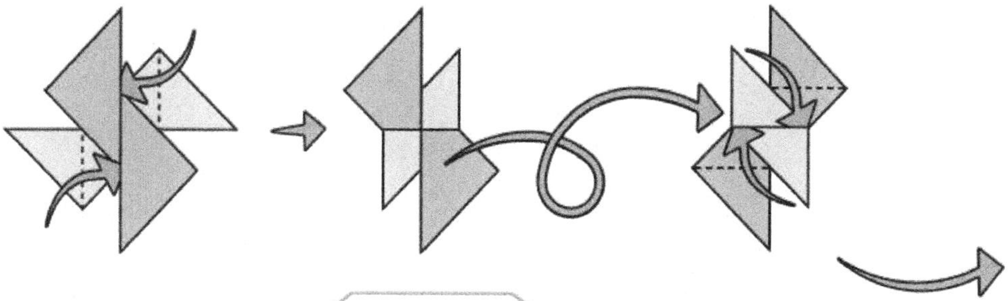

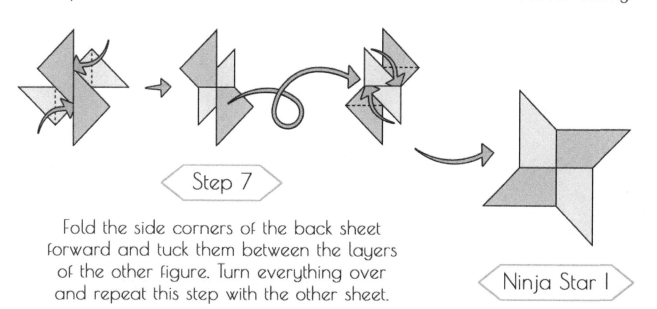

Step 7

Fold the side corners of the back sheet forward and tuck them between the layers of the other figure. Turn everything over and repeat this step with the other sheet.

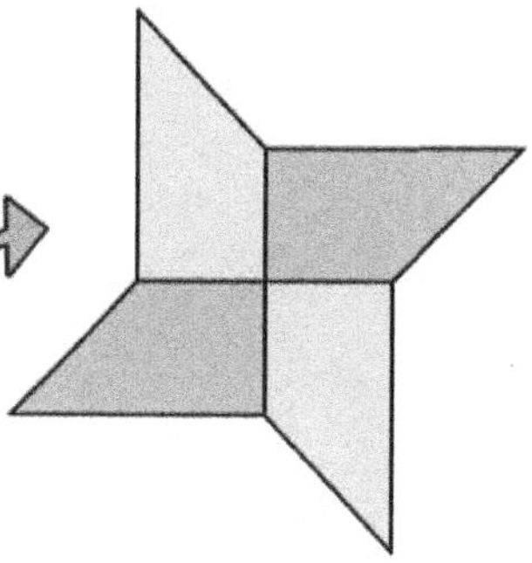

Ninja Star I

Triceratops

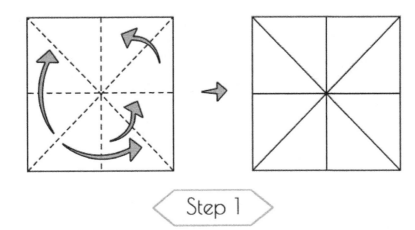

Step 1

Fold in half lengthwise, crosswise, and diagonally, and unfold.

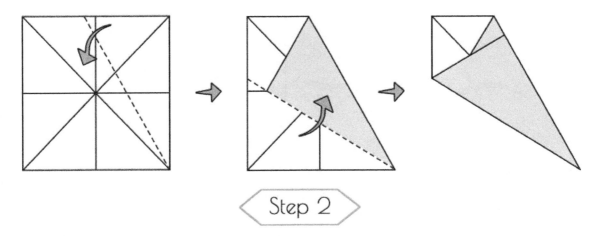

Step 2

Bring the upper right corner to the left side of the horizontal crease.
Then bring the lower left corner to the upper side of the vertical crease

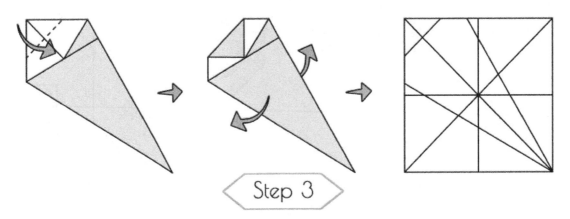

Step 3

Fold the left tip down to the point where the folds from
the previous step meet. Then unfold everything.

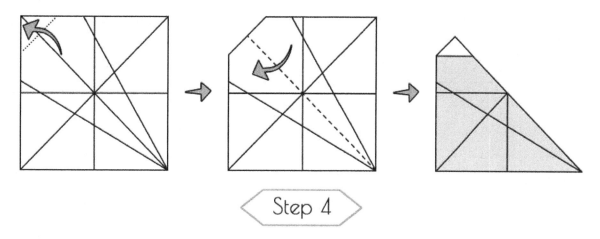

Fold the tip again, this time toward the back along the same crease. Then fold the entire figure diagonally.

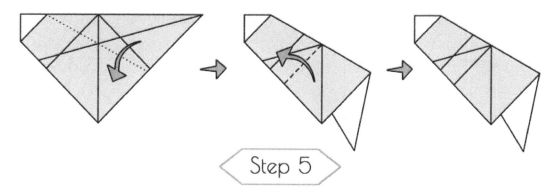

Rotate the figure so the top edge is horizontal, and make an inside reverse fold on the right side of the figure as shown. Then fold so that the lower right corner of the top layer meets the lower left corner, and unfold.

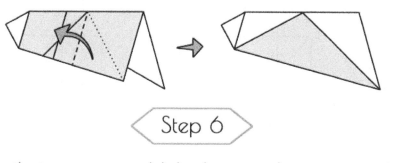

Use that crease to fold the lower right corner of the top layer to the left. You will see that part of the inside reverse fold from the previous step unfolds with it, so flatten until you get a triangular flap.

Triceratops

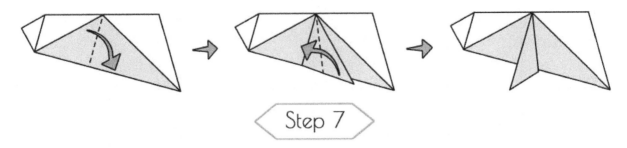

Step 7

Fold the triangular flap back again. Then fold it in half so that its tip sticks out at the bottom edge.

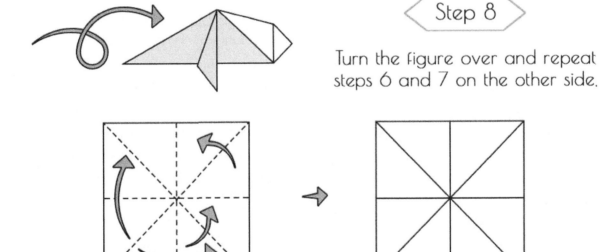

Step 8

Turn the figure over and repeat steps 6 and 7 on the other side.

Step 9

Fold another sheet in half lengthwise, crosswise, and diagonally, and unfold.

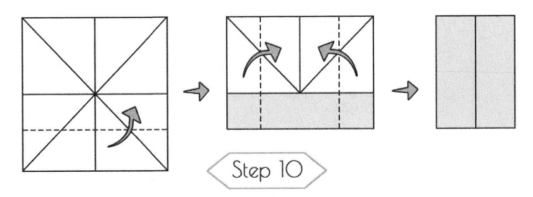

Step 10

Fold the bottom edge up and the side edges inward to the midline.

Triceratops

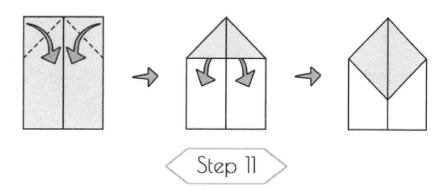

Fold the top corners diagonally inward, then unfold the layer underneath and flatten to get a triangle on each side.

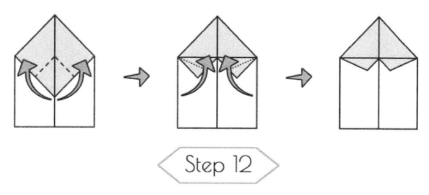

Step 12

Fold diagonally up each side again. Then make an inside reverse fold on each of those side flaps.

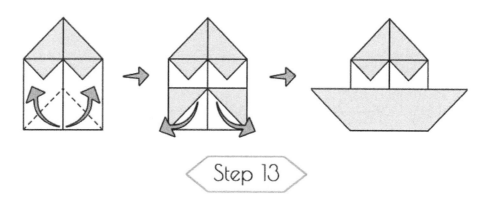

Step 13

Fold the bottom corners diagonally outward. Now carefully separate both sides of the top layer, unfold the layer below and press along the creases you just made (now the layer below should be on top).

93

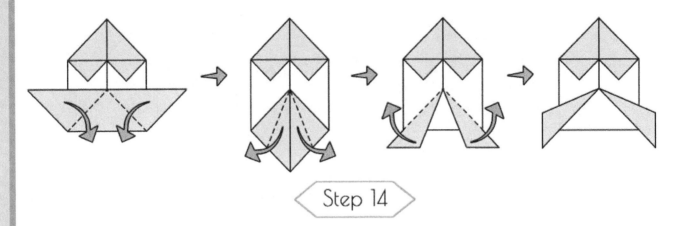

Fold the side corners diagonally down. Then fold them up twice in a row as shown.

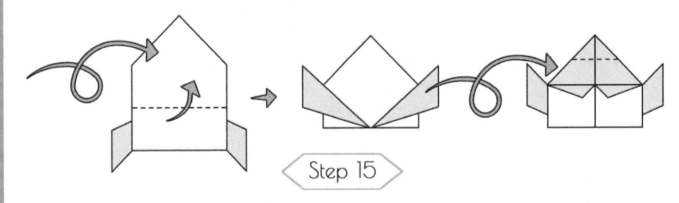

Turn the figure over, then fold it up so that the bottom edge lands right where the triangular shape at the top begins.

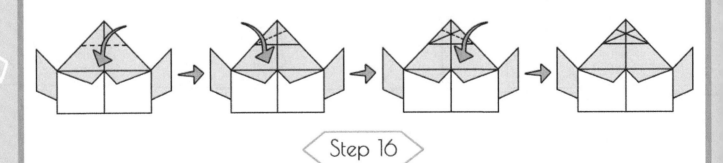

Fold the top tip down in half and unfold. Then fold it to the right, unfold, and to the left, and unfold.

Triceratops

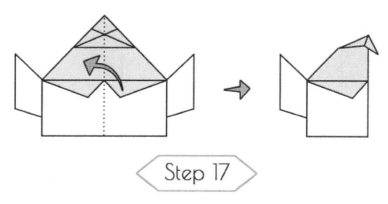

Fold the figure lengthwise in half. At the same time, fold the tip up along the creases from step 16, but only slightly, without pressing it all the way down.

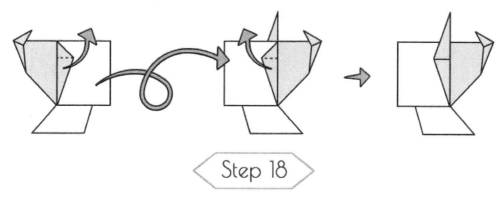

Step 18

Rotate the figure to the side and fold up the triangular flap from step 12. Then turn the figure over and fold the one on the other side up.

Insert the fold on the inside of the head into the flap on the right end of the body to join them!

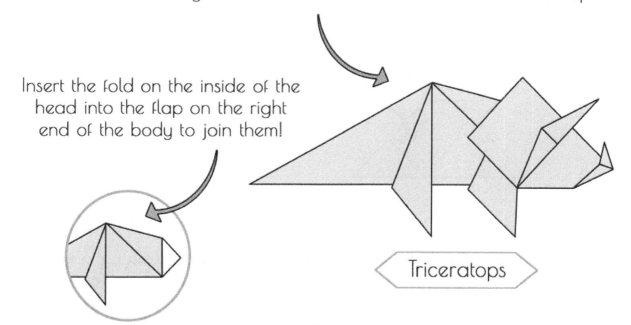

Triceratops

Ninja Star II

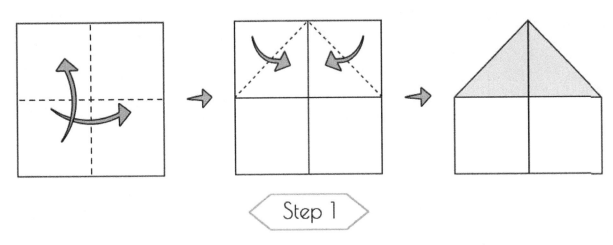

Fold in half lengthwise and crosswise, and unfold. Then fold the top corners forward to the center of the sheet. Repeat this step with 7 more sheets.

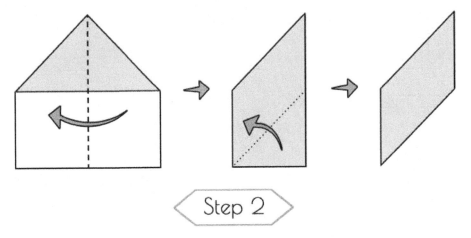

Step 2

Fold in half lengthwise. Then make a diagonal inside reverse fold to tuck the bottom right corner between both layers. Repeat this step with 7 more sheets.

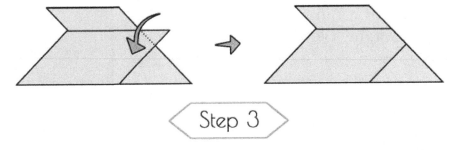

Step 3

Rotate the figure to the left and insert a second figure between the two flaps on the right side so that their bottom edges are aligned. Then fold the tips of the first figure into the flaps of the second so that it stays in place.

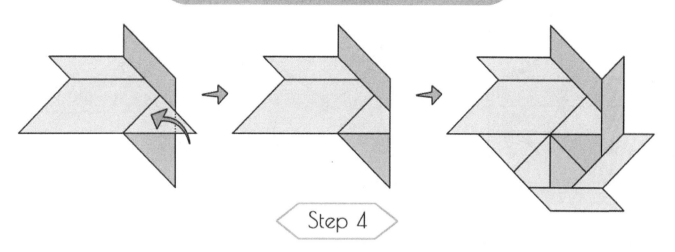

Step 4

Repeat step 3 with a third figure. Keep adding figures until only two are left.

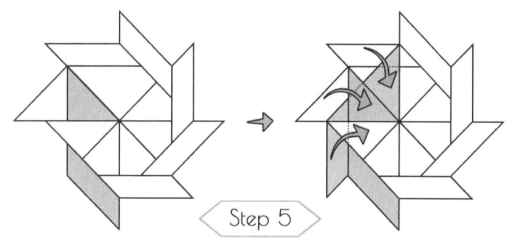

Step 5

Now the tricky part: insert the seventh figure between the flaps of the sixth, but separating its own flaps so that they end over the first figure you placed. Repeat with the eighth figure: insert it between the flaps of the seventh and separate its own so that they end over the first and second figures. Then fold the tips of both figures toward the inside of the corresponding flaps.

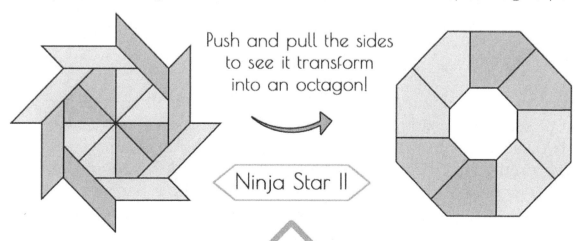

Push and pull the sides
to see it transform
into an octagon!

Ninja Star II

Magic Circle

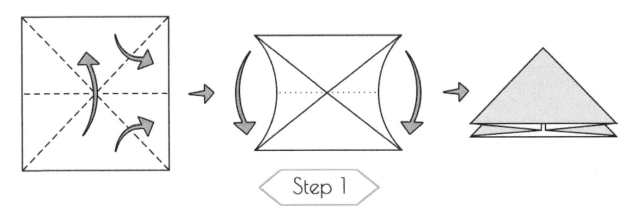

Fold in half crosswise and along the two diagonals, and unfold. Then fold both sides in toward the center and press the edges to make a triangle.

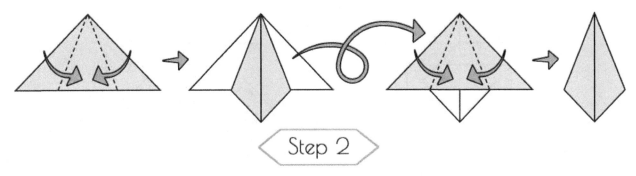

Step 2

Fold the side corners of the top layer toward the midline and press. Turn the figure over and repeat the same step with the back side corners.

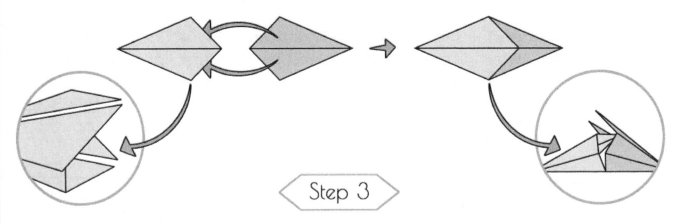

Step 3

Repeat steps 1 and 2 until you have 8 equal figures. Then take two facing each other at the bottom corners. You will see that each corner is made up of two sections with two layers each: insert the tip of each section of the figure on the right between the layers of the tips of the figure on the left. Do this only on one side of the figures, leaving the other side as it was.

Magic Circle

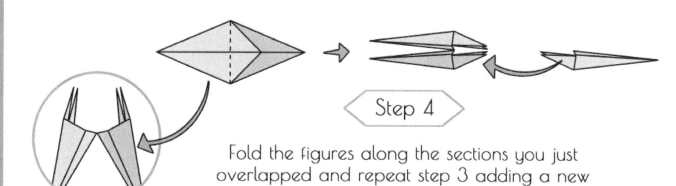

Fold the figures along the sections you just overlapped and repeat step 3 adding a new figure to one of the ends that's still free.

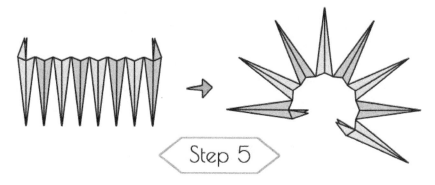

Step 5

Keep adding pieces until they form a row with the ends free. Then form a circle and join the free ends together.

Ready? Flip the circle from the center out to see the magic happen!

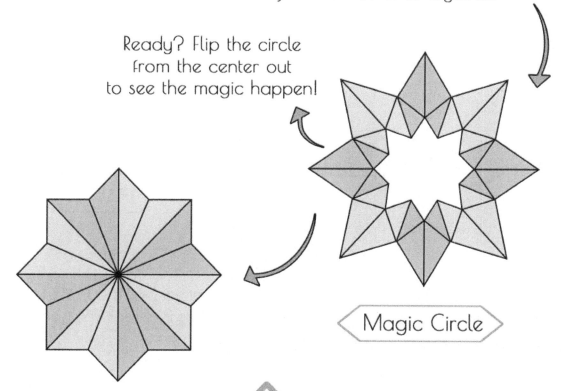

Magic Circle

Water Lily

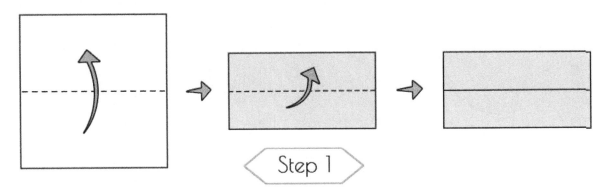

Step 1

Fold in half crosswise. Then fold again crosswise and unfold this part. Repeat this step until you have 16 equal pieces, 8 of them slightly larger than the other 8.

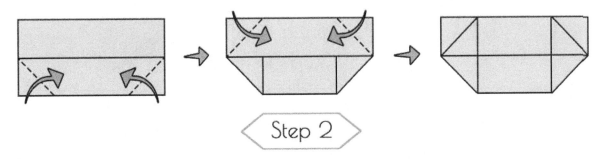

Step 2

Fold the bottom corners diagonally upward. Then fold the top corners, but only from the top layer, diagonally down. Repeat until all 16 figures look the same.

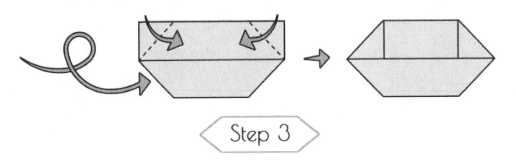

Step 3

Turn the figure over and fold the top corners of the back layer diagonally down. Repeat until all 16 figures look the same.

Water Lily

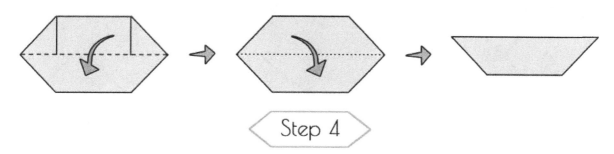

Fold the top half of the front layer forward down. Then fold the top half of the back layer backward down. Repeat until all 16 figures look the same.

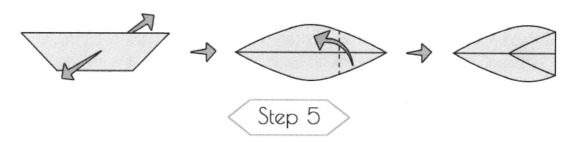

Step 5

Separate both sides of the sheet along the top edge. Then fold one of the side corners inward and press. Repeat for all 16 pieces.

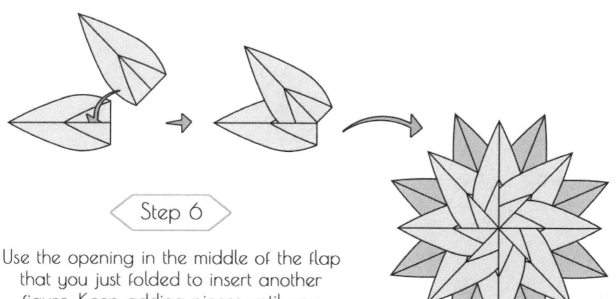

Step 6

Use the opening in the middle of the flap that you just folded to insert another figure. Keep adding pieces until you complete a circle with 8 equal pieces. Then repeat with the 8 pieces that have another size and place the smaller circle on top of the bigger one.

Water Lily

Christmas Tree

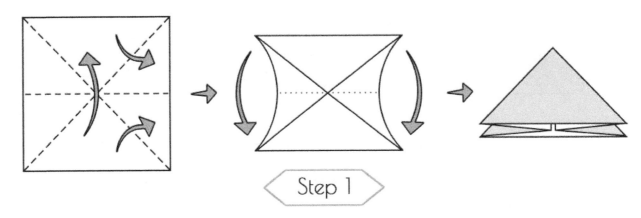

Step 1

Fold in half crosswise and along the two diagonals, and unfold.
Then fold the sides to the center and flatten to get a triangle.
Repeat on three more sheets, each one smaller than the last.

Step 2

Fold the top right side toward the midline and unfold. Then unfold the two
layers of that section following that crease and flatten. Repeat on all sheets.

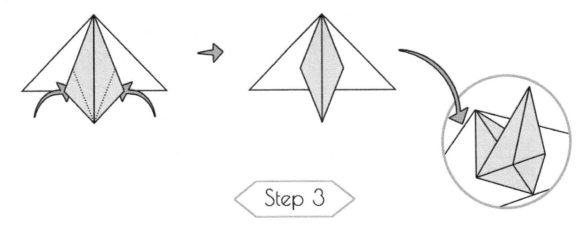

Step 3

Fold the sides in toward the midline, so that the upper edge ends up being
horizontal. Check the 3D view to see how it should look if you fold the
bottom tip up (not part of the process though). Repeat on all sheets.

Christmas Tree

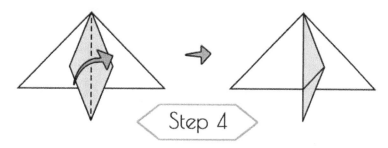

Step 4

Fold that section in half to the right. Repeat on all sheets.

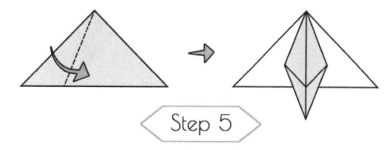

Step 5

Repeat steps 3 through 4 on the top left side. Repeat on all sheets.

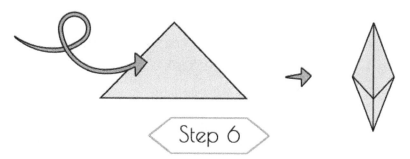

Step 6

Turn the figure over and repeat steps 2 through
4 on the back layer. Repeat on all sheets.

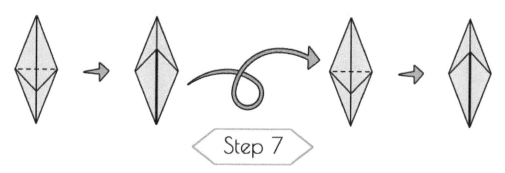

Step 7

Fold up the flap in the center. Then turn the figure over and do
the same on the other side. Note that there is an opening between
the lower sections on both sides of the figure. Repeat on all sheets.

Christmas Tree

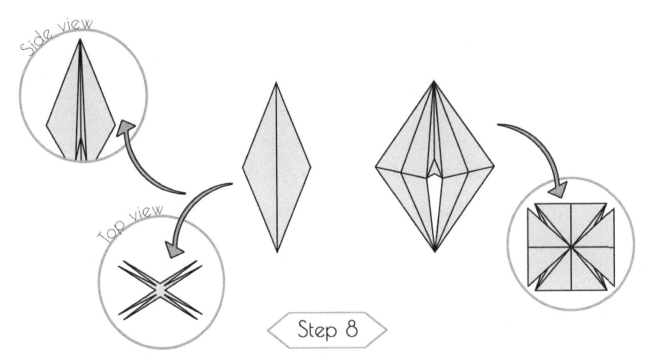

Step 8

At this point the figure has four sides with a flap in the center and four blank sides. Hold the figure so that the flap sides are folded and the blank sides are open. Carefully use a skewer or pencil to insert it through the bottom opening of the figure and pop the blank sides out. Repeat on all sheets.

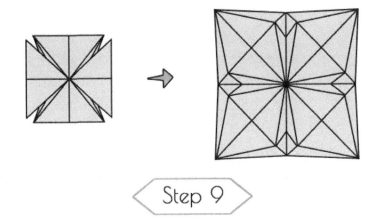

Step 9

Looking at the figure from above, press the center until the figure pops: that top corner will end up pointing in the opposite direction, and the bottom corners will end up pointing up and out. Repeat on all sheets.

Christmas Tree

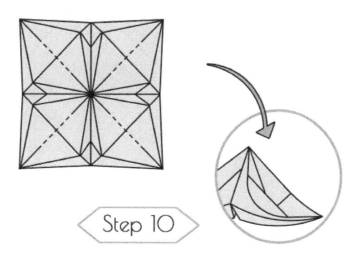

Step 10

Press the middle of the diagonals, so that they form a ridge that sticks out on the opposite side of the figure. Repeat on all the sheets, then flip them over and lay them one on top of the other from largest to smallest.

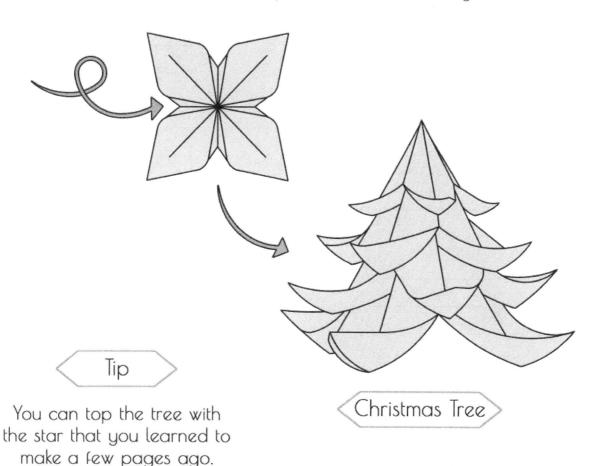

Tip

You can top the tree with the star that you learned to make a few pages ago.

Christmas Tree

Pop-it Triangle

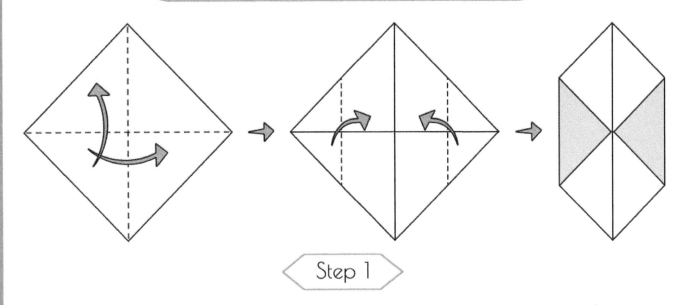

Fold along the diagonals, unfold, and bring the side corners to the midline. Repeat on two more sheets.

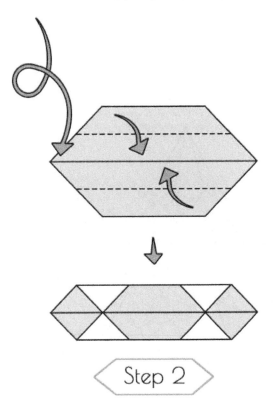

Step 2

Fold the top and bottom edges toward the midline. Repeat on two more sheets.

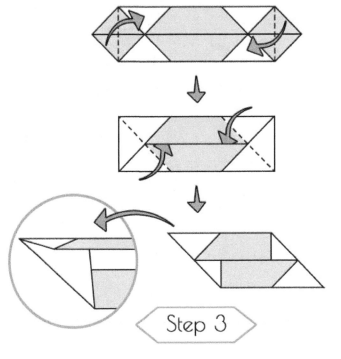

Step 3

Fold the side corners inward. Then fold the lower left and upper right corners diagonally and tuck them under the top layer on the opposite side. Repeat on two more sheets.

106

Pop-it Triangle

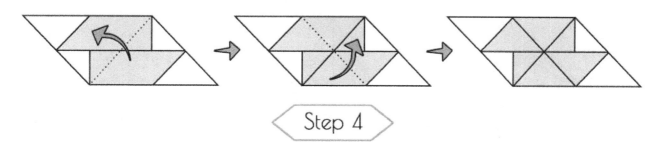

Step 4

Fold the figure diagonally to the left to make a crease and unfold. Then fold to the right to make another crease and unfold. Repeat on the other two sheets.

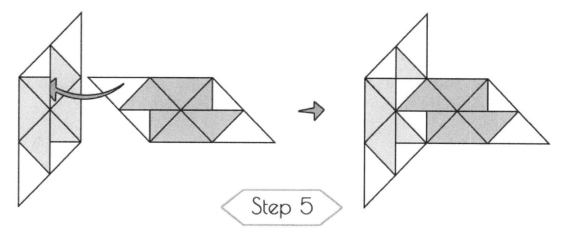

Step 5

Tuck the corner of one figure under the top layer of another as shown, so that they end perpendicular to each other.

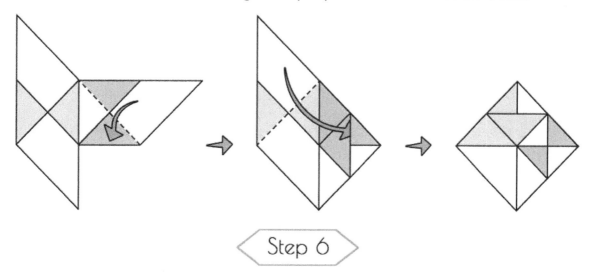

Step 6

Turn everything over and fold the figure on the right diagonally down. Then insert the top corner of the figure on the left just below the tip of the other figure. At the end of this step the entire figure takes a 3D shape.

Pop-it Triangle

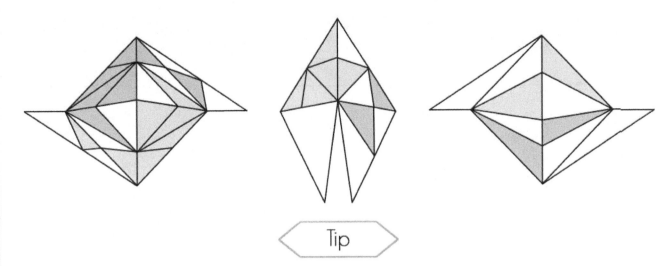

Tip

Before adding the third figure, here's how the layout should look, left to right: from above, from the side, and from below.

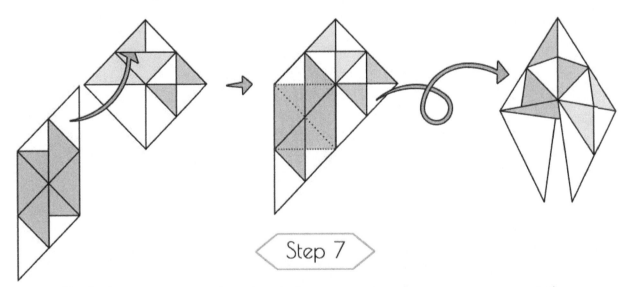

Step 7

Tuck the top tip of the third shape under the top corner of the part that is already assembled. Then fold it so that you can tuck the lower tip under the top corner but on the back side.

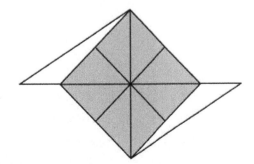

Tip

This is how the figure should look if you turn it over and look at it from below.

Pop-it Triangle

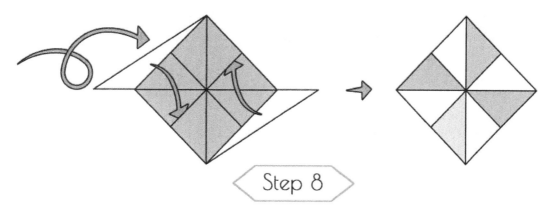

Step 8

Turn the figure over and, looking at its bottom, insert the upper left flap on the left side of the lower corner and the lower right flap on the right side of the upper corner.

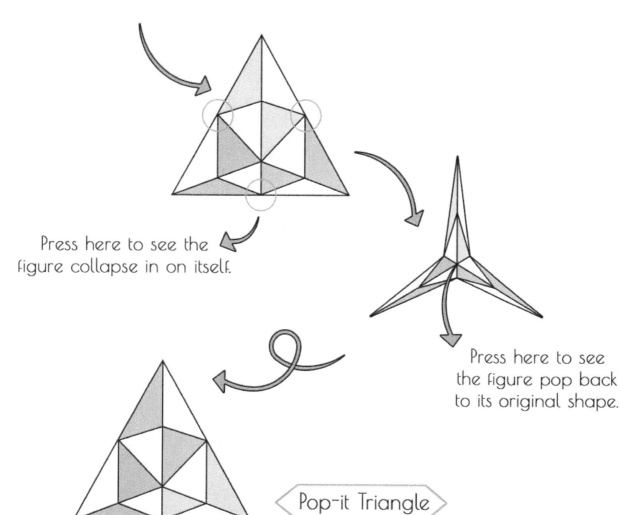

Press here to see the figure collapse in on itself.

Press here to see the figure pop back to its original shape.

Pop-it Triangle

109

Origami
for kids 2

Tall Hat

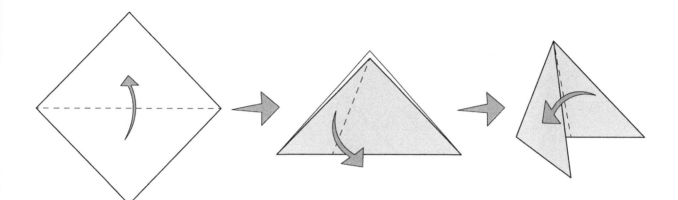

Step 1

Fold the sheet diagonally
up in half.

Step 2

Fold the left corner
in as shown.

Step 3

Fold the right corner
over the left one.

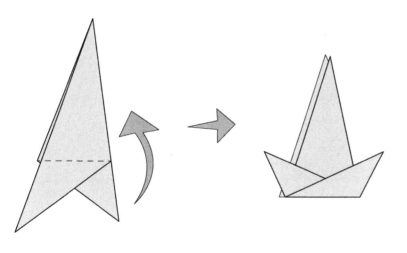

Step 4

Fold both bottom tips up as shown,
then flatten the figure. Slightly separate
both sides of the figure to finish the hat.

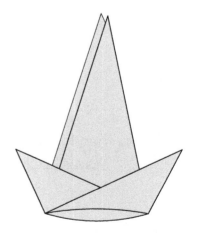

Tall Hat

Cup

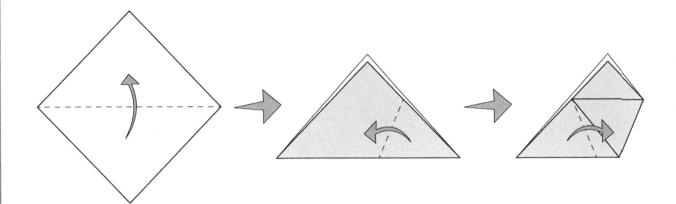

Step 1

Fold the sheet diagonally
up in half.

Step 2

Fold the right corner
in as shown.

Step 3

Fold the right corner
over the left one.

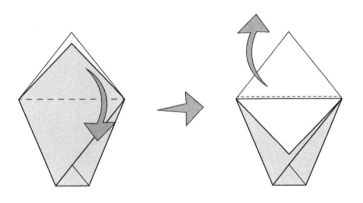

Step 4

Fold the top corner of the top layer forward
down, then fold the top corner of the bottom
layer back down and flatten.

Cup

Envelope

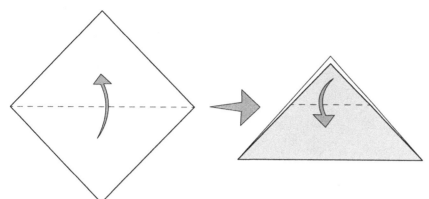

Step 1

Fold the sheet diagonally up in half, then fold the top corner of the top layer forward down as shown.

Step 2

Fold the top corner of the bottom layer forward down over the flap you just made, making sure to leave a small gap between the two folds.

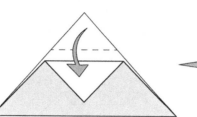

Step 3

Fold the right corner in as shown

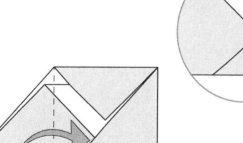

Step 4

Fold the left corner in and tuck it between both layers of the right corner you just folded.

Envelope

113

Ship

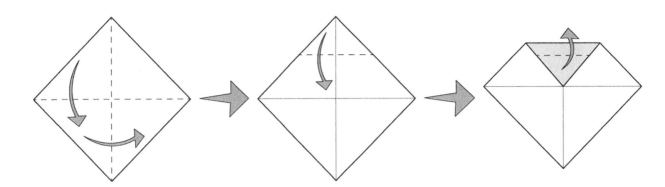

Step 1

Fold the sheet along both diagonals and unfold it.

Step 2

Fold the top corner down to the center of the sheet.

Step 3

Fold the corner back up, leaving a small gap between the two folds.

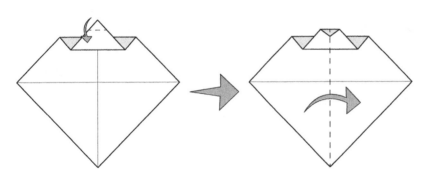

Step 4

Fold the tip down again as shown, then fold the entire figure in half.

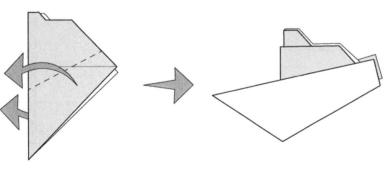

Step 5

Make a crease by folding the figure to both sides along the line shown, then use it to make an outside reverse fold and flatten.

Ship

House

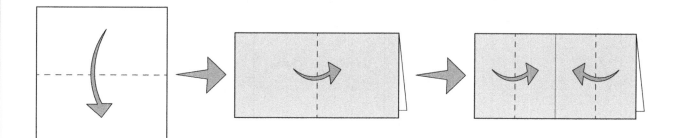

Step 1

Fold the sheet crosswise down in half.

Step 2

Fold in half again as shown and unfold.

Step 3

Bring both side edges to the vertical midline you just made.

Step 4

On the left side, separate both layers of paper until they are completely flat as shown, to do this keep the bottom layer right where it is while you slowly open and flatten the top layer.

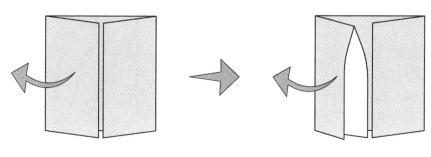

Step 5

Repeat the previous step for the right side.

House

Dress

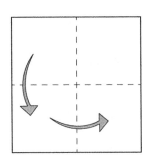 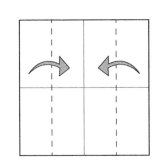 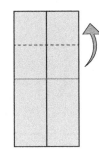

Step 1

Fold the paper sheet in half lengthwise and crosswise. Then unfold it.

Step 2

Bring both side edges to the vertical midline you just made.

Step 3

Fold the top half back in half again as shown.

Step 4

Fold the right side at an angle so that its corner ends past the vertical midline as shown. Then bring the top layer of that corner back again and flatten the figure until you get the drawing below.

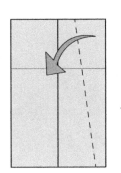 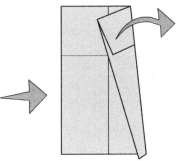

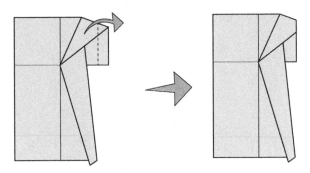

Step 5

Fold the flap you just made vertically back. Then repeat these last two steps for the left side of the figure.

Dress

Chick

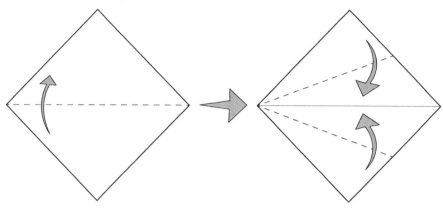

Fold the sheet
diagonally up in half
and unfold. Then bring
the top and bottom
corners to that horizontal
midline as shown.

Step 2

Bring the left corner
in to the edge of the
folds from the previous
step. Then do the same
with the right corner.

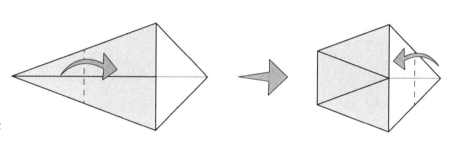

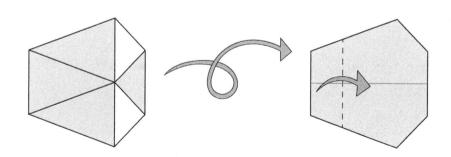

Step 3

Flip the figure over and
fold the left edge
in as shown.

Chick

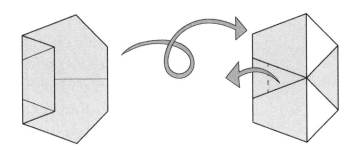

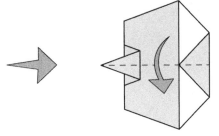

Step 4

Flip the figure over again and fold the tip of the top layer out.

Step 5

Fold the figure down in half.

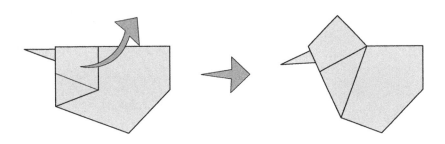

Step 6

Carefully grab the flaps on either side of the figure's left side and gently pull them up until their bottom corners meet the top edge of the figure as shown, then flatten.

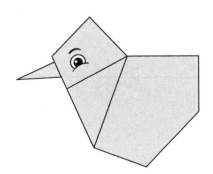

Chick

118

Cupcake

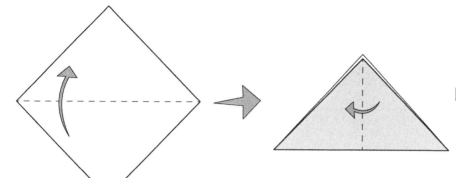

Step 1

Fold the sheet diagonally up in half, then fold it in half again as shown.

Step 2

Fold the tip of the top layer down and then back up, leaving a small gap between the two folds.

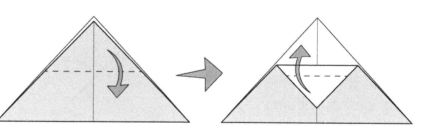

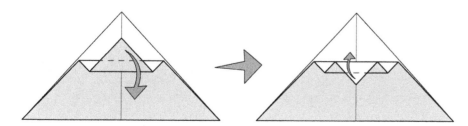

Step 3

Fold the same tip down and then back up again.

119

Cupcake

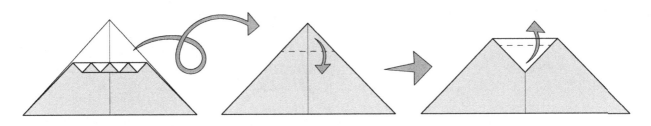

Flip the figure over.

Fold the tip of this layer down and then back up, leaving a small gap between the two folds.

Flip the figure over again, then fold the tip of the bottom layer down over the top layer as shown.

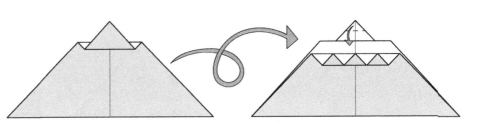

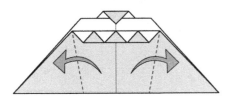

Fold both side corners back as shown and flatten the figure.

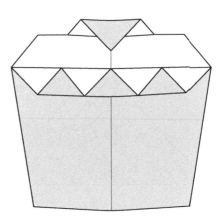

Cupcake

Cicada

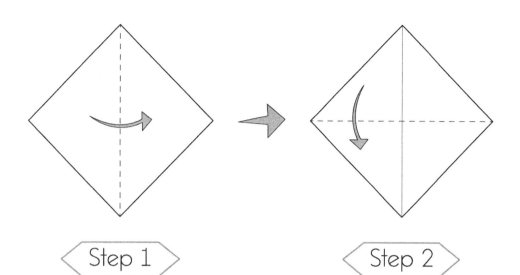

Step 1

Fold the sheet along one of its diagonals and unfold.

Step 2

Now fold the sheet down in half along the other diagonal.

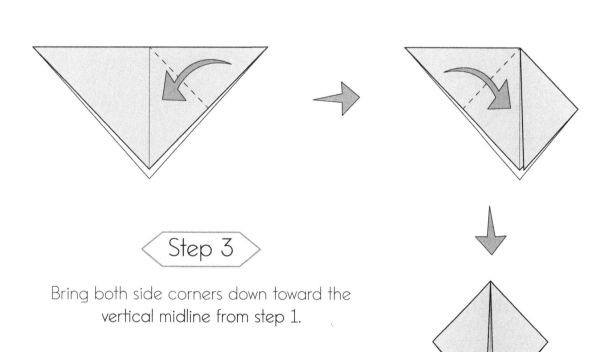

Step 3

Bring both side corners down toward the vertical midline from step 1.

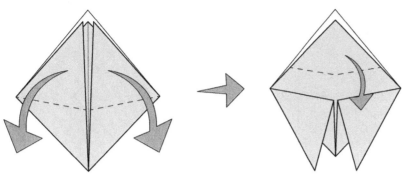

Turn the figure upside down
and fold the flaps from the
previous step down, then
fold the tip of the next
layer of paper down as shown.

Step 5

Fold the last layer of paper
down as well.

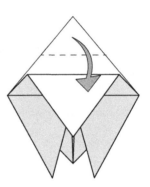

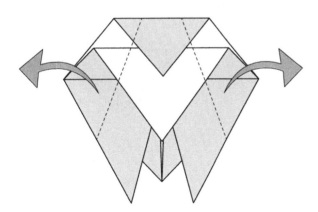

Step 6

Fold both side corners back
at an angle as shown.

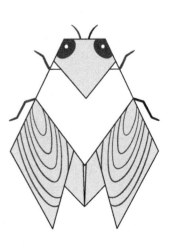

Cicada

Bee

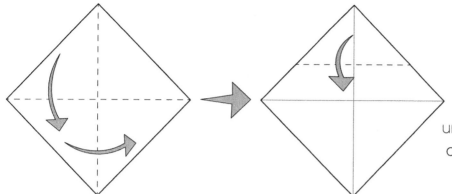

Step 1

Fold the sheet along both diagonals and unfold, then bring the top corner down a little past the horizontal midline.

Step 2

Flip the figure over and bring both side corners down toward the vertical midline.

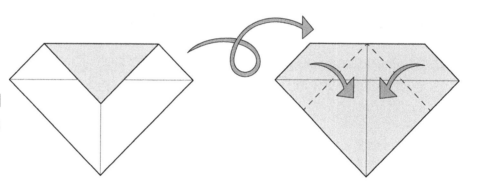

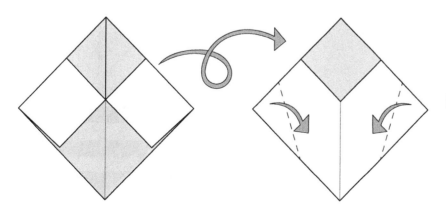

Step 3

Flip the figure over again. Fold and then unfold the side corners as shown to make creases.

123

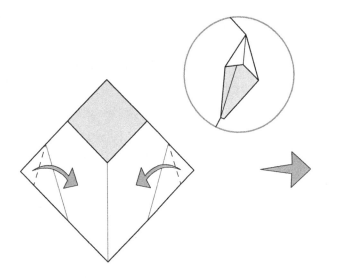

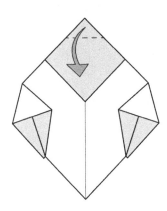

Step 4

Use the creases you just made to separate both layers of paper and fold the top layer forward in. Then flatten the figure and fold the tip down as shown.

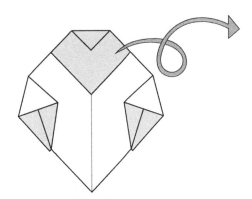

Step 5

Flip the figure over.

Bee

Samurai Helmet

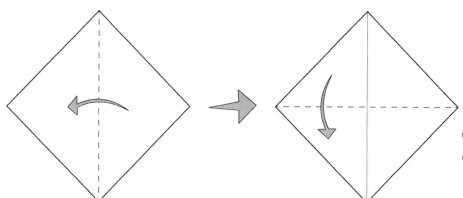

Fold the sheet along its vertical diagonal and unfold, then fold it down in half along the other diagonal.

Step 2

Bring both side corners down toward the vertical midline you just made, then fold them halfway back up as shown.

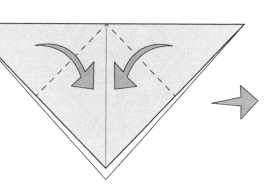

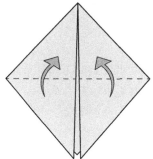

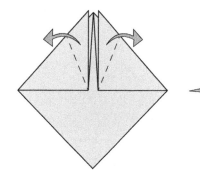

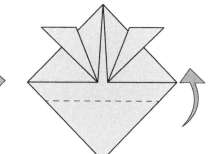

Step 3

Fold the tips of the flaps you just made outward, then fold the bottom corner up as shown.

Samurai Helmet

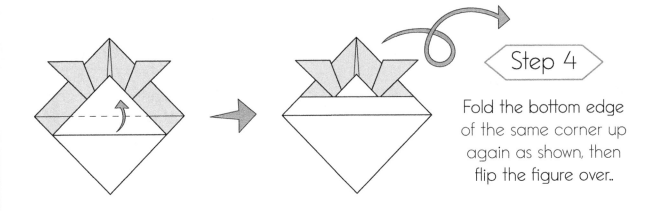

Step 4

Fold the bottom edge of the same corner up again as shown, then flip the figure over..

Step 5

Fold the bottom corner up twice in a row, just like you did on the other side.

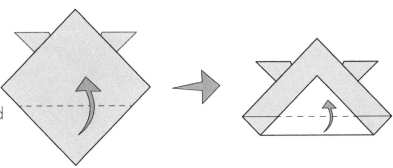

Step 6

Flip the figure over.

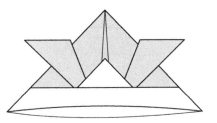

Samurai Helmet

Dracula

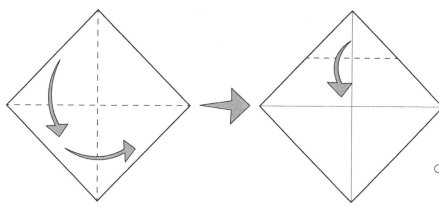

Fold the sheet along both diagonals and unfold, then bring the top corner down to the center of the sheet, where the two creases meet.

Step 2

Fold both side corners in at an angle as shown, then flip the figure over.

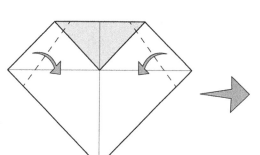 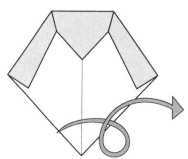

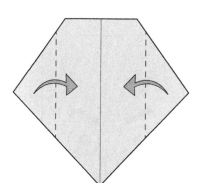 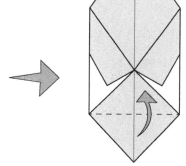

Step 3

Bring both side corners in toward the vertical midline, then bring the bottom corner up to meet them.

Dracula

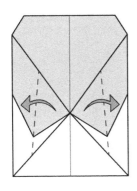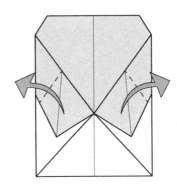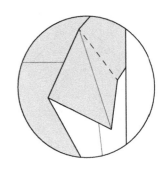

Step 4

Fold both corners back out as shown, then unfold them to make two creases.

Step 5

Use those creases you just made to open the top layer and fold it out as shown to make Dracula's ears.

Step 6

Fold both bottom corners up along the bottom edge of the ears as shown.

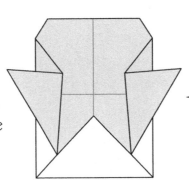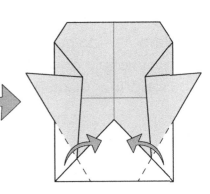

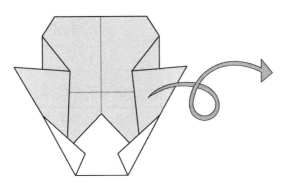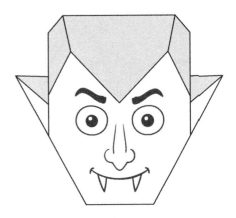

Step 7

Flip the figure over.

Dracula

Mushroom

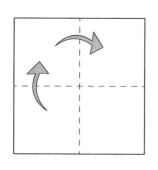 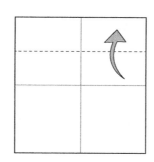 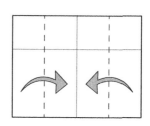

Step 1

Fold the paper sheet in half lengthwise and crosswise. Then unfold it.

Step 2

Fold the top edge backward to the horizontal midline.

Step 3

Fold both side edges in toward the vertical midline.

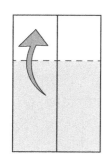 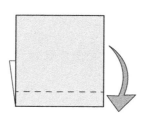 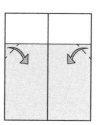

Step 4

Fold the bottom of the figure up along he horizontal midline from Step 1.

Step 5

Now fold the same section back down, leaving a small gap between the two folds.

Step 6

Fold the corners of the top layer down as shown, then unfold them.

Mushroom

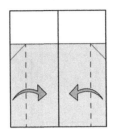 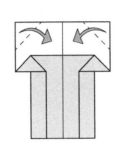

Use the creases you just made to fold the sides of the top layer in as shown. As you fold in the sides, flatten the top until you get a triangle on each side. Then fold the top corners down.

Step 8

Fold the bottom corners up.

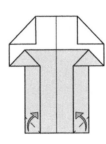 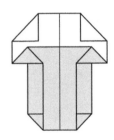

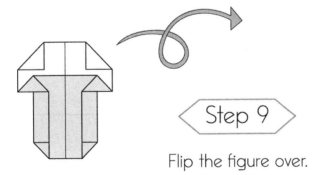

Step 9

Flip the figure over.

Mushroom

130

Lantern

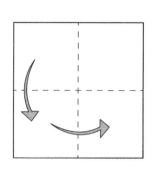 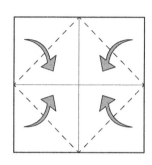 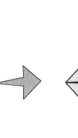 

Step 1

Fold the paper sheet in half lengthwise and crosswise. Then unfold it.

Step 2

Bring all corners to the center of the sheet where the two creases from previous step meet.

Step 3

Flip the figure over.

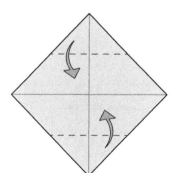 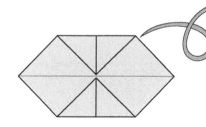 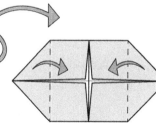

Step 4

Bring the top and bottom edges to the center of the figure as well, then flip the figure over again.

Step 5

Now fold the side corners in to the center of the figure.

Lantern

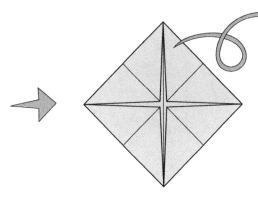

Step 6

Repeat Step 2, that is, bring all corners to the center of the figure, then flip the figure over.

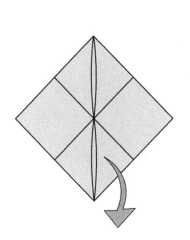

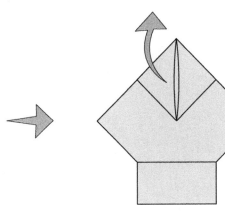

Step 7

You will see that the bottom corner is made up of two flaps, open them carefully while pulling them down and flatten to get a rectangle. Repeat the process for the top corner.

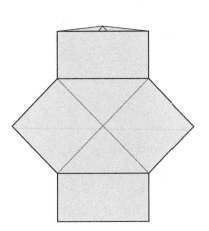

Lantern

Strawberry

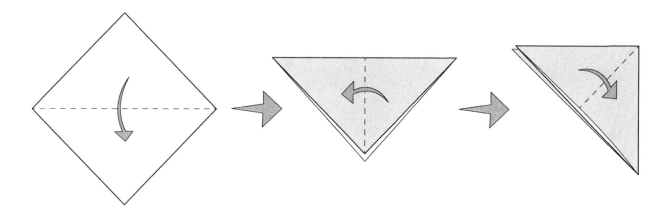

Step 1
Fold the sheet diagonally down in half.

Step 2
Fold the figure in half.

Step 3
Fold the top layer diagonally down and unfold it to make a crease.

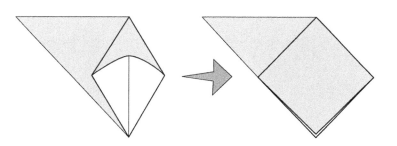

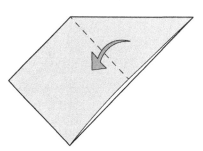

Step 4
Pull this top layer to the right along the crease you just made and flatten as shown.

Step 5
Flip the figure over and repeat steps 3 and 4.

Strawberry

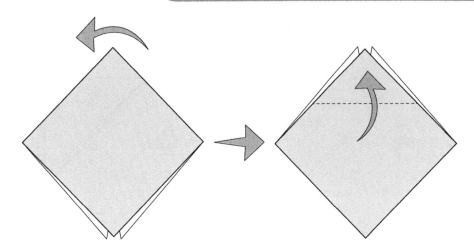

Turn the figure upside down and fold the tip of the top layer backward as shown.

Step 7

Now fold the tips of the layer just below forward over the top layer, then fold the side corners backward as shown.

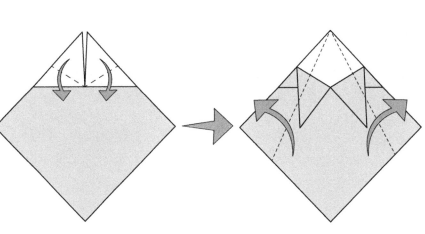

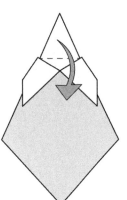

Step 8

Fold the top corner down over the top layer.

Strawberry

134

Jack-O'-Lantern

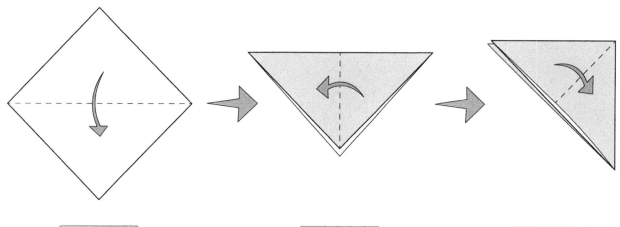

Step 1

Fold the sheet diagonally down in half.

Step 2

Fold the figure in half.

Step 3

Fold the top layer diagonally down and unfold to make a crease.

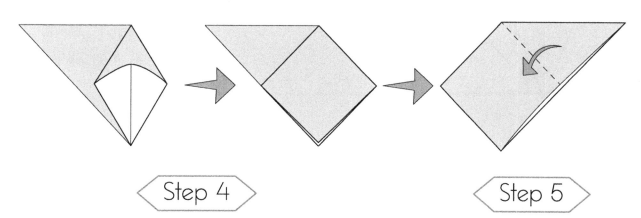

Step 4

Pull this top layer to the right along the crease you just made and flatten as shown.

Step 5

Flip the figure over and repeat steps 3 and 4.

Jack-O'-Lantern

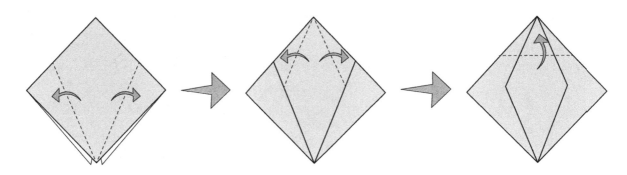

Step 6

Fold the bottom of the side corners of the top layer backward.

Step 7

Now fold the top of the side corners of the same layer backward as well.

Step 8

Fold the upper corner of the figure back.

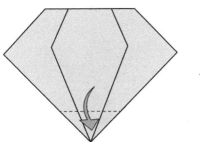

Step 9

Repeat the previous step for the bottom corner.

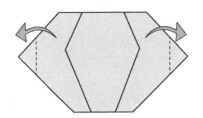

Step 10

Do the same for the side corners.

Jack-O'-Lantern

Sunglasses

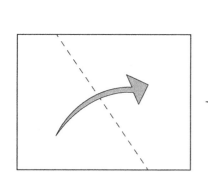

Take an A4 sheet and bring the bottom left corner up until it meets the top right corner and flatten it.

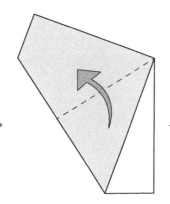

Step 2

Fold the figure up in half as shown.

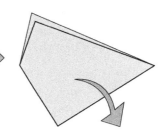

Step 3

Unfold everything you've done so far.

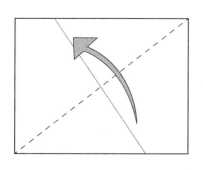

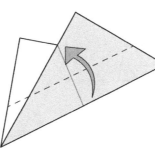

Step 4

Now fold the bottom right corner up until the bottom edge of the sheet meets the crease from Step 1. Then fold the new bottom edge up to the point where the two layers of paper form a V shape as shown.

Sunglasses

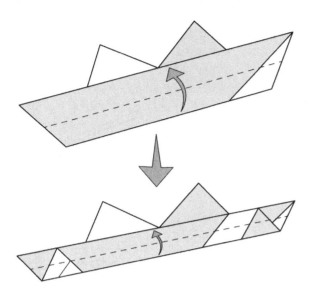

Step 5

Fold the bottom edge back
up twice in a row.

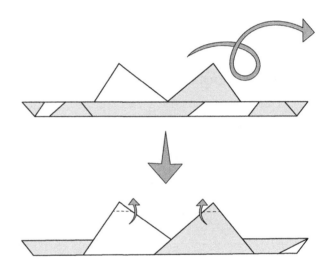

Step 6

Flip the figure over and fold the
tips of the V-shape back.

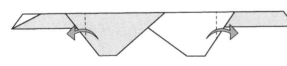

Step 7

Rotate the figure as shown
and fold both sides halfway back.

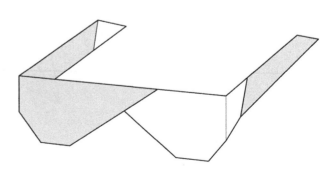

Sunglasses

Ring

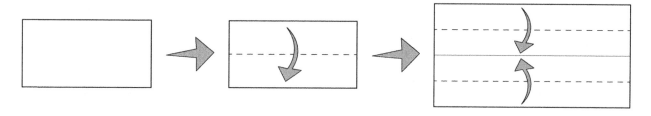

Take a square sheet and cut in half, then fold one of the pieces in half and unfold it.

Step 2

Bring the top and bottom edges to the crease you just made.

Step 3

Fold the figure in half to the left.

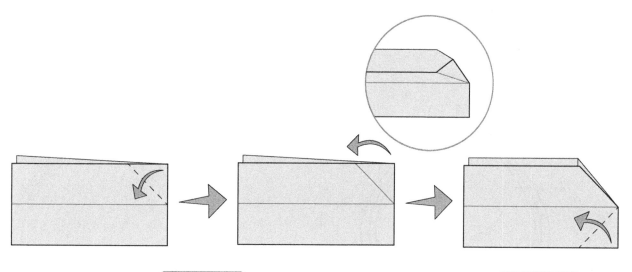

Step 4

Fold the top right corner diagonally down and unfold it to make a crease. Then use that crease to make an inside reverse fold as shown.

Step 5

Repeat the previous step for the bottom right corner.

139

Ring

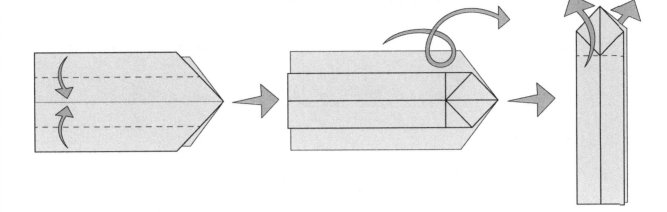

Step 6

Bring the top and bottom edges of the top layer to the midline, flip the figure over, and repeat on the other side. Now rotate the figure and fold both 'arms' halfway up as shown.

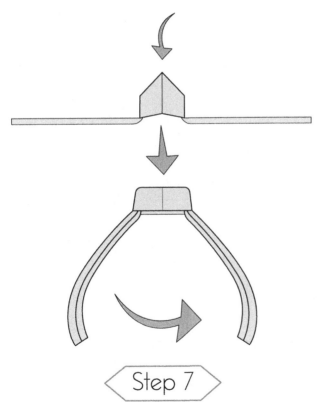

Step 7

Push the center of the figure to flatten it, then curve the 'arms' until you can fit the end of one inside the other to lock them in place.

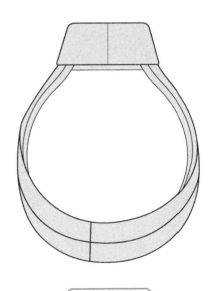

Ring

Big House

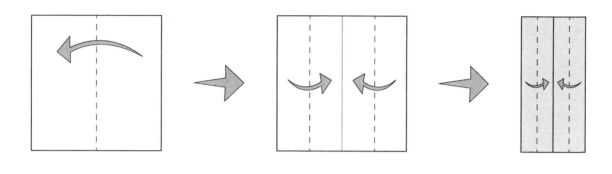

Step 1

Fold the paper sheet lengthwise and unfold it.

Step 2

Bring both side edges in toward the vertical midline you just made, then fold them again.

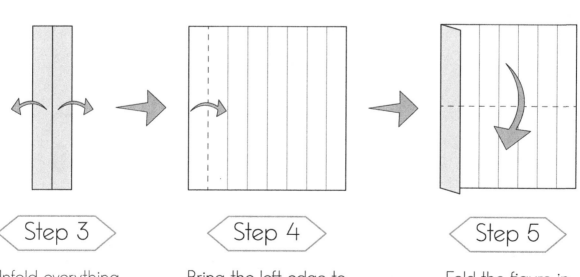

Step 3

Unfold everything.

Step 4

Bring the left edge to the second vertical crease as shown.

Step 5

Fold the figure in half crosswise.

Big House

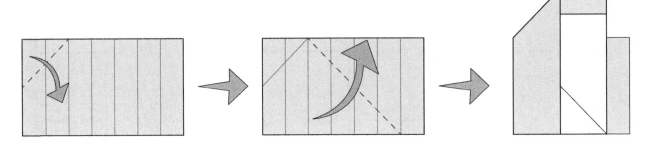

Step 6

Fold the upper left corner diagonally down to make a crease and unfold it.

Step 7

Bring the top layer of the figure along the diagonal line shown, using the crease from the previous step to flatten the figure.

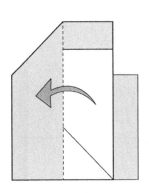 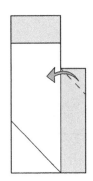

Step 9

Fold the top layer on the right side in. While separating both layers of paper on that side, flatten its top until it forms a triangle.

Step 8

Fold the left side of the figure backward as shown.

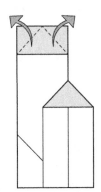

Step 10

Fold the corners on top backwards to form a triangle.

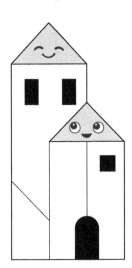

Big House

Little Bird

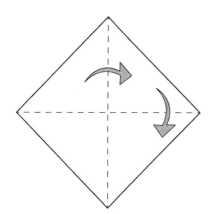

Fold the sheet along both diagonals and unfold.

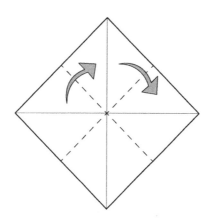

Step 2

Now fold it lengthwise and crosswise, then unfold.

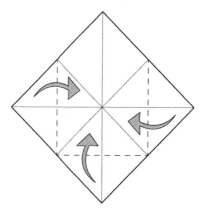

Step 3

Bring the bottom and side corners to the center of the sheet where all the creases meet, leaving the top corner unfolded.

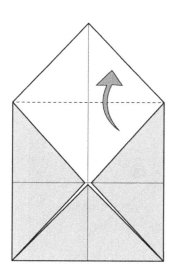

Step 4

Fold the top corner, but backward this time.

Step 5

Now bring all corners to the center of the sheet.

Step 6

Flip over the figure.

Little Bird

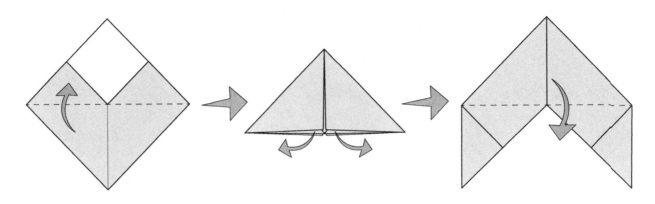

Step 7

Fold the figure up
in half.

Step 8

Pull the corners you will see
in the middle of the figure
right under the top layer.

Step 9

Bring the top corner
back down.

Step 10

Fold the figure forward in
half, while pulling the flap at
the top out so that it ends
up sticking out from the
folded figure.

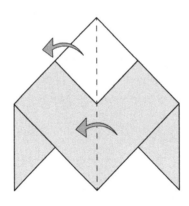

Step 11

In the bottom right corner
you will see a flap on its
middle layer. Pull it out to
make the bird's tail.

Little Bird

Pinwheel

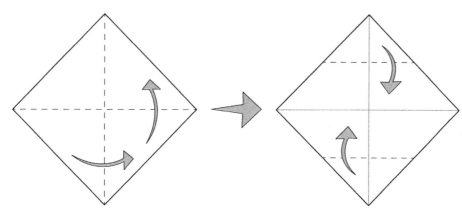

Fold the sheet along both diagonals and unfold. Then bring the top and bottom corners to the center of the sheet where the two creases meet.

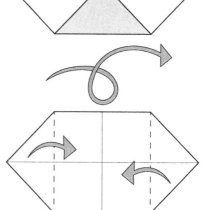

Step 2

Flip the figure over and bring both side corners to the center of the sheet as well.

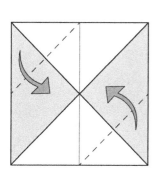 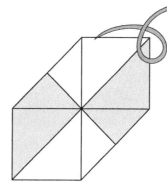

Step 3

Fold the top left and bottom right corners to the center of the sheet, then flip the figure over.

145

Pinwheel

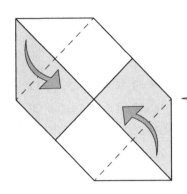 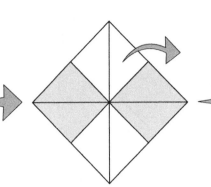 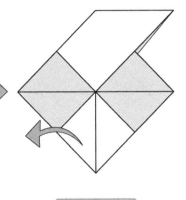

Step 4

Fold the top left and bottom right corners to the center of the sheet again.

Step 5

If you open up the top layer on the right side of the top corner a little bit, you'll see that there's a flap just below it. Pull it out and flatten it to make one of the pinwheel blades.

Step 6

Repeat the previous step on the left side of the bottom corner.

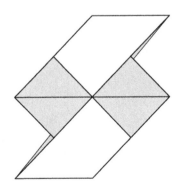

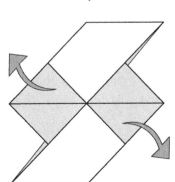

Step 7

Flip the figure over and repeat the previous two steps on that side to make the remaining two blades.

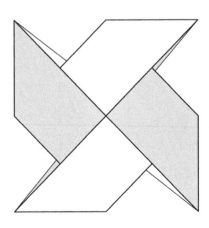

Pin Wheel

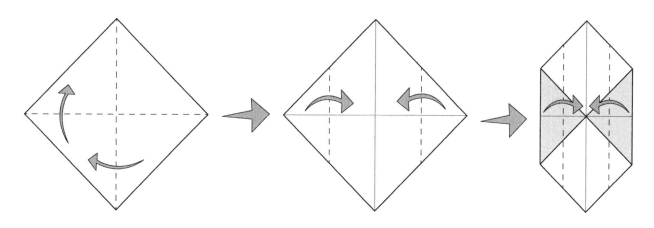

Step 1

Fold the sheet along both diagonals and unfold.

Step 2

Bring both side corners to the center of the sheet, where the two creases meet.

Step 3

Now fold the side edges to the center of the sheet.

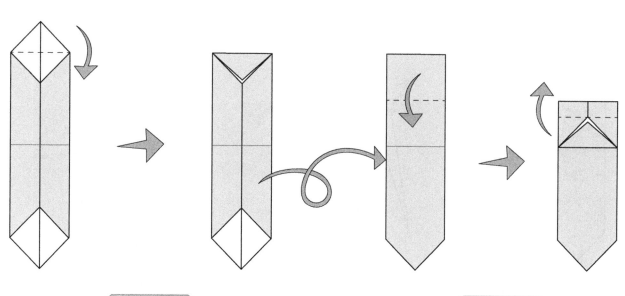

Step 4

Fold the top corner down as shown, then flip the figure over.

Step 5

Fold the top edge down to the midline and then up again, leaving a small gap between the two folds.

Tie

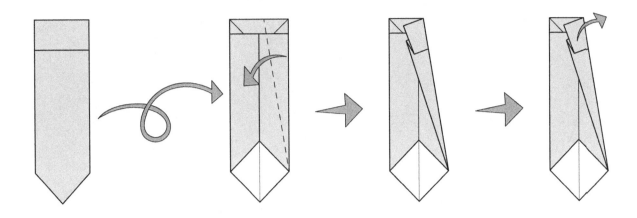

⟨ Step 6 ⟩

Flip the figure
over.

⟨ Step 7 ⟩

Fold the right side diagonally inward as shown.
Then fold its top corner back out and flatten.

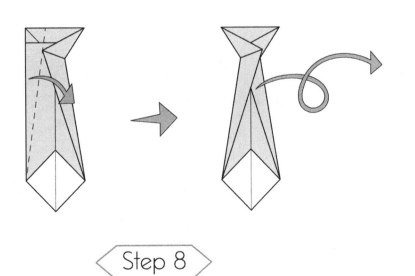

⟨ Step 8 ⟩

Repeat the previous step on the left
side, then flip the figure over.

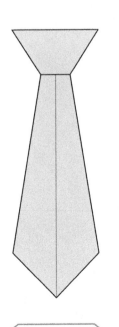

⟨ Tie ⟩

Whale

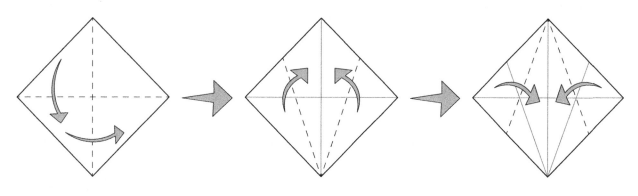

Step 1

Fold the sheet along both diagonals and unfold.

Step 2

Fold the bottom edges of both sides inward to the midline as shown, then unfold it.

Step 3

Now repeat for the top edges of both sides.

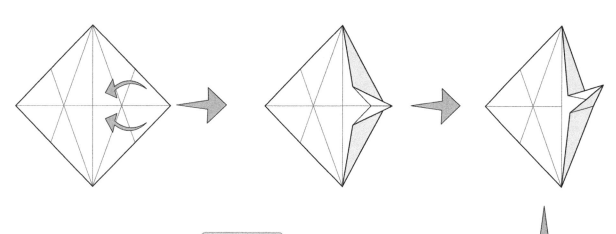

Step 4

You'll see that the creases from Step 2 and 3 form an X. Fold the right corner in along the inner creases of that X. (Longest ones). The shorter creases of the X will form a flap that sticks out, fold it up and flatten. Then flip the figure over.

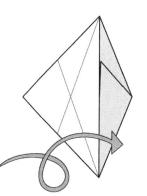

Whale

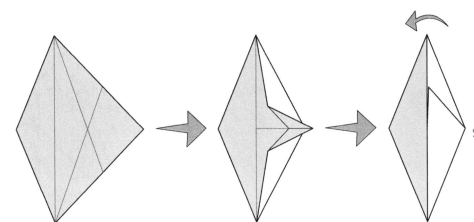

Step 5

Repeat the previous step on this side, then rotate the figure counterclockwise.

Step 6

Fold the flap down, then fold the left corner back as shown.

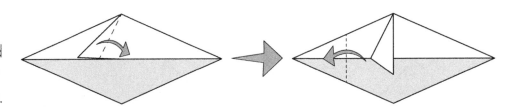

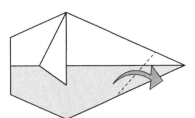

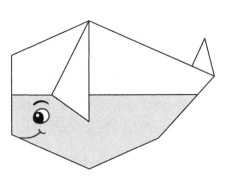

Step 7

Fold the right corner diagonally back as shown to make the tail.

Whale

150

Chair

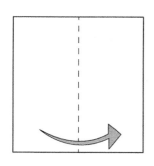

Step 1

Fold the paper in half lengthwise and unfold it.

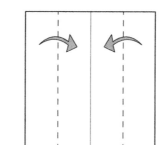

Step 2

Bring both side edges to the vertical midline.

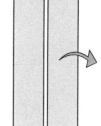

Step 3

Unfold the right edge.

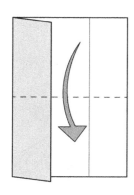

Step 4

Fold the figure down in half.

Step 5

Fold th upper right corner diagonally down and unfold to make a crease.

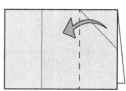

Step 6

Bring the top layer of the right side in along the crease you just made and flatten.

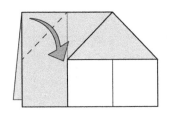 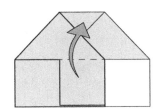 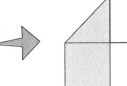 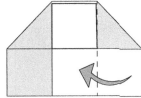

Step 7

Repeat steps 5 and 6 on the left side.

Step 8

After steps 5, 6 and 7 there are two overlapping flaps right in the middle of the figure. Fold them up as shown.

Step 9

Fold the right side in as shown.

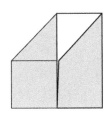 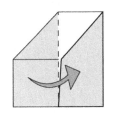

Step 10

Now fold the left side in as shown.

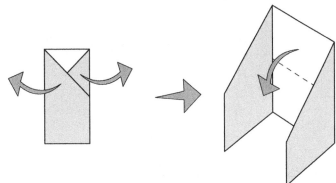 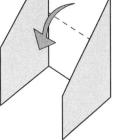 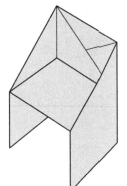

Step 11

Unfold both sides halfway out, then unfold the flaps in the middle on the figure from Step 8 halfway down.

Chair

Table

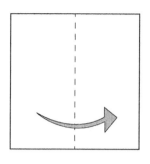 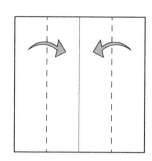 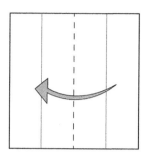

Step 1

Fold the paper in half lengthwise and unfold it.

Step 2

Bring both side edges to the vertical midline and unfold.

Step 3

Fold the sheet in half again.

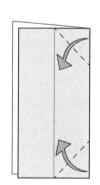 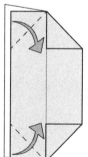 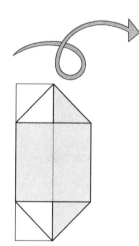

Step 4

Fold the upper right corner diagonally down and the bottom right corner diagonally up as shown.

Step 5

Repeat the previous step on the top layer of the left side.

Step 6

Flip the figure over.

Table

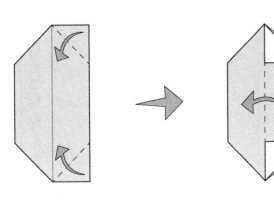

Step 7

Fold the corners of this side in the same way, then fold the top layer of the right side in as shown.

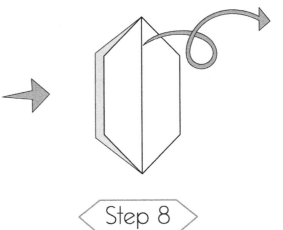

Step 8

Flip the figure over.

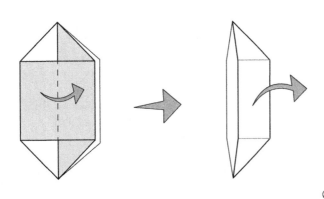

Step 9

Fold the figure in half. Then separate both layers of the figure along the left edge while pushing the top and bottom corners into the space between them. Open the layers and push the corners until all the walls of the figure end up being perpendicular to each other.

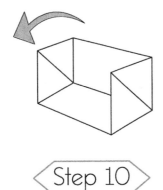

Step 10

Rotate the figure until it matches the illustration.

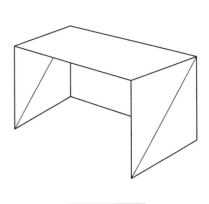

Table

154

Water Bomb

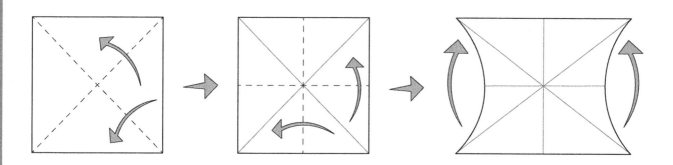

Step 1

Fold the sheet along both diagonals and unfold it.

Step 2

Now fold it lengthwise and crosswise, then unfold.

Step 3

Bring the bottom edge up to meet the top edge, while you fold both sides in to make a triangle.

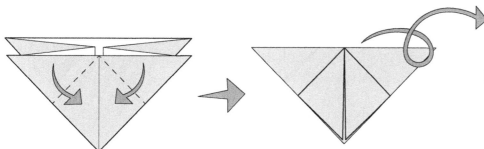

Step 4

Fold the side corners of the top layer diagonally down as shown, then flip the figure over.

Step 5

Fold these side corners diagonally down as well, then fold the sides of the layer in as shown.

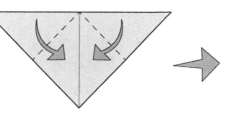

155

Water Bomb

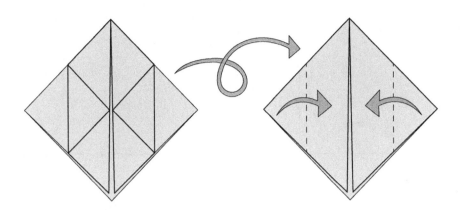

Step 6

Flip the figure over and fold these side corners in as well.

Step 7

Fold the flaps at the bottom up and tuck them under the flaps you just made. Then repeat on the back side.

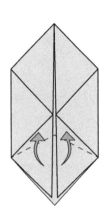 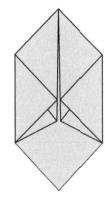

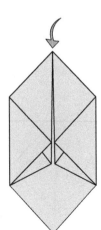

Step 8

Fill the figure with air through the top tip and the water bomb will be ready.

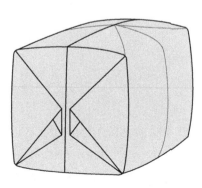

Waterbomb

Nodding Dog

Tip

You will need 2 square
sheets to make this
Nodding Dog.

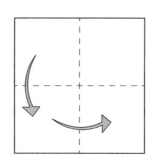

Step 1

Fold one of the paper
sheets in half lengthwise
and crosswise, then unfold.

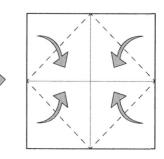

Step 2

Bring all the corners to
the center of the sheet.

Step 3

Rotate the figure, then fold it
diagonally down to make
the triangle that will be
Dog's body.

Step 4

Fold the tip of right corner in to
make the dog's tail. The body is
ready, let's move on to the head.

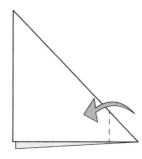

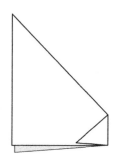

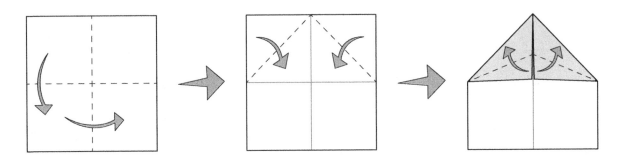

Nodding Dog

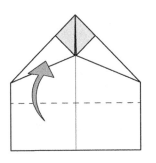

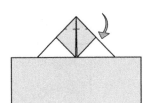

Step 5

Fold the second paper sheet in half lengthwise and crosswise, then unfold.

Step 6

Fold both corners diagonally down.

Step 7

Fold those flaps halfway up, so that their bottom edge meet the sides of the figure as shown.

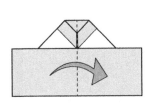

Step 8

Fold the bottom edge up to meet the folds from the previous step as shown, then fold the top tip down.

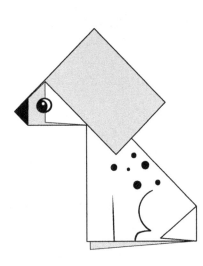

Step 9

Fold the figure backward in half and insert the body between both layers as shown. Gently press the nose and you will see how the head moves up and down.

Nodding Dog

Crown

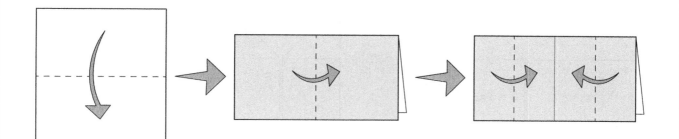

Step 1

Fold the paper
in half crosswise.

Step 2

Fold the figure in half
and unfold it to make
a crease.

Step 3

Fold both side edges
in to the vertical midline
you just made.

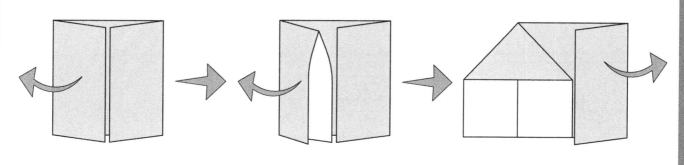

Step 4

Bring the top layer of the left flap back
out and flatten the top to make a triangle.

Step 5

Repeat on the right side.

Crown

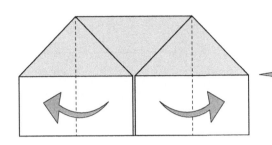

Step 6

Fold both sides backwards as shown.

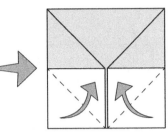

Step 7

Fold both bottom corners of the top layer diagonally up to make a triangle.

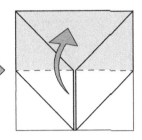

Step 8

Fold the triangle up as shown.

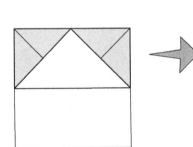

Step 9

Repeat Step 7 and 8 on the back side of the figure.

Step 10

Now separate the front and back bottom edges while gently pushing the middle layer on top of the figure.

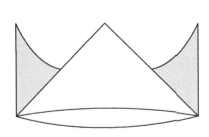

Crown

Hen

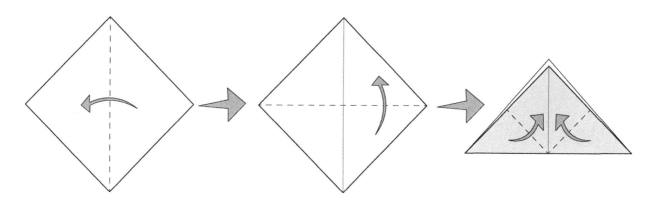

Step 1

Fold the sheet diagonally to the left and unfold it.

Step 2

Then fold it diagonally up in half to make a triangle.

Step 3

Bring both side corners up to the vertical midline.

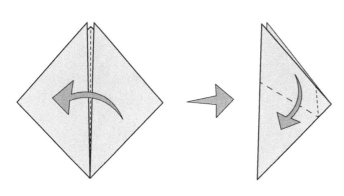

Step 4

Fold the left half of the figure back, then fold the tip of the right corner and unfold it to make a crease. Now use that crease to bring the top layer of the top corner down until you get something like the illustration below.

Step 5

Flip the figure over and repeat for the other side.

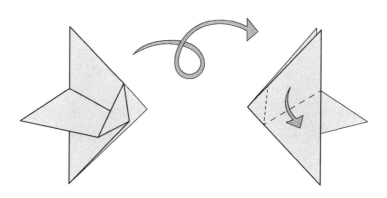

Hen

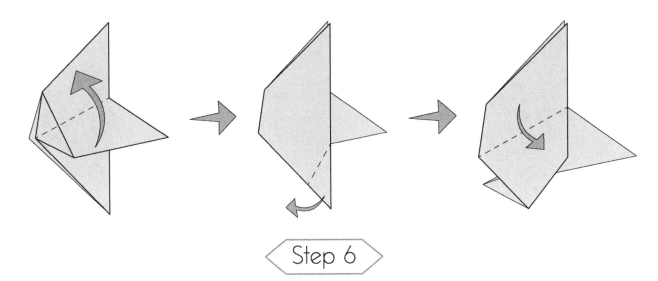

Step 6

Fold this side back up as shown to make an inside reverse fold at the bottom corner, then fold the top layer down again.

Step 7

Fold the tip of the top layer down at an angle as shown.

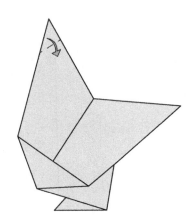

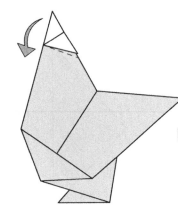

Step 8

Make an inside reverse fold at the tip of the bottom layer to make the hen's beak.

Hen

Dove

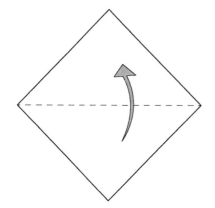

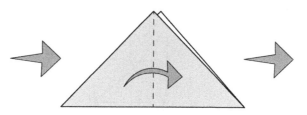

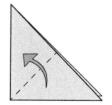

Step 1

Fold the sheet diagonally up in half.

Step 2

Fold the triangle you just made in half.

Step 3

Fold the top layer diagonally up.

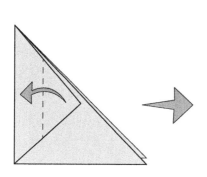

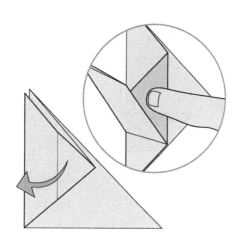

Step 4

Fold out the corner you just made right in the middle of the figure, then use it to make an inside reverse fold.

Step 5

Fold the top layer down as shown, then flip the figure over.

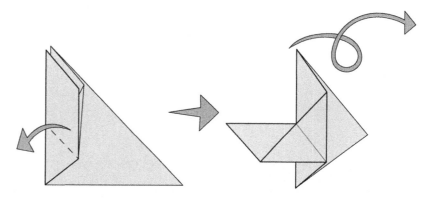

Dove

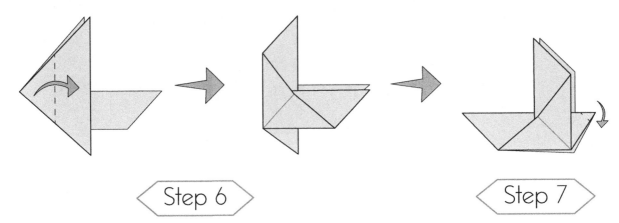

Step 6

Repeat step 3 through 5 on the other side, then rotate the figure counterclockwise.

Step 7

Make an inside reverse fold on the right corner.

Step 8

Fold the left corner in half as shown, then unfold it to make a crease. Pull that crease forward down to make the tail and flatten.

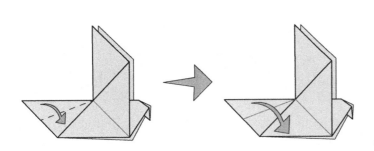

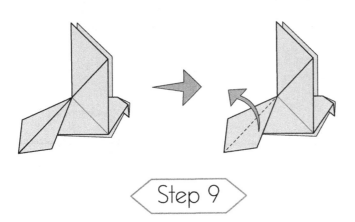

Step 9

Fold half of that tail backward as shown.

Dove

Rocket

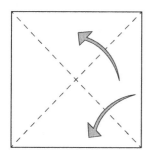  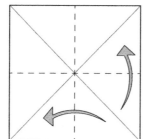 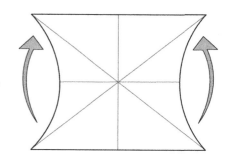

Step 1

Fold the paper sheet diagonally and unfold it.

Step 2

Fold the paper sheet crosswise and lengthwise and unfold it.

Step 3

Bring the top edge down to meet the **bottom edge**, while you fold both sides in to make a triangle.

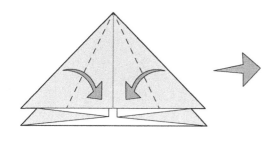 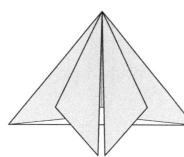

Step 4

Fold both side corners down as shown.

Step 5

Fold the side corners of the flaps you just made in to the vertical midline.

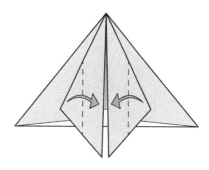

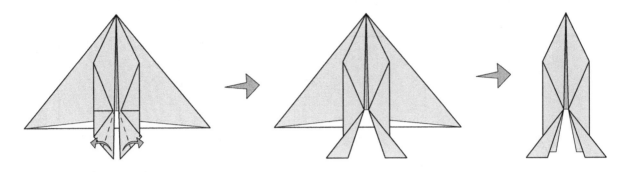

Step 6

Fold the bottom tips of those same flaps
outward so their edges meet the
folds from the previous step.

Step 7

Repeat steps 4 to 6
on the other side of
the figure.

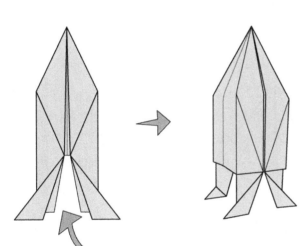

Step 7

Then open it carefully to
shape your rocket.

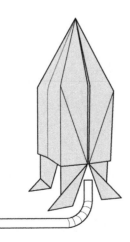

Step 8

Insert a straw into the
bottom of the rocket and
blow to see it fly!

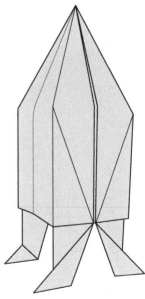

Rocket

Rabbit

Tip

You will need 2 square
sheets to make this rabbit.

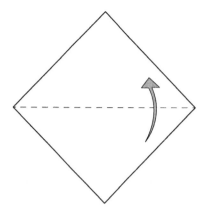

Step 1

Fold one of the sheets
diagonally up in half.

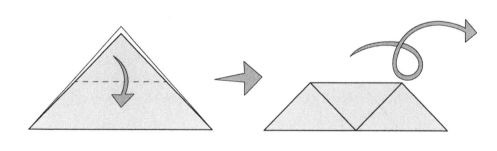

Step 2

Fold the triangle
down in half again,
then flip the figure
over.

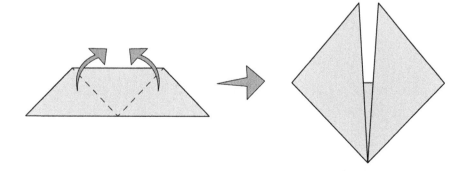

Step 3

Fold both side
corners up at an
angle as shown.

167

Rabbit

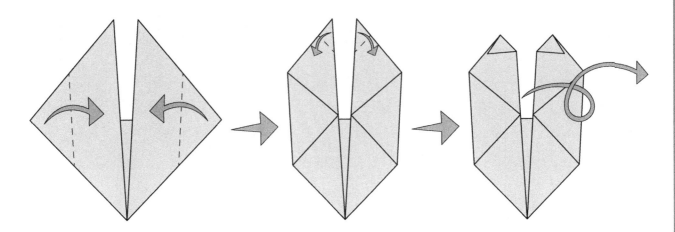

Step 4

Fold the side corners inward until they meet the inner edges of the flaps you just made.

Step 5

Fold the top tips down as shown, then flip the figure over.

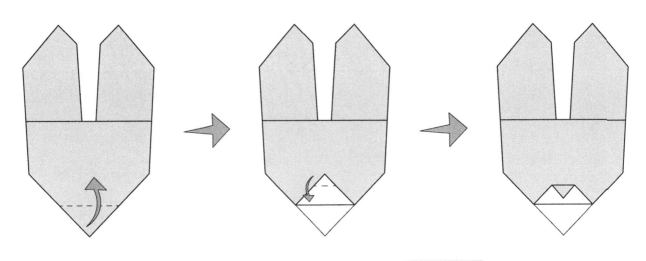

Step 6

Fold the top layer of the bottom corner up as shown.

Step 7

Fold the tip back down to make the rabbit's nose. The rabbit's head is ready, let's move on to its body.

Rabbit

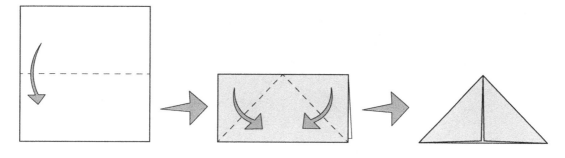

Step 8

Fold the second paper sheet in half crosswise.

Step 9

Fold the top corners diagonally down to make triangle.

Step 10

Fold both side corners down as shown, then fold them up so their tips stick out from the sides.

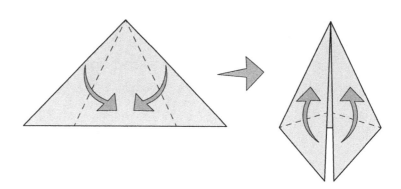

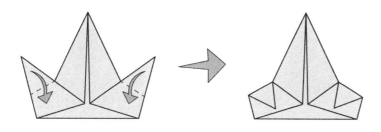

Step 11

Fold the side corners back down as shown. Then tuck the top corner into bottom edge of the head and the rabbit is ready.

Rabbit

Ghost

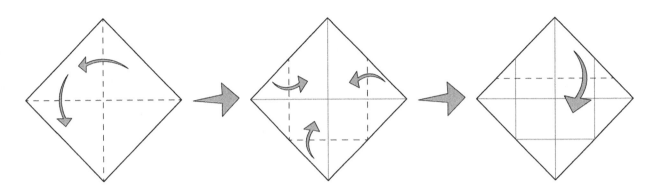

Step 1

Step 2

Step 3

Fold the sheet along both diagonals and unfold it.

Bring the bottom and side corners to the center of the sheet and unfold again.

Fold the top corner down to meet the **crease made by the bottom** corner as shown.

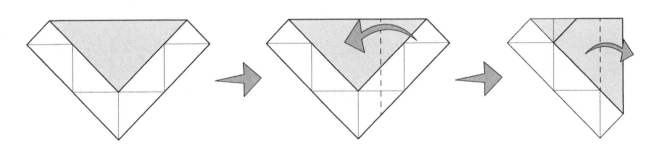

Step 4

Step 5

Fold the right corner in to meet the crease made by the left corner on step 2.

Fold the right corner back out at the midline as shown.

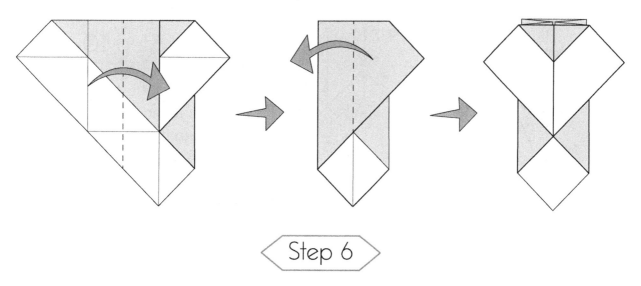

<Step 6>

Repeat steps 4 and 5 for the left side of the figure.

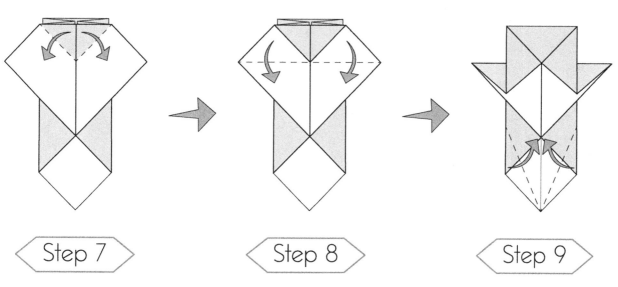

<Step 7>

Fold the top corners
of the top layer
diagonally down as
shown and unfold.

<Step 8>

Fold the top layer of the
figure down as shown,
using the creases you just made
to flatten the layer just below.

<Step 9>

Fold the bottom sides
up to the vertical midline.

Ghost

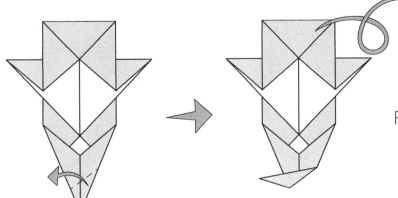

Fold the bottom corner to the side at an angle as shown, then flip the figure over.

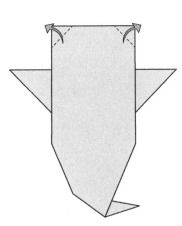

Step 11

Fold the top corner diagonally back as shown.

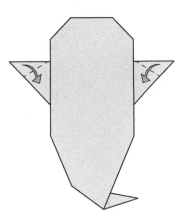

Step 12

Fold the side corners down at an angle as shown. The ghost is ready!

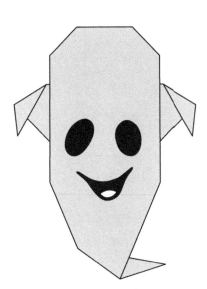

Ghost

Heart Envelope

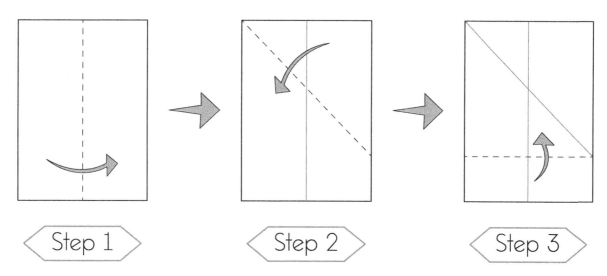

Step 1

Take an A4 sheet and fold it in half lengthwise, then unfold it.

Step 2

Fold the upper right corner diagonally down and unfold it to make a crease.

Step 3

Fold the bottom edge up at the point where the crease you just made meets the right edge.

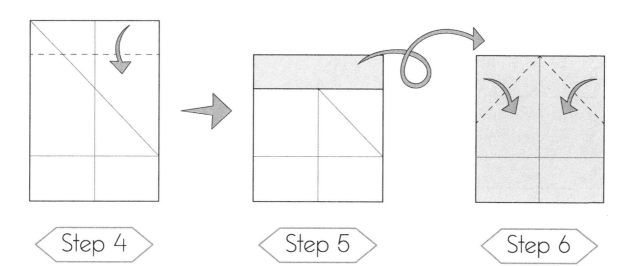

Step 4

Fold the top edge down at the point where the crease from step 2 meets the vertical midline.

Step 5

Flip the figure over.

Step 6

Fold both top corners diagonally down.

Heart Envelope

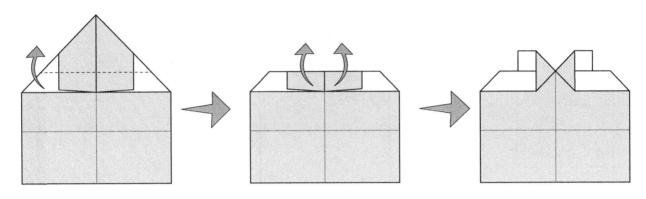

Fold the top corner
backward as shown.

Open the flaps on the top layer and flatten to
make two triangles as shown.

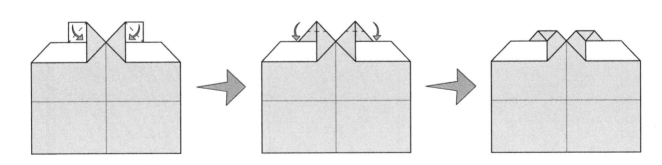

Fold the outside corners
of those flaps diagonally
down.

Fold the top tips down in half.

Heart Envelope

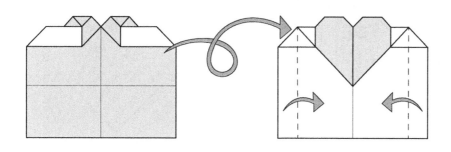

Flip the figure over, then fold both side edges in as shown.

Step 12

Fold the heart-shaped flap up, then fold the bottom of the figure up in half.

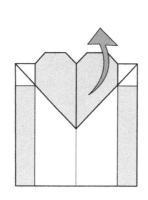 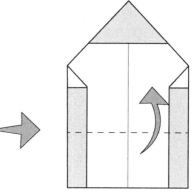

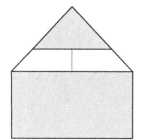 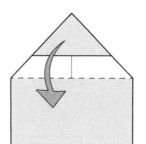

Step 13

Fold the heart-shaped flap back down.

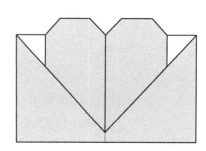

Heart Envelope

Pecking Crow

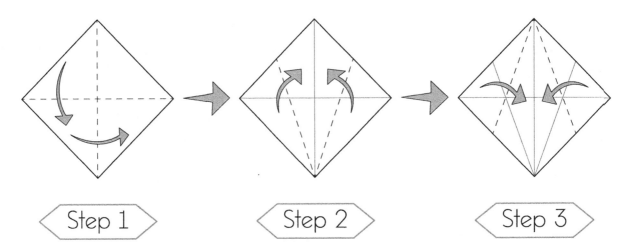

Step 1

Fold the sheet along both diagonals and unfold.

Step 2

Bring the bottom sides up to the vertical midline you just made and unfold.

Step 3

Repeat with the top sides.

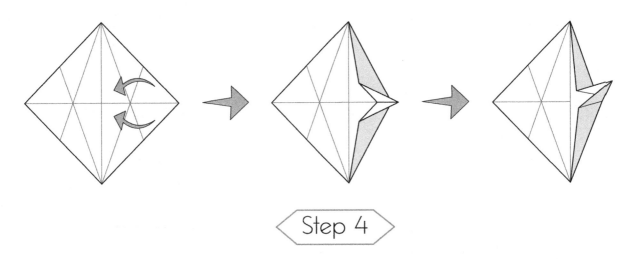

Step 4

You'll see that the creases from steps 2 and 3 form an X on each side of the figure. Fold the right corner i along the inner creases of that X (the longest ones). The shorter creases of the X will form a flap that sticks out, fold it up and flatten.

Pecking Crow

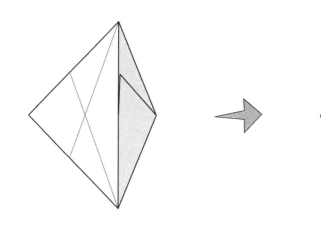 

Step 5

Repeat the previous step for the left side, then fold the figure up in half as shown.

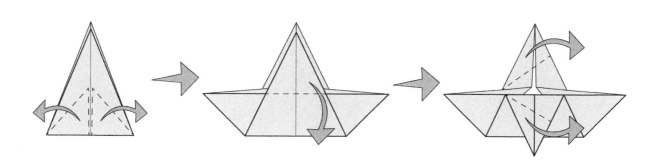

Step 6

Pull the flaps under the top layer you just folded outward (see dotted lines) and flatten.

Step 7

Fold the top corner of the top layer down as shown.

Step 8

Fold both corners to the right as shown.

Pecking Crow

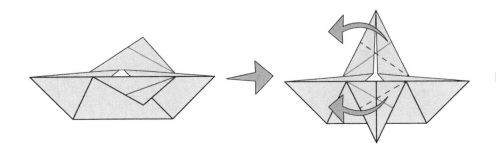

Unfold both corners
and fold them to
the left now, then
unfold again.

Step 10

Use those creases to valley
fold both corners as shown
(just like you did on step 4)

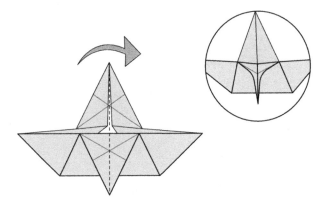

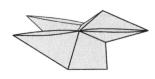 

Tip

Fold the sides of the figure backward
to see how the crow's beak closes and unfold
them to see it open again.

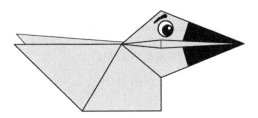

Pecking Crow

178

Moving Lips

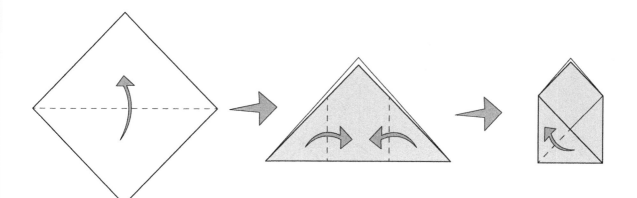

Step 1

Fold the sheet diagonally up to make a triangle.

Step 2

Fold the triangle into three equal parts, so that when you fold the side corners in, they overlap perfectly as shown. Make sure the left corner sits on top of the right corner.

Step 3

Fold the top layer (left corner from the previous step) up in half.

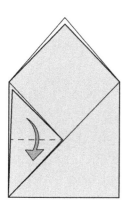 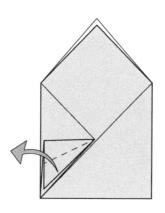 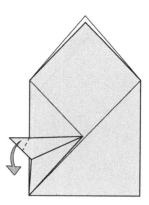

Step 4

Fold the same flap down in half as shown.

Step 5

Fold it up again in half.

Step 6

Fold its tip down to meet the edge of the figure as shown.

Moving Lips

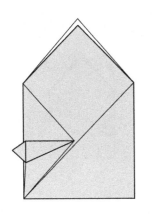 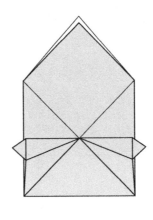

Step 7

Repeat steps 3 through 6 on the right side of the figure, then unfold everything you've done so far.

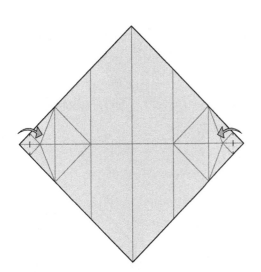

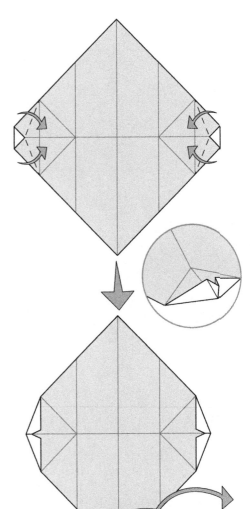

Step 8

From now you're going to use all the creases you've made so far. Fold the side tips inward as shown, then use the X-shaped creases to fold those corners inward again. Pinch the flap that will stick out on both sides to flatten it. Flip the figure over.

Moving Lips

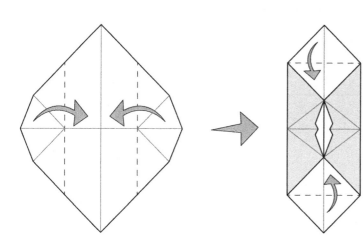

Fold both sides in along the vertical creases on either side of the midline, these are the lips. Then fold the top and bottom corners to match these folds you just made.

Step 10

Fold the top and bottom edges until they meet the edges of the lips.

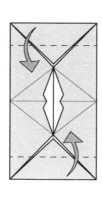 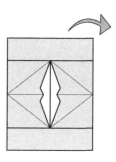

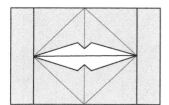

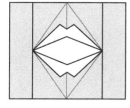

Step 11

Now that the lips are ready, grab the figure by its sides and fold it back and forth to see how they open and close!

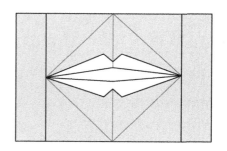

Moving Lips

181

Chinese Boat

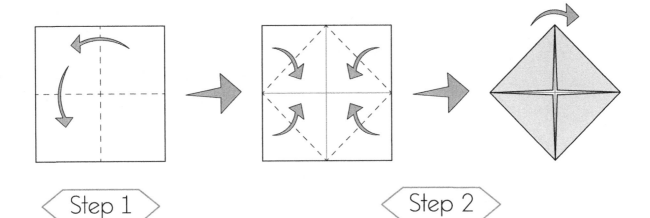

Step 1

Fold the sheet in half lengthwise and clockwise then unfold.

Step 2

Bring all the corners in to the center of the sheet (where the two crease from the previous step meet)

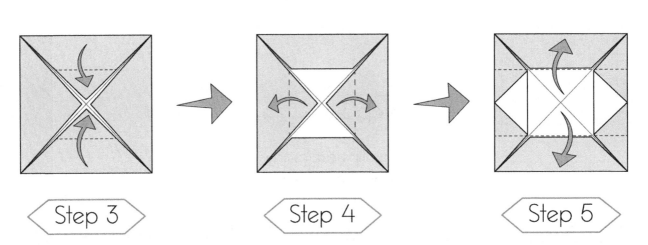

Step 3

Fold the top and bottom corners in half backward as shown.

Step 4

Fold the side corners back out in half as shown.

Step 5

Fold the sheet along both diagonals and unfold. Then bring the top and bottom edges to meet the center of the sheet at the back of the figure.

Chinese Boat

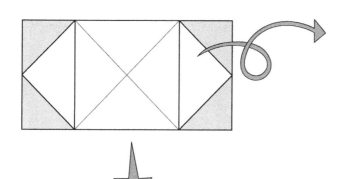

Flip the figure over.

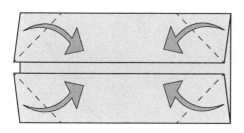

Step 7

Fold all the corners diagonally inward as shown.

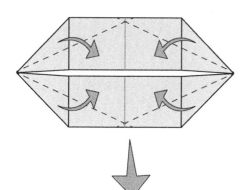

Step 8

Fold the corners on the left side to the horizontal midline, then repeat for the right side. You will see that the flaps on the right side slightly overlap those on the left side.

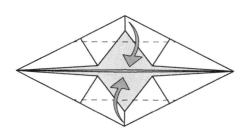

Step 9

Bring the top layer of the top and bottom corners to the horizontal midline as shown.

Chinese Boat

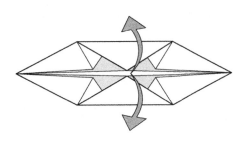 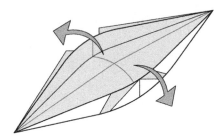

Step 10

This is the tricky part of this design, but don't worry, it's easy and you can do it! Stick a finger under each side of the horizontal midline and separate them to completely turn the entire figure inside out. Then flip the figure over.

 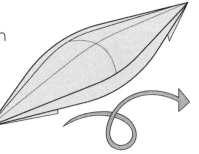

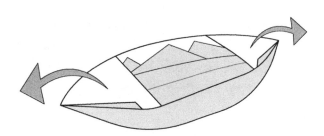

Step 11

Carefully pull the flaps that you will see in each corner of the figure to finish shaping your boat.

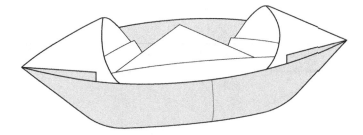

Sampan

Dinosaur

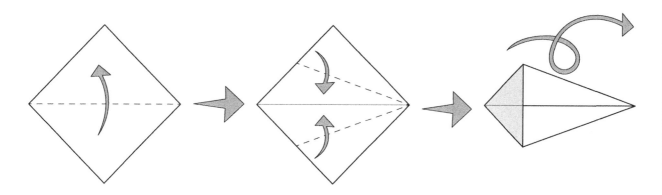

Step 1

Fold the sheet diagonally
up in half and unfold.

Step 2

Bring the top and bottom
corners to the horizontal
midline as shown.

Step 3

Flip the figure over.

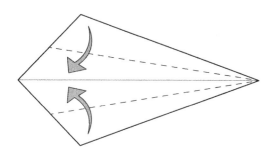

Step 4

Bring the top and bottom corners
to the horizontal midline again
as shown.

Step 5

Unfold the flaps you made
on step 2 and flatten.

Step 6

Now bring those same flaps to
the horizontal midline.

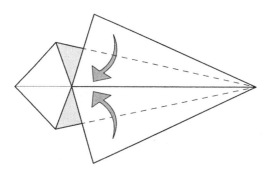

185

Dinosaur

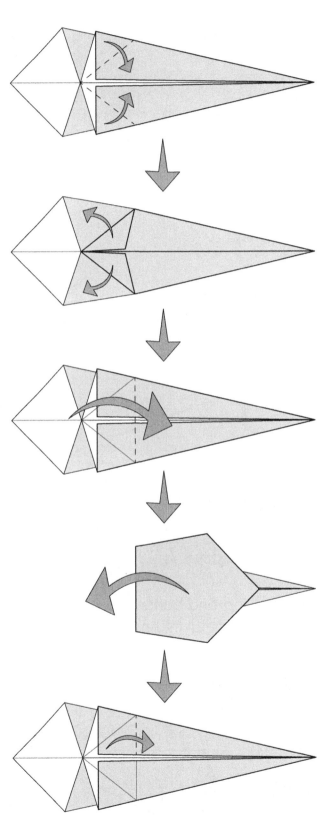

Step 7

Bring the top and bottom corners of the top layer to the horizontal midline.

Step 8

Unfold both corners.

Step 9

Fold the entire figure to the right at the point marked by the creases from the previous step as shown.

Step 10

Unfold it.

Step 11

Let's focus on the top half of the figure: Open the bottom corner of the top layer to the right using the crease from step 7 to make a triangle then flatten.

Dinosaur

Step 12

Repeat the previous step on the bottom half of the figure.

Step 13

Fold the top and bottom corners of the back layer forward to the horizontal midline, then unfold.

Step 14

Now repeat steps 11 and 12 for these corners.

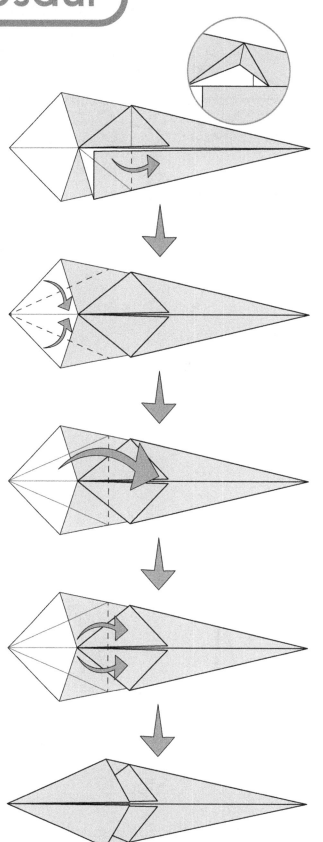

Dinosaur

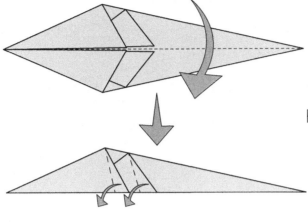

Fold the figure back up in half, then fold the flaps in the middle of the figure so that their edges end up vertical and their tips stick out from the bottom of the figure.

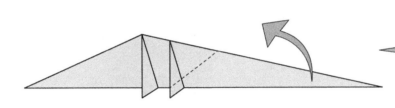

Fold the right side up as shown and unfold it to make a crease, then use it to make an inside reverse fold.

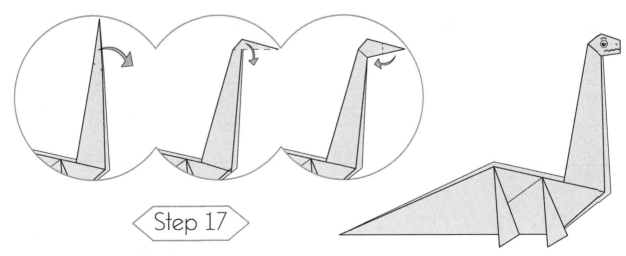

Now make an outside reverse fold on top of that same section to make dinosaur's head. Then fold the tip inward as shown.

Dinosaur

188

Hat

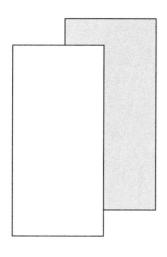

You will need two sheets to make this cap. Sheets should be twice as tall as they are wide, for example, 10 x 20 cm.

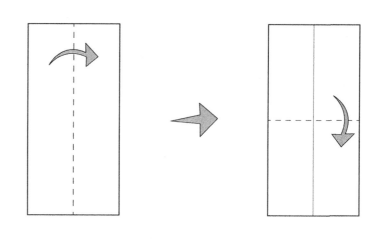

Step 1

Fold the paper in half lengthwise and unfold it to make a crease. Then fold the sheet in half crosswise.

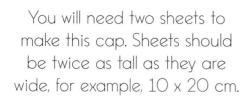

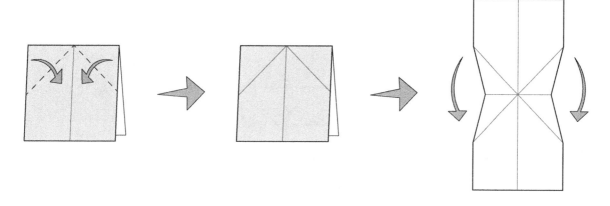

Step 2

Fold both top corners diagonally down and unfold them to make creases, then unfold the entire figure.

Step 3

Fold the figure down in half and use the creases from the previous step to fold those corners in to make a triangle at the top of the figure.

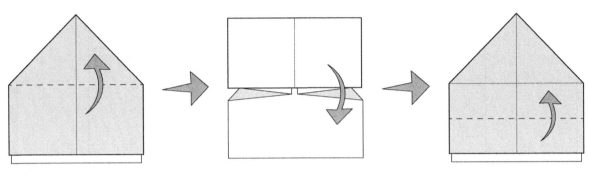

Step 4

Fold the top layer of the bottom edge up as shown, then unfold it to make a crease.

Step 5

Fold the same edge back up to meet the crease you just made.

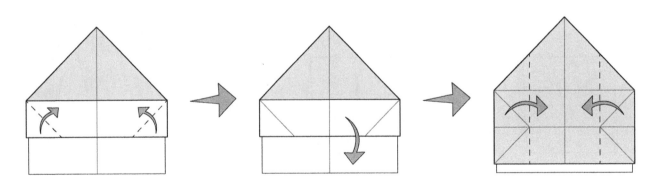

Step 6

Fold the corners of the flap you just made diagonally, then unfold them. Bring that edge back down as shown.

Step 7

Bring both side edges of the top layer in to the vertical midline.

Hat

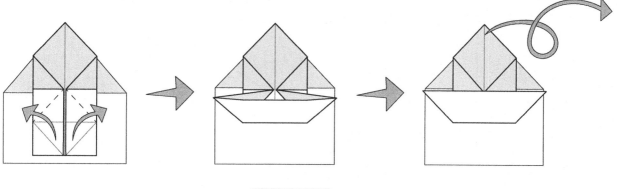

Use the creases you made in step 6 to bring the corners out as shown and flatten. Flip the figure over and repeat everything on the other side.

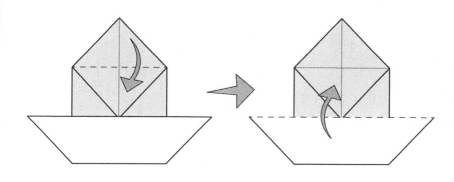

Step 9

Fold the top corner down and unfold it. Then bring the bottom edge of both sides of the figure up as shown.

Step 10

Pull both layers of the figure apart while pushing the top corner down to flatten it and shape the cap.

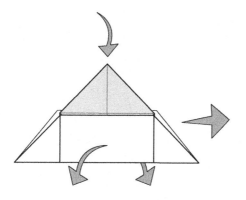
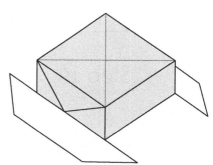

Hat

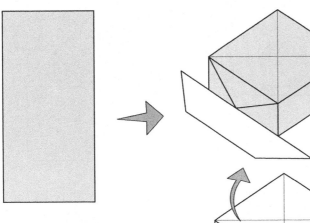

Step 11

Take the other sheet and repeat all the steps so far.

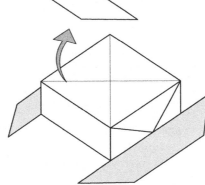

Step 12

Rotate this figure and insert it under the first figure you made, making sure the flaps of both figures are on different sides as shown.

Step 13

Fold one of the corners of the upper figure as shown.

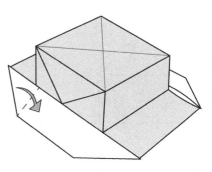

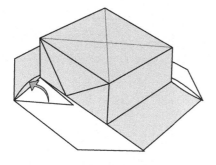

Step 14

Now tuck that corner into the corner of the figure below as shown. Repeat for all corners.

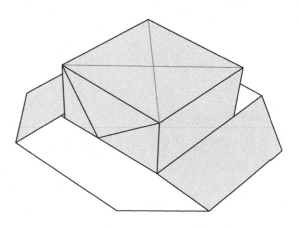

Cap

Chatterbox

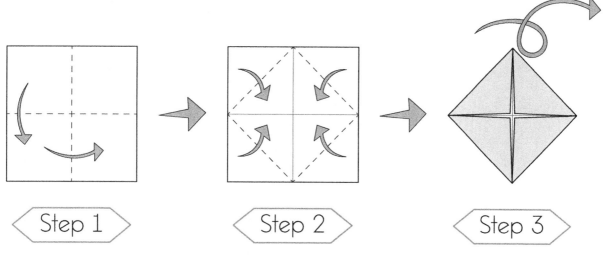

Step 1

Fold the paper sheet
in half lengthwise and
crosswise. Then unfold it.

Step 2

Bring all corners to the
center of the sheet.

Step 3

Flip the figure over.

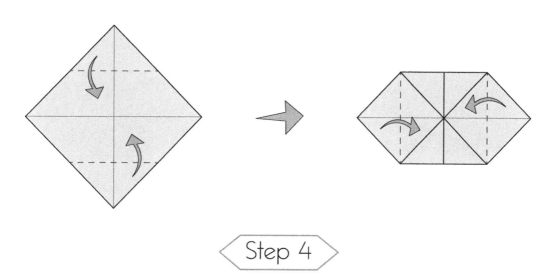

Step 4

Bring all corners to the center of sheet again and flatten it.

Chatterbox

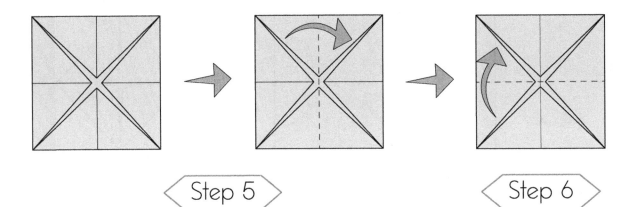

Step 5

Fold the figure in half lengthwise and unfold it to make a crease.

Step 6

Now fold the figure in half crosswise.

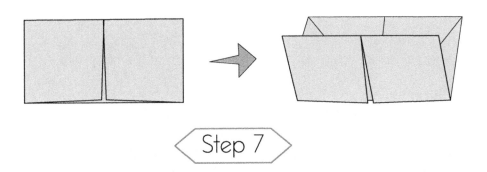

Step 7

Insert your fingers into the flaps in each corner and your chatterbox is ready to play!

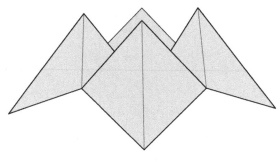

Chatterbox

Chatterbox Games

Now that your chatterbox is ready, it's the funniest moment: let's decorate it and play! The good thing about your chatterbox is that you can decorate it however you like and use as many colors as you want. Once you have a colorful chatterbox you can use it to play fun games at home with friends and family, during car trips, birthday parties, holidays... Even on your own just for fun!

The chatterbox has 3 layers or levels where you can color or write:

- The outer side of the flaps where you insert your fingers to open and close it, which is the visible part when it's completely closed and which will be the 'top layer' from now on.

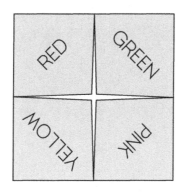

- The inner side of those flaps that is only visible when you open the chatterbox a little and that will be the 'middle layer'.

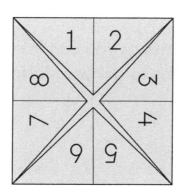

Chatterbox Games

- The layer below all of the above, which is only visible if you lift the inner side of the flaps and which will be the 'bottom layer'.

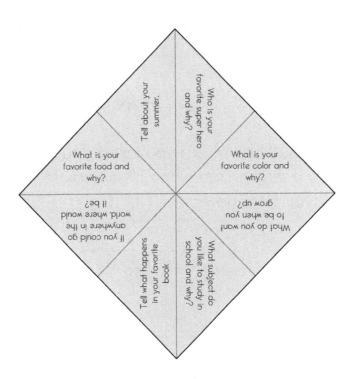

On the top layer you can use different colors, patterns, shapes... Anything you can think of! In the middle layer you can put numbers or drawings related to the theme of the game you choose, for example, animals or flowers. And on the bottom layer write actions or questions to have fun and have a great time with your friends or family.

You can play as many games as you can think of with your chatterbox, so here are just a few examples to get you started and the rest is up to your imagination!

Chatterbox Games

Game #1: Nature

- Top layer: Draw different flowers, leaves or seeds on each flap.
- Middle layer: Write numbers from 1 to 8 or draw insects.
- Bottom layer: Write actions for each number or drawing, here are some ideas.

  - Find 3 birds.
  - Look for 3 different insects.
  - Find leaves of 3 different colors.
  - Look for the perfect pet rock.
  - Feel the grass with your bare feet.
  - Hug a tree.
  - Run between two trees 3 times.
  - Find a tree with rough bark and a smooth one.

Game #2: Animals

- Top layer: Draw different animals or their fur patterns.
- Middle layer: Write numbers or draw animal tracks.
- Bottom layer: Write actions for each number or drawing, here are some ideas.

  - Bark like a dog.
  - Jump like a frog.
  - Walk slowly like a snail.
  - Sing like a rooster.
  - Moo like a cow.
  - Meow like a cat.
  - Pretend you can fly like a bird.
  - Jump around like a monkey.

Chatterbox Games

Game #3: Exercise

- Top layer: Draw people exercising or gym stuff.
- Middle layer: Write numbers or sports.
- Bottom layer: Write actions for each number or drawing, here are some ideas.

    - Jump 10 times.
    - Run around the house or the park.
    - Stand on one foot for 10 seconds.
    - Run on the spot for 20 seconds.
    - Dance for 30 seconds.
    - Do 10 jumping jacks.
    - Good luck! No exercise for you.
    - Walk backwards until your next turn.

Game #4: What would you do....?

- Top layer: Draw question marks of different colors or things related to the questions.
- Middle layer: Write numbers, letters, shapes...
- Bottom layer: Write questions that start with 'what would you do...?' for each number or drawing, here are some ideas.

    - What would you do if you could go anywhere?
    - ... If you could only eat one thing for the rest of your life?
    - ... If you had a lot of money right now?
    - ... If you had to choose between having a dog or a cat?
    - ... If you had to choose chocolate or vanilla ice cream forever?
    - ... If you could have whatever you want for dinner?
    - ... If you could fly?
    - ... If you could breathe underwater?

Chatterbox Games

Here's how to play:

1. Ask someone to choose one of the colors or patterns on one of the flaps on the top layer.
2. Open and close the chatterbox by spelling that color or object. For example, if you drew a cow's fur open and close it spelling c-o-w, or if you colored it yellow open and close it spelling y-e-l-l-o-w.
3. Ask that person to choose one of the numbers or drawings on the middle layer.
4. Open it to reveal what they have to do!

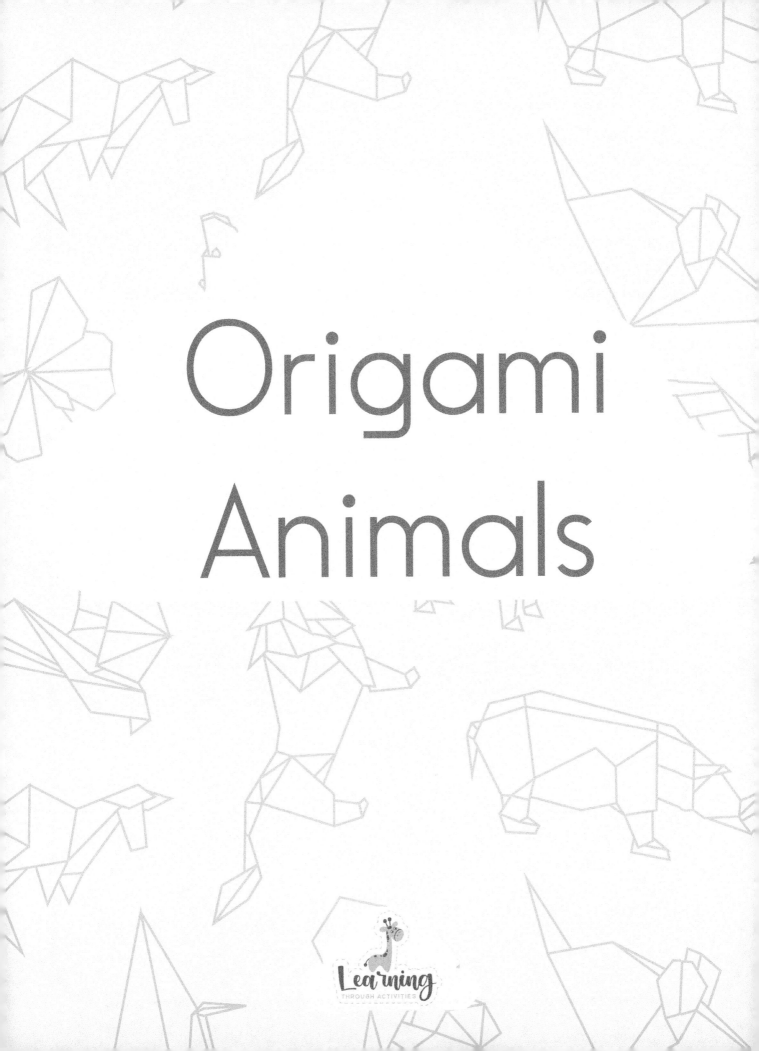

Origami
Animals

Owl

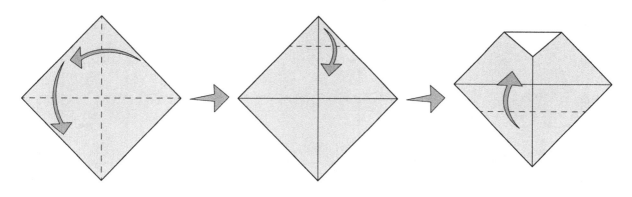

Step 1

Fold the sheet along both diagonals and unfold it.

Step 2

Fold the top corner halfway down as shown, then bring the bottom corner up to meet that tip.

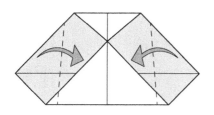

Step 3

Fold both sides in to the vertical midline at a small angle.

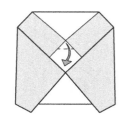

Step 4

Fold the tip in the middle of the figure down a little.

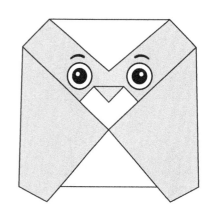

Owl

Bear

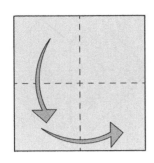 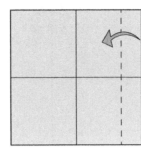  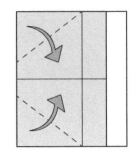

Step 1

Fold the sheet in half lengthwise and crosswise, then unfold it.

Step 2

Fold the right edge inward as shown.

Step 3

Bring the top and bottom left corners to the horizontal midline as shown.

Step 4

Bring the top and bottom right corners in to the vertical midline, then fold them back out at a small angle as shown.

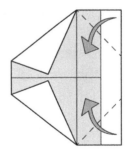 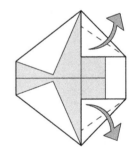

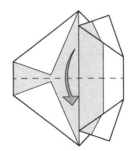

Step 5

Fold the figure down in half.

Bear

Polar Bear

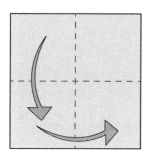 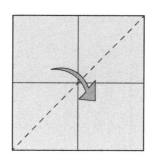 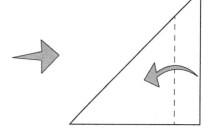

Step 1

Fold the sheet in half lengthwise and crosswise, then unfold it.

Step 2

Fold the sheet in half along one of its diagonals.

Step 3

Fold the right edge inward as shown, then unfold it.

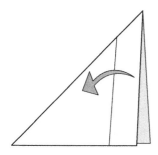 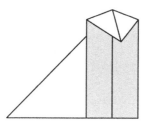

Step 4

Now fold the top layer of the right edge along that crease you just made. As you do that, flatten the top corner as shown.

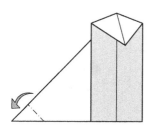 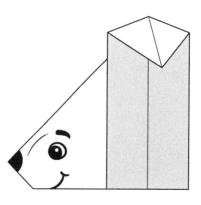

Step 5

Fold the left corner backward at a small angle.

Polar Bear

Monkey

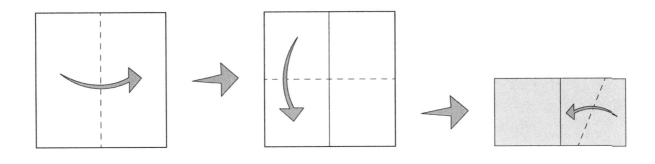

Step 1

Fold the sheet in half lengthwise, the unfold it.

Step 2

Now fold the sheet down in half, then fold the right edge inward at a slight angle and unfold it to make a crease.

Step 3

Use that crease you just made to fold the top layer of the right edge. As you do that, flatten the top corner and fold inward the corners of both layers as shown.

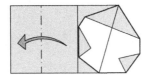

Step 4

Fold the left side of the figure backward in half.

Monkey

Pig

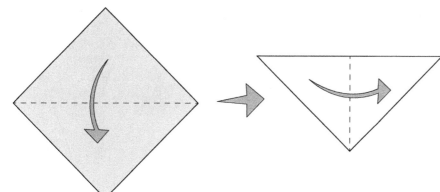

Step 1

Fold the figure diagonally down to make a triangle. Then fold that triangle in half and unfold it to make a crease.

Step 2

Pull just the top layer to the right along the crease you just made and flatten as shown.

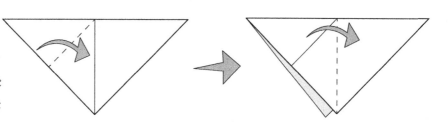

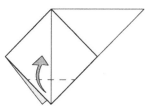 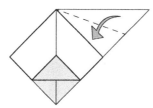 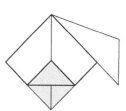

Step 3

Fold the tip of the top layer of the bottom corner up to make the pig's nose, then fold the right corner down at an angle as shown.

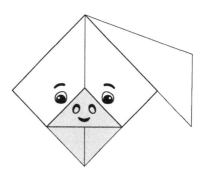

Pig

Woodpecker

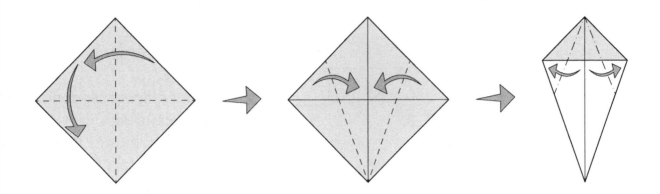

Fold the sheet along both
diagonals, then unfold it.

Step 2

Bring the bottom of both
sides in to the vertical
midline as shown.

Step 3

Now fold the top of
both sides backward
to meet the vertical
midline as well.

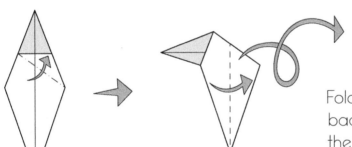

Step 4

Fold the top of the figure diagonally
back and down as shown. Then fold
the vertical section back in half and
flip the figure over.

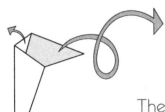

Step 5

There's flap in the upper left corner,
unfold it and flip the figure over again.

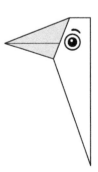

Woodpecker

Bat

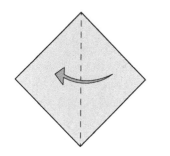

Fold the sheet along one of its diagonals and unfold it.

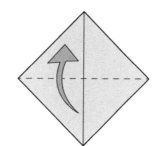

Step 2

Now fold it up in half along the other diagonal to make a triangle.

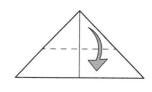

Step 3

Fold the top corner down so it sticks out the bottom edge as shown.

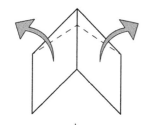

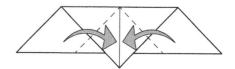

Step 4

Fold both sides diagonally down to the vertical midline, then fold them back out at a small angle as shown. Then flip the figure over.

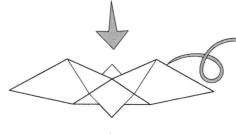

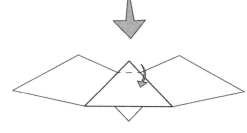

Step 5

Fold the tip of the top corner down.

Bat

207

Sheep

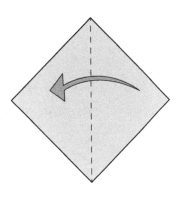

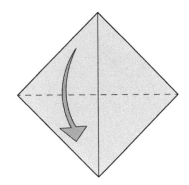

Step 1

Fold the sheet along one of
its diagonals and unfold it.

Step 2

Now fold it down in half
along the other diagonal to
make a triangle.

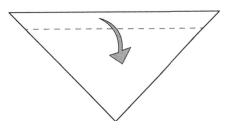

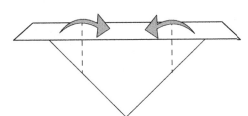

Step 3

Fold the top edge down
a bit as shown.

Step 4

Fold both side corners in so
they overlap a little.

Sheep

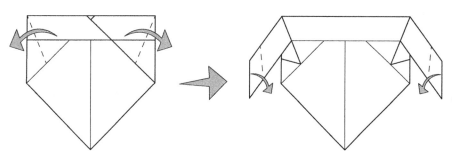

Step 5

Fold both sides back out at a small angle, then fold the tips of both sides inward as shown.

Step 6

Flip the figure over.

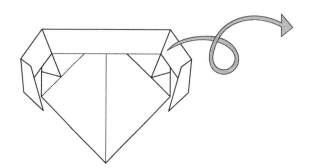

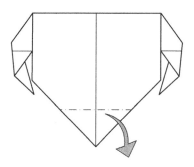

Step 7

Fold the bottom corner backward.

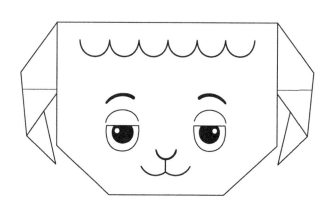

Sheep

Ladybug

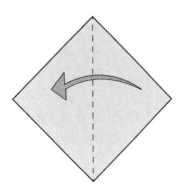 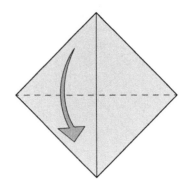

Step 1

Fold the sheet along one of
its diagonals and unfold it.

Step 2

Now fold it down in half along
the other diagonal to make a
triangle.

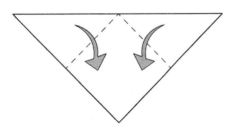 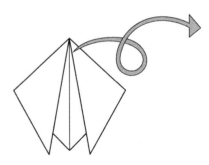

Step 3

Bring both top corners down to the
vertical midline, leaving a small gap
between them.

Step 4

Flip the figure over.

Ladybug

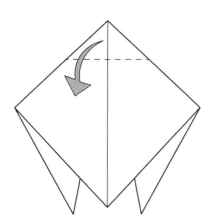 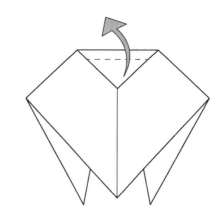

Fold the top corner down as shown.

Now fold it back up, leaving a small gap between both folds.

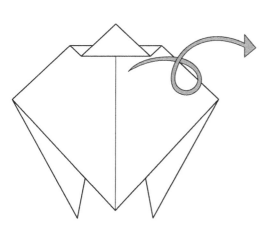 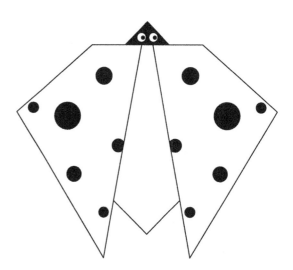

Flip the figure over.

Ladybug

Duck

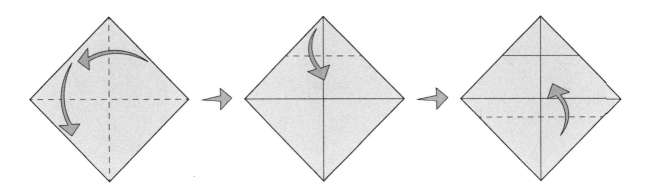

<**Step 1**>

Fold the sheet along both diagonals, then unfold it.

<**Step 2**>

Fold the top corner down to the horizontal midline and unfold it to make a crease.

<**Step 3**>

Bring the bottom corner up to the crease you just made.

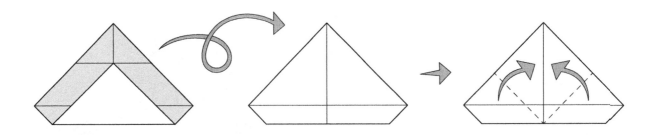

<**Step 4**>

Flip the figure over.

<**Step 5**>

Fold both side corners up to the vertical midline.

Duck

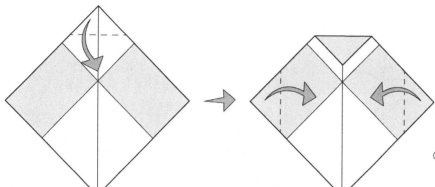

Step 6

Fold the top corner down and the side corners inward as shown.

Step 7

Flip the figure over and fold the tip in the middle of the figure backward.

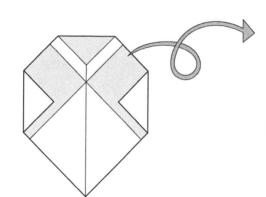

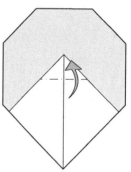

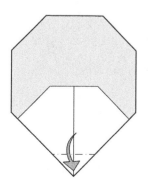

Step 8

Fold the bottom corner backward as well.

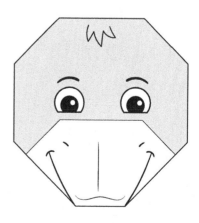

Duck

Penguin

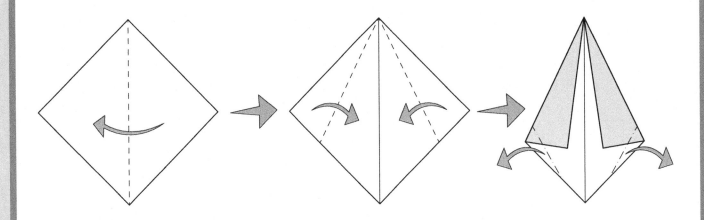

Step 1

Fold the sheet along one of its diagonals and unfold it.

Step 2

Bring the top of both side corners down to the vertical midline, leaving a small gap between them.

Step 3

Fold the tips of both side corners backward as shown.

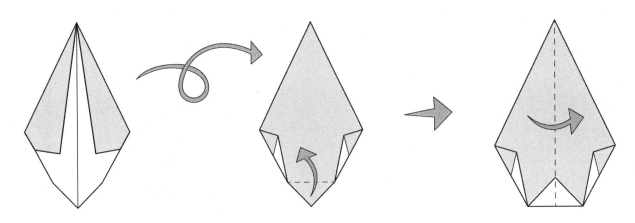

Step 4

Flip the figure over and fold the bottom corner up.

Step 5

Fold the figure in half.

Penguin

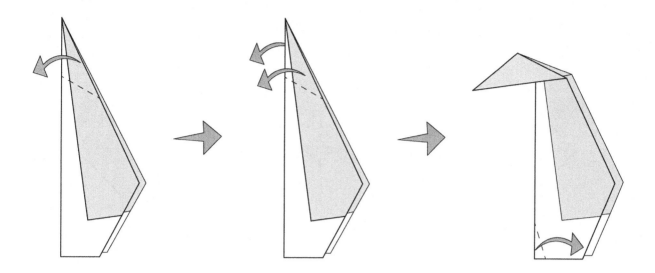

Step 6

Fold the top corner down at a small angle and unfold it to make a crease. Now use that crease to make an outside reverse fold.

Step 7

Fold the bottom corner inward and tuck it between both layers of the figure.

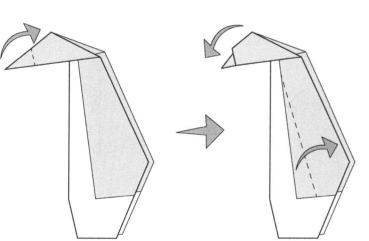

Step 8

Fold the top left corner backward and then out again. Then fold the flap on the top layer out to make the penguin's flipper.

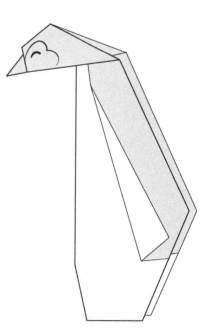

Penguin II

215

Rabbit

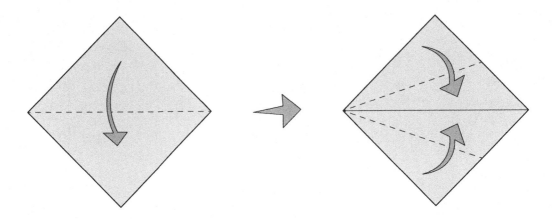

Fold the sheet horizontally along one of its diagonals and unfold it.

Step 2

Bring the top and bottom corners to that crease you just made.

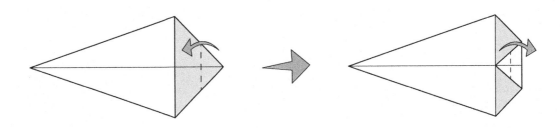

Step 3

Fold the right corner in to meet the flaps from the previous step.

Step 4

Now fold it back out until the tip sticks out the right edge.

Rabbit

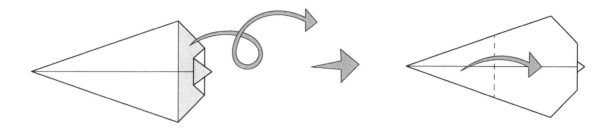

Step 5

Flip the figure over and fold it to the right in half. Make sure the left corner meets the right edge.

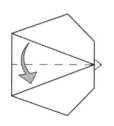 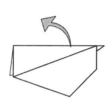

Step 6

Fold the figure backward in half and pull the top layer to the position shown below.

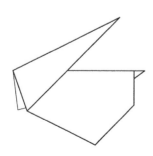

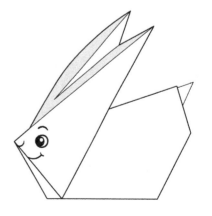

Rabbit

Gorilla

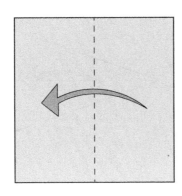 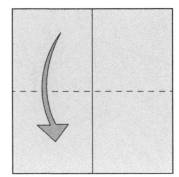

Step 1

Fold the sheet in half lengthwise, then unfold it.

Step 2

Now fold the sheet in half crosswise.

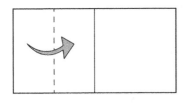 

Step 3

Bring the left edge in to the vertical midline and unfold it. Then fold the upper left corner diagonally down and unfold it.

Step 4

Use the creases you just made to open the top layer and flatten it as shown.

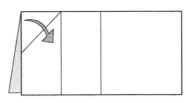 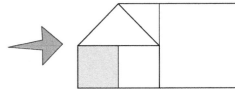

Gorilla

Step 5

Fold the top layer back to the left, then fold the right side of the figure diagonally down as shown.

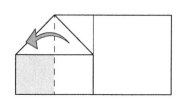 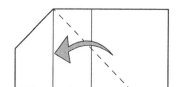

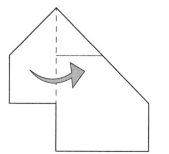 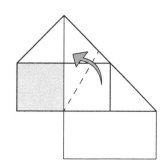

Step 6

Open again the top layer of the left edge, make sure to place it on top of the right side that you folded in the previous step. Then fold that same flap upward at a small angle as shown.

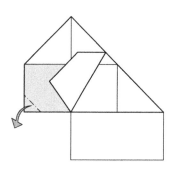

Step 7

Fold the left corner backward as shown.

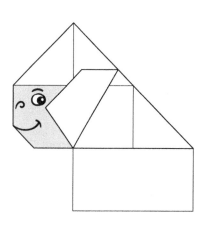

Gorilla

Puppy

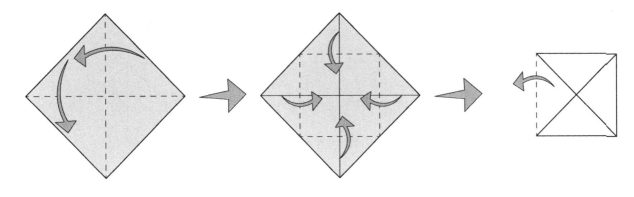

Step 1

Fold the sheet along both diagonals, then unfold it.

Step 2

Bring all the corners to the center of the sheet.

Step 3

Unfold the left corner.

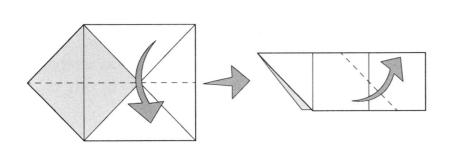

Step 4

Fold the figure down in half. Then fold it diagonally up as shown and unfold it to make a crease.

Step 5

Pull just the top layer to the right along the crease you just made and flatten the top as shown.

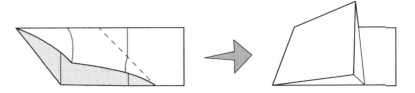

Puppy

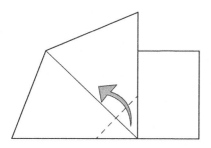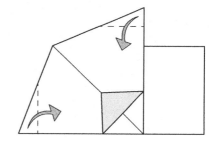

Step 6

Fold the bottom right corner of the flap you just made as shown.

Step 7

Fold the tips of the bottom left and upper right corners inward as shown.

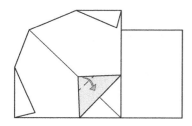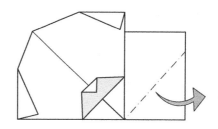

Step 8

Fold the tip of the bottom right corner back down. Then fold the right side of the figure diagonally back as shown.

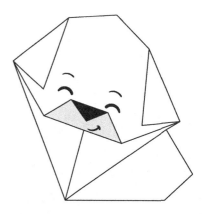

Puppy

Cow

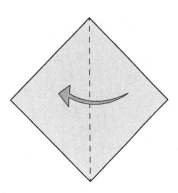

Step 1

Fold the sheet along one of its diagonals and unfold it.

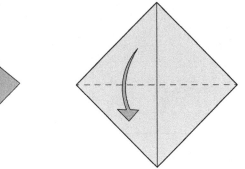

Step 2

Now fold it down in half along the other diagonal to make a triangle.

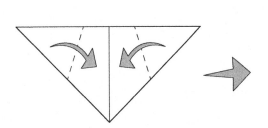

Step 3

Fold both side corners in so they overlap.

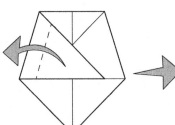

Step 4

Fold one of the flaps back out at a slight angle as shown.

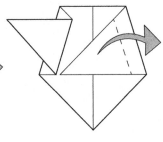

Step 5

Repeat for the other flap.

Cow

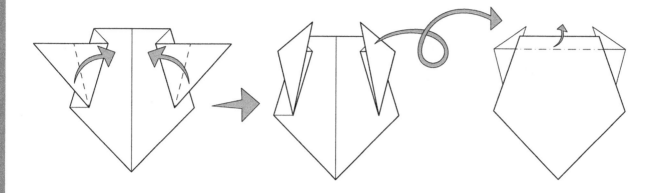

Step 6

Fold both flaps back in, so that their tips stick out over the top edge of the figure. Flip the figure over.

Step 7

Fold the top edge backward.

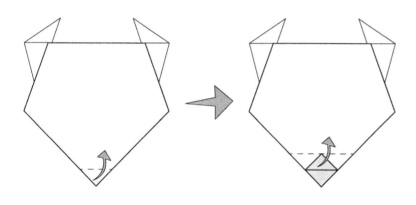

Step 8

Fold the top layer of the bottom corner up twice in a row.

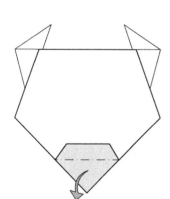

Step 9

Fold the bottom corner backward as shown.

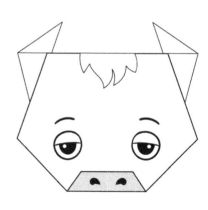

Cow

Pigeon

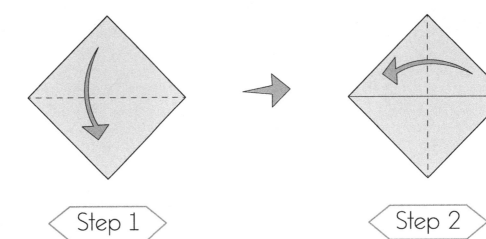

Fold the sheet down along one of
its diagonals and unfold it.

Now fold it to the left along the other
diagonal to make a triangle.

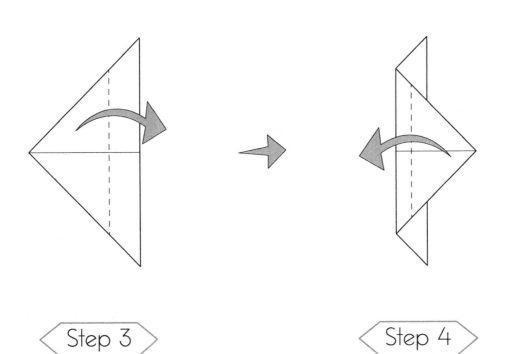

Fold the left corner to the right
until it sticks out halfway through
the right edge.

Fold the top layer back to the left,
leaving a small gap between both folds.

Pigeon

Step 5

Fold the figure forward in half, then fold both sides of the bottom of the figure up at a small angle as shown.

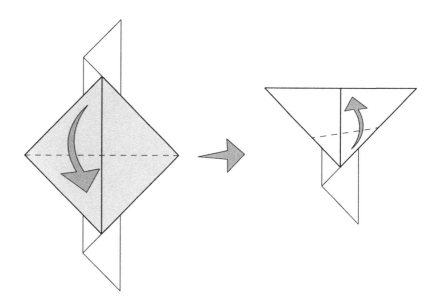

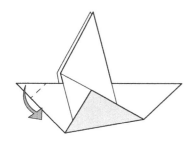

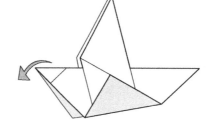

Step 6

Fold the left corner down and unfold it to make a crease, then use it to make an inside reverse fold.

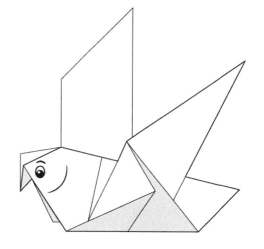

Pigeon

Elephant

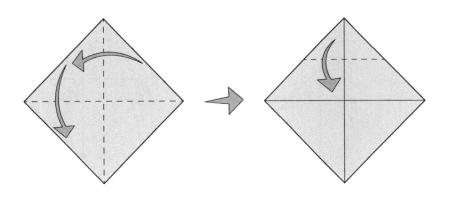

Step 1

Fold the sheet along both diagonals and unfold it. Then bring the top corner down to the center of the sheet.

Step 2

Fold the bottom of both side corners inward so they overlap, then fold one of the corners diagonally out again as shown.

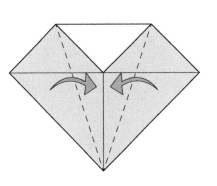 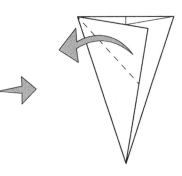

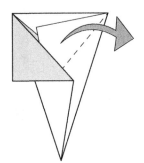 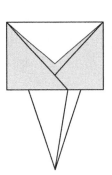

Step 3

Fold the other corner diagonally out as well.

Elephant

Step 4

Fold the bottom corner up to meet the upper edge, then fold it back down leaving a small gap between both folds.

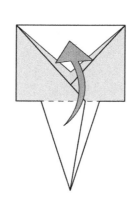 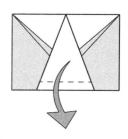

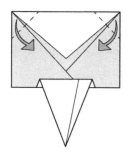 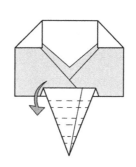

Step 5

Fold both top corners diagonally down as shown. Then fold the bottom corner up and down 4 times in a row, leaving small gaps between all the folds to make a zig-zag pattern.

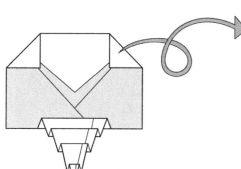

Step 6

Flip the figure over.

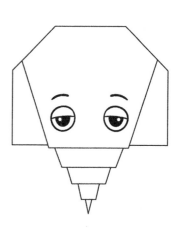

Elephant

Swan

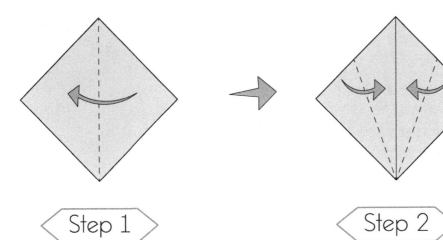

Fold the sheet vertically along one of its diagonals and unfold it.

Step 2

Bring the bottom of both side corners to the vertical midline.

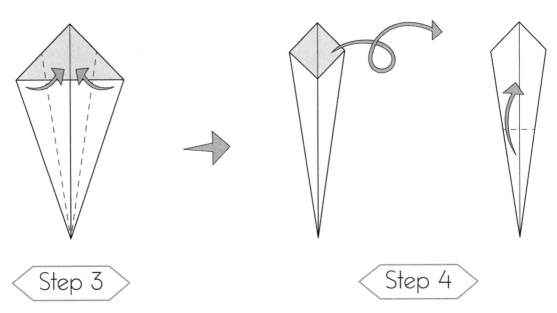

Step 3

Bring the bottom of both side corners again to the vertical midline.

Step 4

Flip the figure over and fold it up in half.

Swan

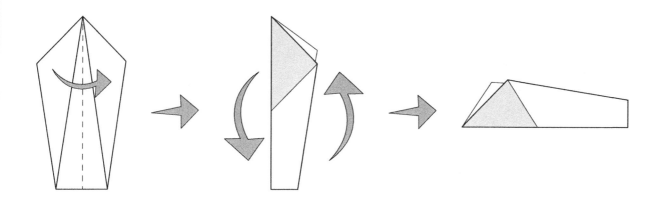

Fold the figure to the right in half.

Rotate the figure to match the illustration.

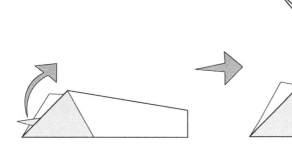

Pull the tip between the two outer layers of the figure halfway up and make an inside reverse fold as shown.

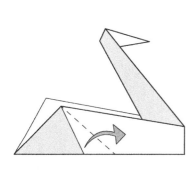

Fold the top layer on both sides of the figure as shown.

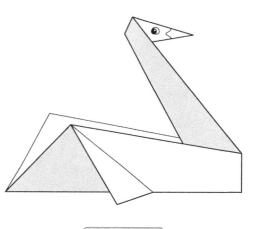

Swan

Fox

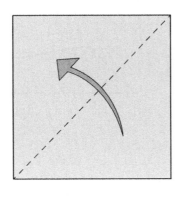

Step 1

Fold the sheet up to the left along one of its diagonals and unfold it.

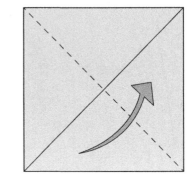

Step 2

Now fold it up to the right along the other diagonal.

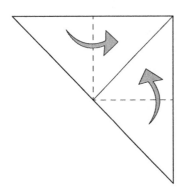 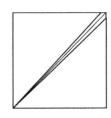

Step 3

Bring the upper left and bottom right corners to the upper right corner as shown.

230

Fox

 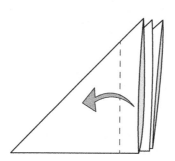 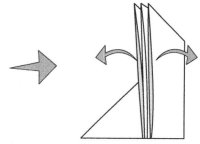

Step 4

Fold the figure diagonally backward as shown.

Step 5

Fold the right edge inward as shown.

Step 6

The flap you just made has two layers. Now fold just the top layer back to the right and flatten the flap between them as shown.

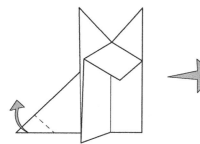 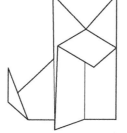

Step 7

Fold the left corner up at a small angle.

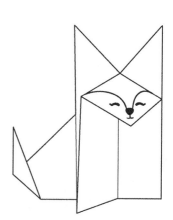

Fox

Koala

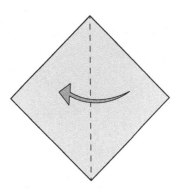 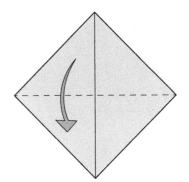

Step 1

Fold the sheet vertically along one of its diagonals and unfold it.

Step 2

Now fold it down in half along the other diagonal to make a triangle.

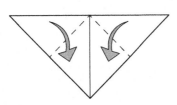 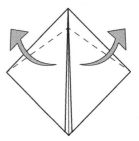

Step 3

Bring both side corners down to the vertical midline.

Step 4

Fold them back up at a small angle as shown.

Koala

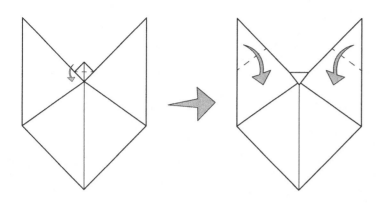

Fold the tip in the middle of the figure down over the flaps you just made to lock them in place. Then fold the top corners down at a small angle.

Step 6

Flip the figure over.

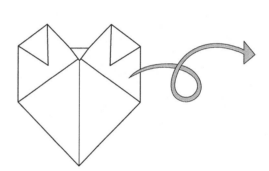

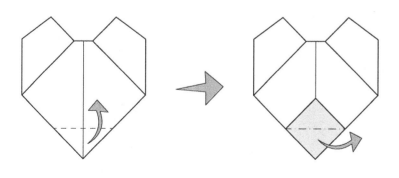

Step 7

Fold the top layer of the bottom corner up, then fold the bottom layer backward.

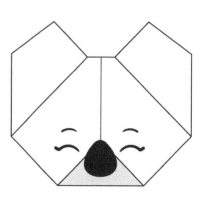

Koala

233

Tiger

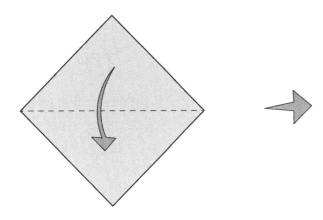 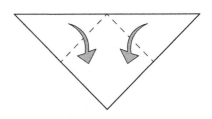

Fold the sheet down in half along one of its diagonals to make a triangle.

Step 2

Bring both side corners down to the center of the figure.

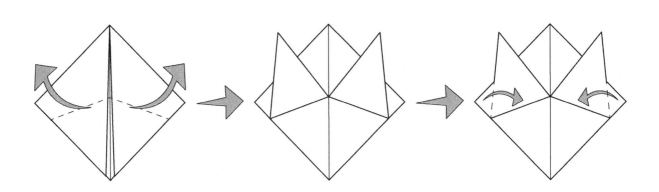

Step 3

Fold them back up almost in half as shown.

Step 4

Fold both side corners over the flaps you just made to lock them in place.

Tiger

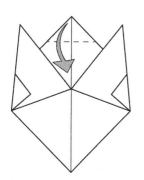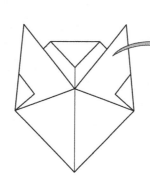

Step 5

Fold the top corner down as shown, then flip the figure over.

Step 6

Fold the top layer of the bottom corner up, then fold the bottom layer backward.

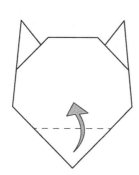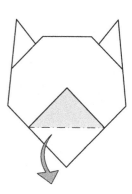

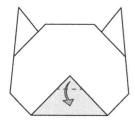

Step 7

Fold the tip of the top layer back down.

Tiger

235

Dog

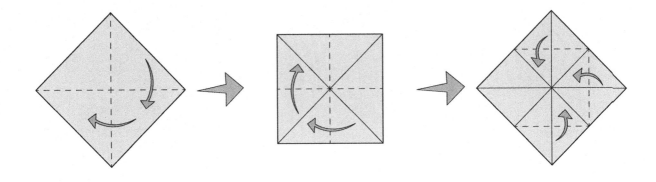

Step 1

Fold the sheet along both diagonals and unfold it.

Step 2

Now fold it in half lengthwise and crosswise, then unfold it.

Step 3

Bring the top, right and bottom corners in to the center of the figure.

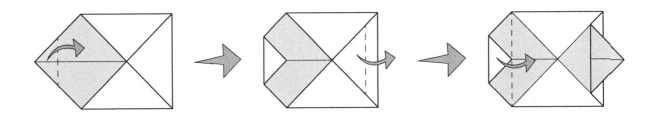

Step 4

Fold the left corner halfway in.

Step 5

Fold the right corner back out, leaving a small gap between its two folds. Then fold the left corner inward again as shown.

Dog

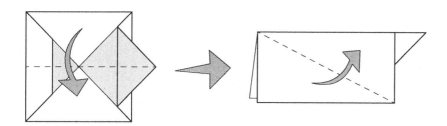

Step 6

Fold the figure down in half, then fold the top layer diagonally up.

Step 7

Pull out the flap that is just below the fold you just made, then repeat on the other side of the figure.

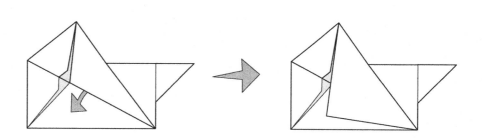

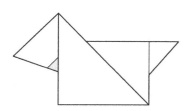

Step 8

There's small corner tucked between both layers of the left corner of the figure, pull it out and flatten it.

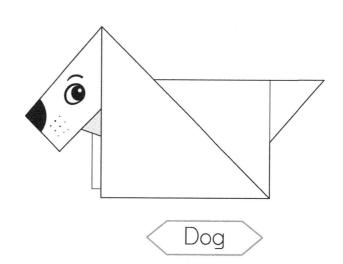

Dog

Crab

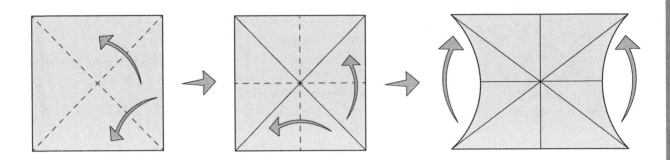

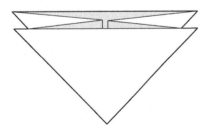

Step 1

Fold the sheet along both diagonals and unfold it.

Step 2

Now fold it in half lengthwise and crosswise, then unfold it.

Step 3

Bring the bottom edge up to meet the top edge, while folding the sides toward the vertical midline to make a triangle.

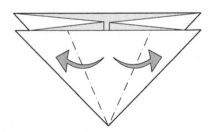

Step 4

Fold the side corners of the top layer backward, leaving a small gap between them.

Crab

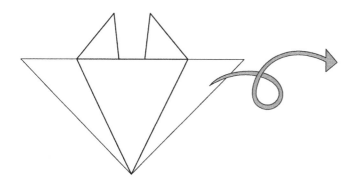 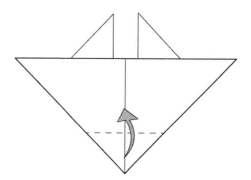

Flip the figure over.

Fold the bottom corner
up as shown.

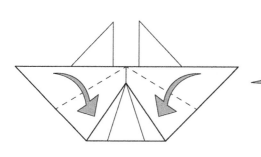 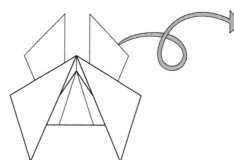

Fold both side corners down so that they
stick out on either side of the bottom edge.
Then flip the figure over.

Crab

Bull

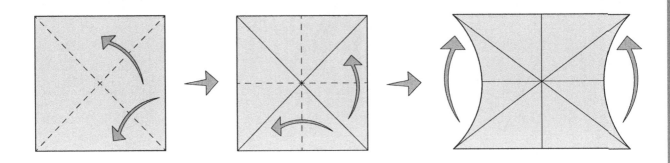

Step 1

Fold the sheet along both diagonals and unfold it.

Step 2

Now fold it in half lengthwise and crosswise, then unfold it.

Step 3

Bring the bottom edge up to meet the top edge, while folding the sides toward the vertical midline to make a triangle.

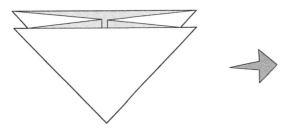

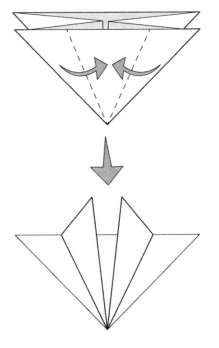

Step 4

Fold the side corners of the top layer inward, leaving a small gap between them.

Bull

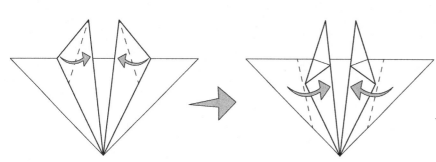

Fold the sides of those flaps you just made diagonally down as shown. Then fold both sides of the bottom layer over them until their tips meet.

Step 6

Fold them back out, leaving a small gap between both folds as shown. Then fold the bottom corner up as shown.

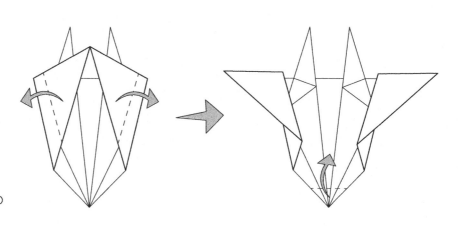

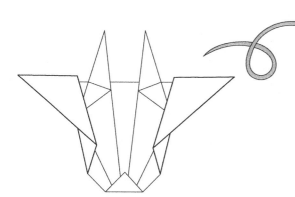

Step 7

Flip the figure over.

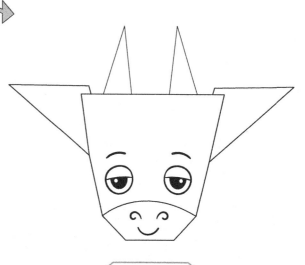

Bull

241

Chameleon

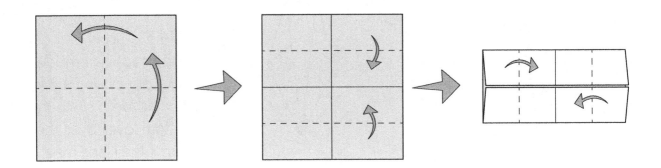

Step 1

Fold the sheet in half lengthwise and crosswise, then unfold it.

Step 2

Bring the top and bottom edges to the horizontal midline.

Step 3

Bring both side edges to the vertical midline and unfold them to make creases.

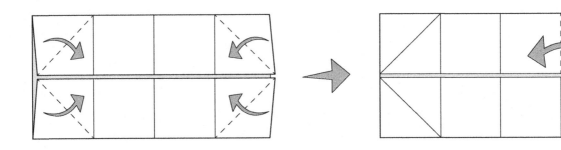

Step 4

Fold all corners diagonally inward and unfold them to make creases.

Step 5

Pull the top layer of the upper right corner to the left along the creases you just made. Then repeat for the other corners.

242

Chameleon

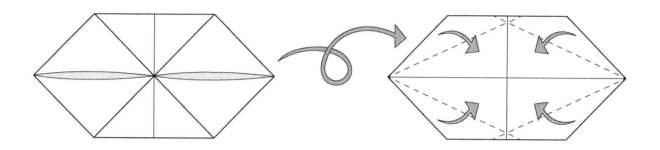

Step 6

Flip the figure over, then bring the top and bottom corners to the horizontal midline. make sure they end up overlapping each other.

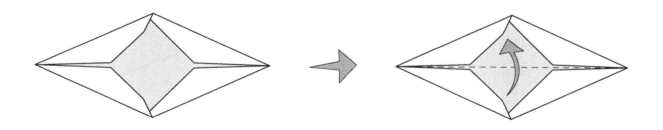

Step 7

Fold the figure up in half.

Chameleon

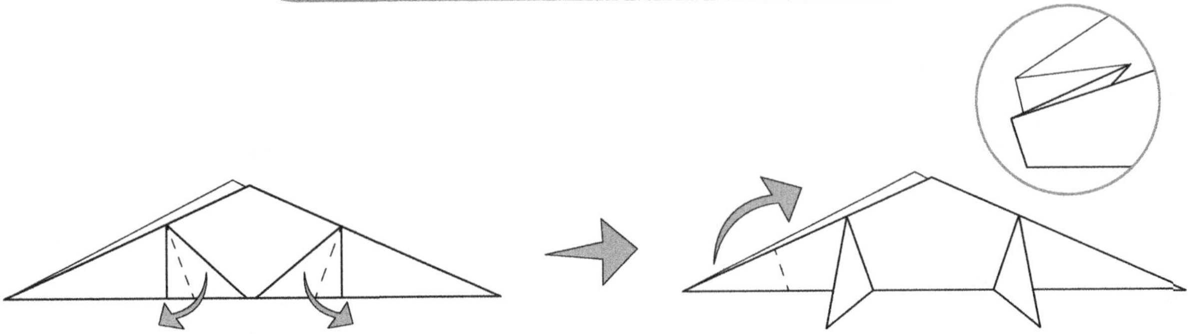

Step 8

Fold the flaps in the middle of the figure out. Then make an inside reverse fold at the left corner of the figure.

Step 9

Make an outside reverse fold at the right corner of the figure.

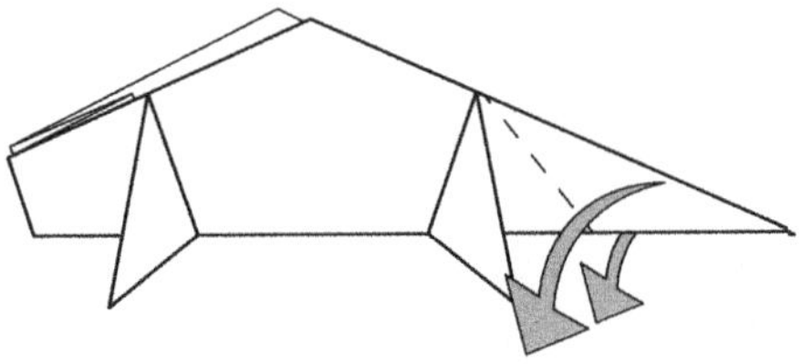

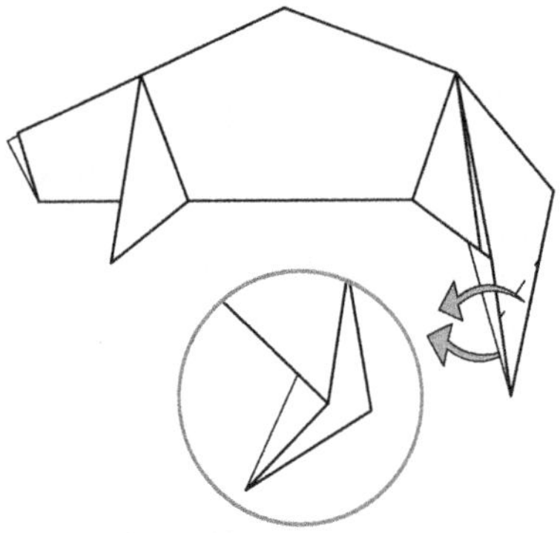

Step 10

Then make an inside reverse fold at the tip of the same corner.

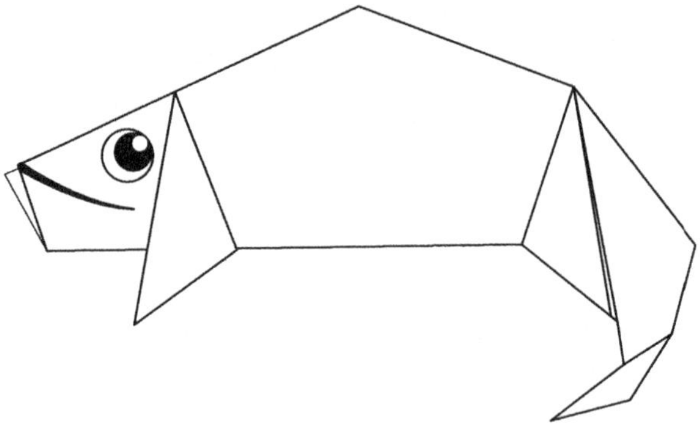

Chameleon

Fish

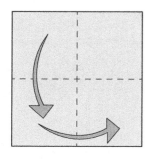 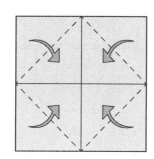 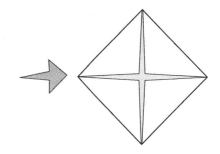

Step 1

Fold the sheet in half lengthwise and crosswise, then unfold it.

Step 2

Bring all the corners to the center of the sheet.

Step 3

Unfold everything.

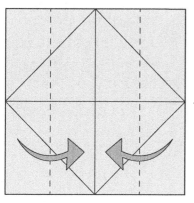  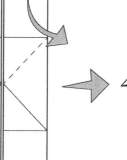 

Step 4

Bring both side edges to the vertical midline.

Step 5

Use the diagonal creases from step 2 to bring the top corners out. As you do that, the bottom layer will fold down, flatten it out as shown. Then repeat for the bottom corners.

Step 6

Fold the bottom flaps diagonally down toward the vertical midline.

Step 7

Fold the bottom right flap diagonally up to the left, so that its right edge ends up horizontal. Then fold it back to the right as shown.

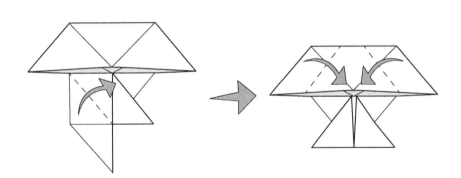

Step 8

Repeat the previous step for the bottom left flap. Then fold both top flaps down so that their top edge ends up vertical.

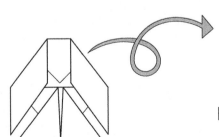

Step 9

Flip the figure over and rotate it.

Fish

Wild Duck

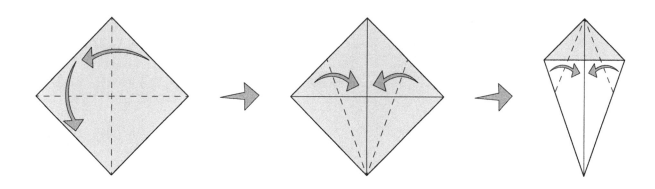

Step 1

Fold the sheet along both diagonals and unfold it.

Step 2

Bring the bottom of both sides in to the vertical midline as shown. Then fold the top of both sides in to the vertical midline as well and rotate the figure.

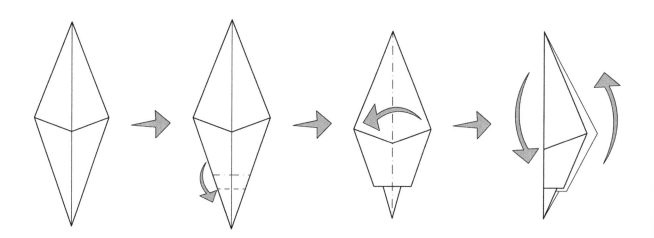

Step 3

Fold the bottom corner backward up and then down again, leaving a small gap between both folds.

Step 4

Fold the figure backward in half and rotate it to the left.

247

Wild Duck

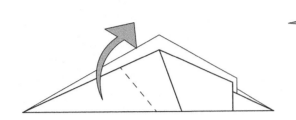

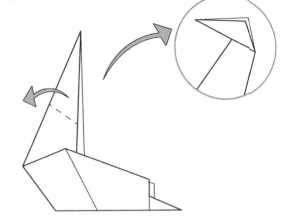

Fold the left side of the figure up and unfold it to make a crease, then use it to make an inside reverse fold.

Make an outside reverse fold at the tip of that same section.

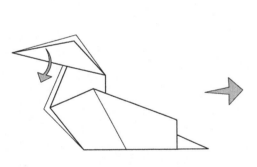

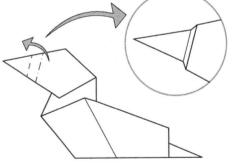

Step 7

Open up both layers of the outside reverse fold you just made. Fold its tip in and out again, leaving a small gap between both folds as shown.

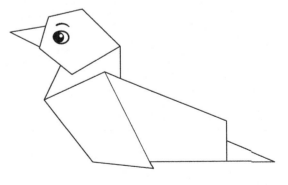

Wild Duck

Horse

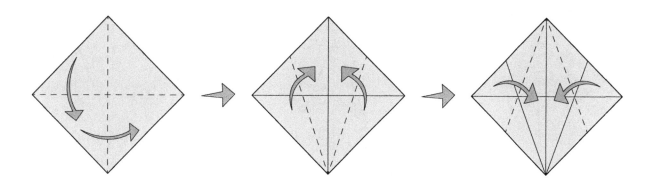

Step 1

Fold the sheet along both diagonals and unfold it.

Step 2

Bring the bottom of both sides in to the vertical midline and unfold.

Step 3

Now bring the top of both sides in to the vertical midline and unfold again.

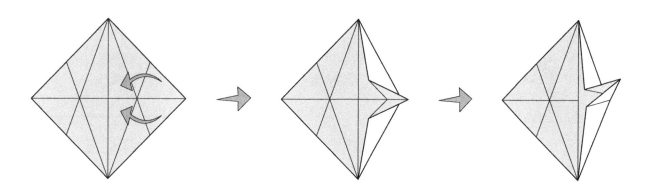

Step 4

Use those creases you just made to fold the right side of the figure. You will see a small flap form in the center of the fold, flatten it up as shown.

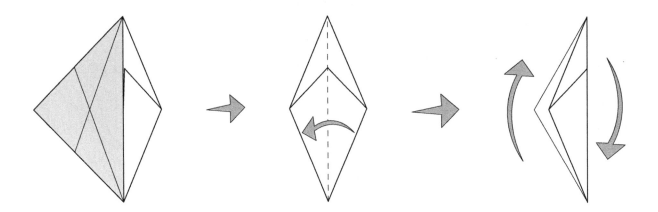

Step 5

Repeat for the left side of the figure, Then fold it backward
in half and rotate it to the right.

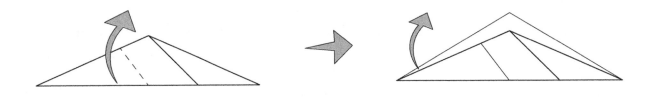

Step 6

Fold the left side of the figure up and unfold it to make a crease, then
use it to make an inside reverse fold.

Horse

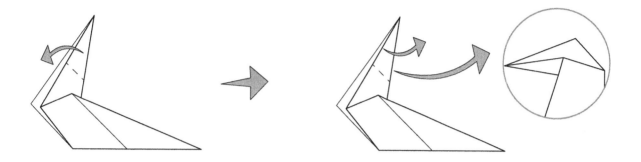

Step 7

Fold the tip of that same section down and unfold it to make a crease, then use it to make another inside reverse fold.

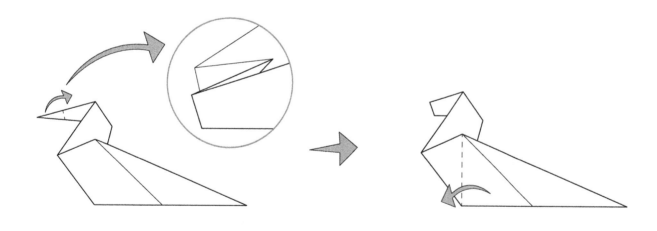

Step 8

Tuck the tip between both layers of the inside reverse fold. Then fold the flaps on both sides of the figure to the left.

Horse

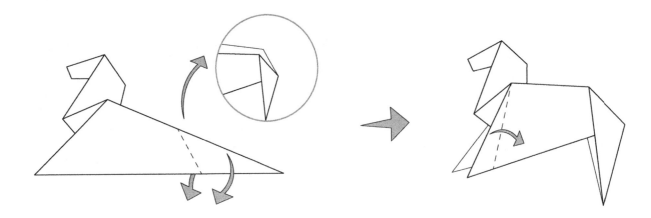

Step 9

Fold the right side of the figure down and unfold it to make a crease, then use it to make an outside reverse fold. Fold the edges of the flaps that you unfolded in the previous step back again.

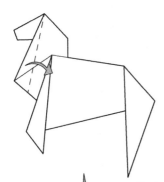

Step 10

Fold the left side of the figure backward as shown, then make an inside reverse fold in the back legs so that both sets of legs are the same length.

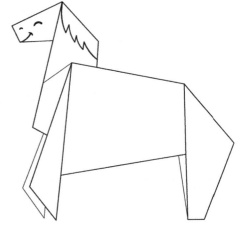

Horse

Whale

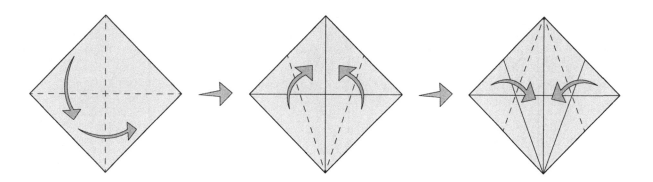

Step 1

Fold the sheet along both diagonals and unfold it.

Step 2

Bring the bottom of both sides in to the vertical midline and unfold.

Step 3

Now bring the top of both sides in to the vertical midline and unfold again.

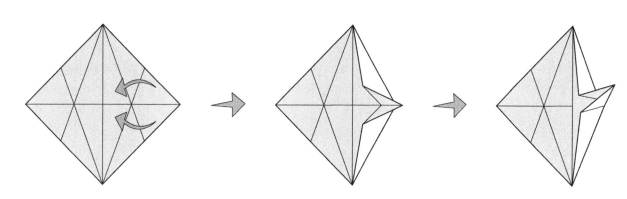

Step 4

Use those creases you just made to fold the right side of the figure.
You will see a small flap form in the center of the fold, flatten it up as shown.

253

Whale

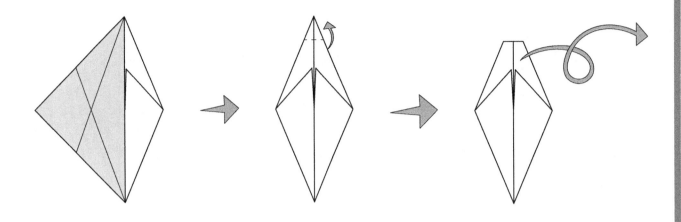

Repeat for the left
side of the figure.

Fold the top corner backward and
flip the figure over.

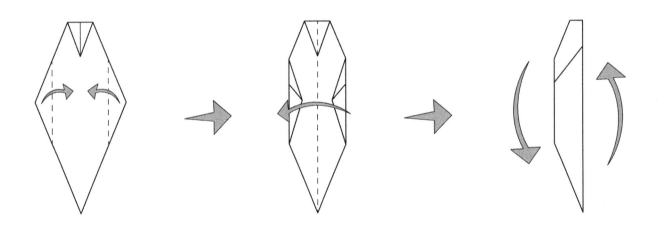

Fold both side corners inward as shown, then fold the figure
to the left in half. Rotate it to the left.

Step 8

Fold the flap on the top layer down so that it sticks out the bottom edge.

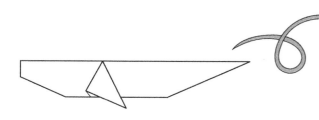 

Step 9

Flip the figure over and fold the flap on the other side too.

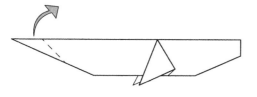 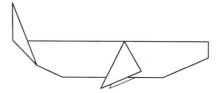

Step 10

Make an outside reverse fold on the left side of the figure.

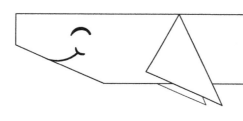

Whale

Origami Boxes

Box

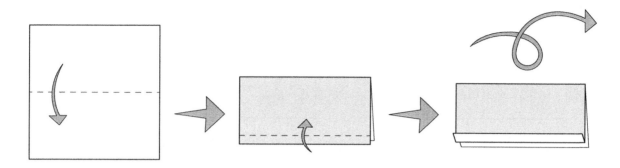

Step 1
Fold the paper sheet down in half.

Step 2
Fold the bottom edge up just a little to make a flap.

Step 3
Flip the figure over and repeat the previous step on the other side.

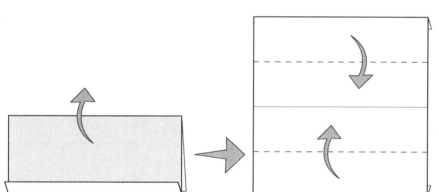

Step 4
Unfold the paper sheet as shown, then bring the top and bottom edges to the horizontal midline.

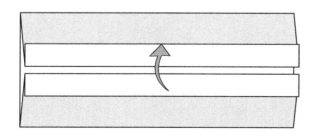

Step 5
Unfold the lower flap.

Box

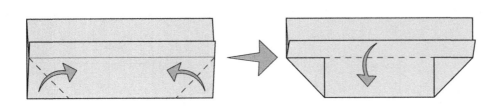

Step 6

Fold the bottom corners diagonally up, then fold the flap back down.

Step 7

Repeat steps 5 and 6 for the upper flap and corners. Then fold sides and unfold them as shown.

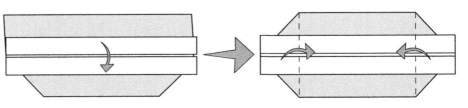

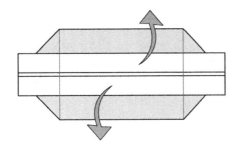

Step 8

Separate the top and bottom halves of the figure while folding the sides back following the creases from the previous step to shape your box.

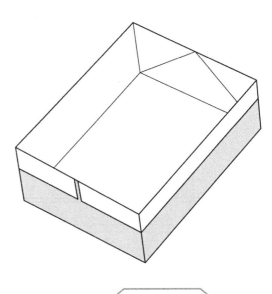

Box

Triangle Box

Tip

You will need 3 paper sheets
for this Triangular Box

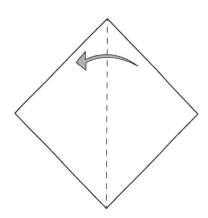

Step 1

Fold the sheet diagonally
in half and unfold.

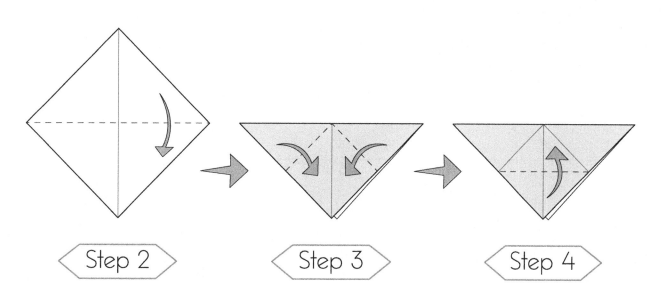

Step 2

Fold it diagonally down
in half to make a triangle.

Step 3

Fold both side corners
down to the vertical
midline, then unfold.

Step 4

Fold the bottom corner
up to meet the top edge,
then unfold.

Triangle Box

Step 5

Repeat steps 1 through 4 for the other two paper sheets.

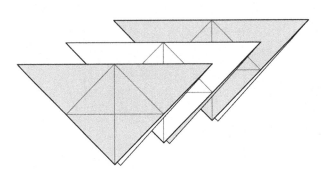

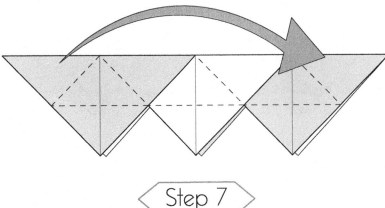

Step 6

Take two sheets and insert one of them between the two layers of the other as shown.

Step 7

Take the 3rd sheet and insert it in the same way to have all three figures in a row. Then close the figure until the two free ends touch and tuck one inside the other.

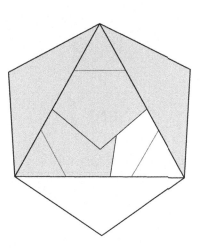

Triangle Box

Pencil Case

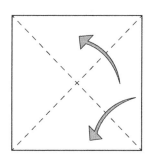

Step 1

Fold the paper sheet diagonally and unfold it.

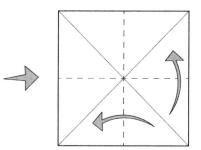

Step 2

Fold the paper sheet crosswise and lengthwise and unfold it.

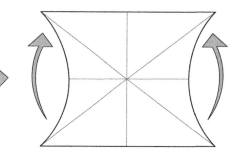

Step 3

Bring the bottom edge up to meet the top edge, while you fold both sides in to make a triangle.

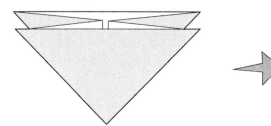

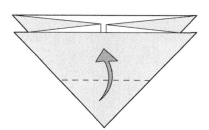

Step 4

Fold the figure up in half and unfold to make a crease, then bring the bottom corner up to that crease.

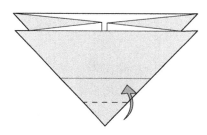

Pencil Case

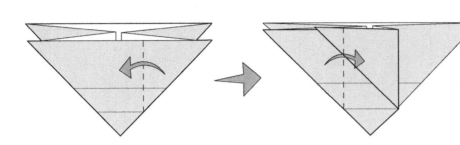

Fold the top layer of the right corner in as shown, then fold the top layer of the left corner over it.

Step 6

Fold the left corner back out so that its edge ends up vertical, then tuck the tip under the right corner you folded in the previous step.

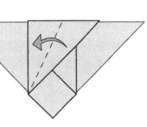

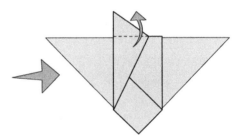

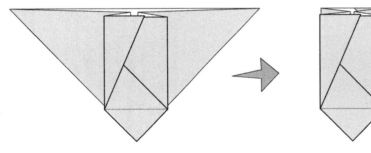

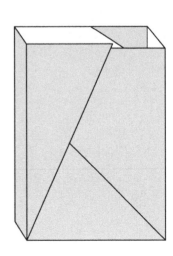

Step 7

Flip the figure over and repeat steps 5 and 6 on the other side, then slowly open the figure until the bottom flattens and the case is ready.

Pencil Case

Cat Box

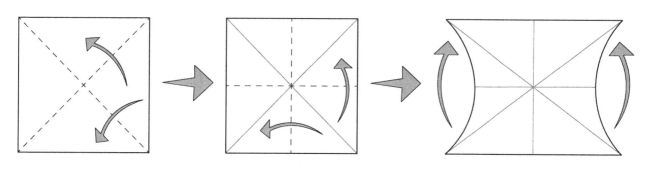

Step 1

Fold the sheet along both diagonals and unfold it.

Step 2

Now fold it lengthwise and crosswise, then unfold.

Step 3

Bring the bottom edge up to meet the top edge, while you fold both sides in to make a triangle.

Step 4

Bring the top layer of the side corners in to the vertical midline, then unfold them. Now fold the bottom corner up along the line that joins those creases you just made, then unfold.

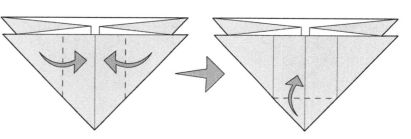

Step 5

Fold the top layer on both sides diagonally inward as shown and unfold to make creases. Then use the creases from the previous step and the ones you just made to pull both sides inward to form a pocket on each side.

Cat Box

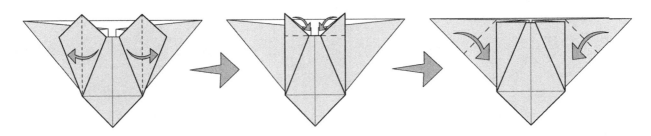

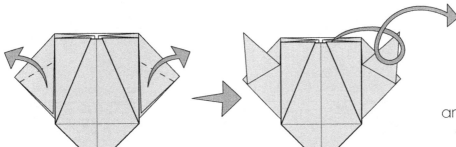

Step 6

Fold the outer half backwards as shown.

Step 7

Tuck the tips sticking out at the top between the layers of the figure.

Step 8

Fold both sides of the bottom layer diagonally down as shown.

Step 9

Fold them back up at an angle so they stick out the sides, then flip the figure over.

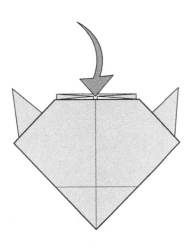

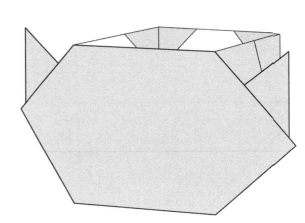

Step 10

Now open the figure from the inside out through the top while flattening the bottom.

Cat Box

Cube

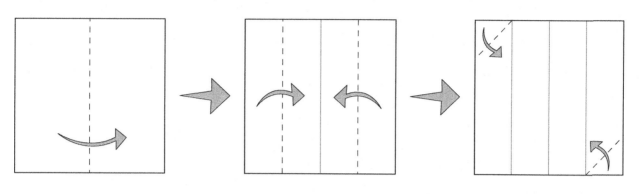

Step 1

Fold the sheet
lengthwise in half
as shown and unfold it.

Step 2

Bring both side edges in to
the vertical midline, then
unfold them.

Step 3

Fold the top left and
bottom right corners
diagonally as shown.

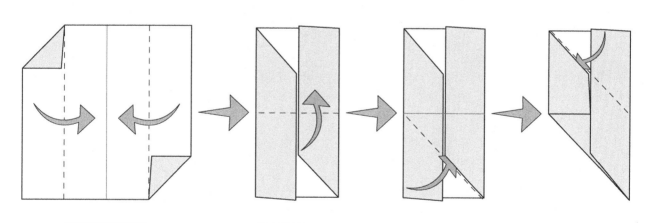

Step 4

Bring both side edges
in to the vertical
midline again.

Step 5

Fold the figure
in half crosswise
and unfold it

Step 6

Fold the bottom left corner
diagonally up and tuck it
under the flap on the right side.
Then fold the top right corner
diagonally down and tuck it
under the flap on the left side.

Cube

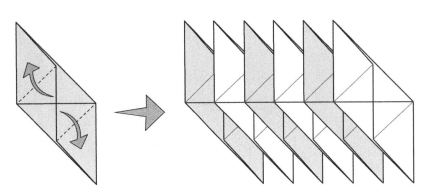

Step 7

Fold both ends until they end up being perpendicular to the center of the figure. Repeat all steps so far until you have 6 of the same figures.

Step 8

Tuck 5 of the pieces inside each other as shown in the picture.

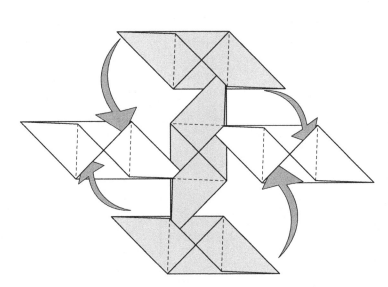

Step 9

Take the last piece and place it on the free side of the cube, tucking its ends into the appropriate sides as shown.

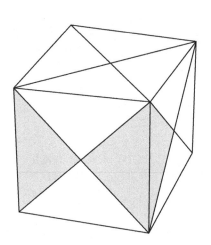

Cube

266

Dice

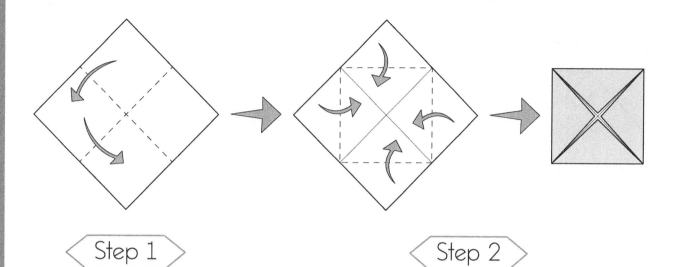

Step 1

Fold the paper sheet crosswise and lengthwise and unfold it.

Step 2

Bring all corners in to the center of the sheet.

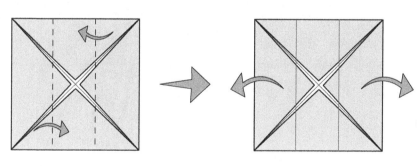

Step 3

Fold the figure lengthwise in three equal parts. Then unfold both side corners back to its original place.

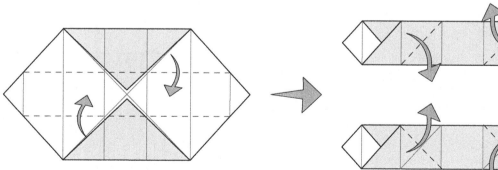

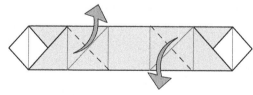

Step 4

Fold the figure crosswise in three equal parts. Make sure they overlap each other.

Step 5

Fold the figure diagonally in the sections shown and unfold.

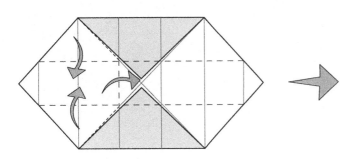

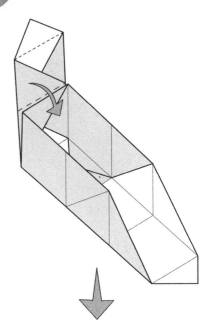

Step 6

Undo the crosswise folds from step 4, then fold both side edges up along the creases from steps 4 and 5. Fold the corner that sticks out down over the folds you just made to lock the sides in place as shown.

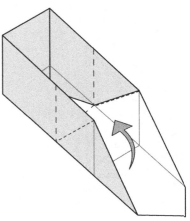

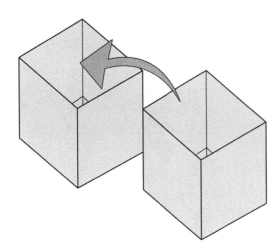

Step 7

Repeat all the steps to make another slightly smaller box and tuck it inside the first box to finish your dice.

Dice

Star Box

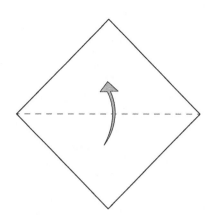

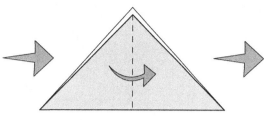

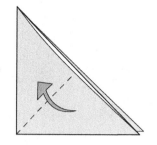

Step 1

Fold the sheet
diagonally up in half.

Step 2

Fold the triangle in
half to the right.

Step 3

Fold the top layer
diagonally up and
unfold it to make
a crease.

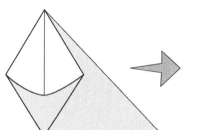

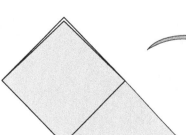

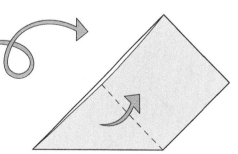

Step 4

Pull this top layer to the left along the crease
you just made and flatten as shown.

Step 5

Flip the figure over and
repeat steps 3 and 4.

269

Star Box

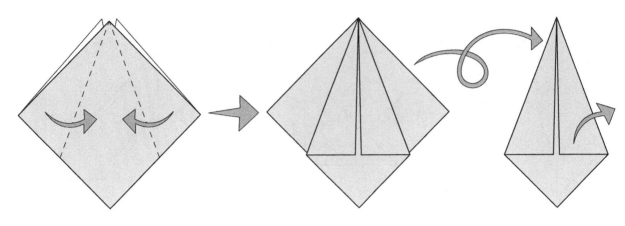

Fold the side corners of the top layer down to the center of the figure.

Flip the figure over and repeat the previous step on the other side. Then open both layers of the right flap and flatten.

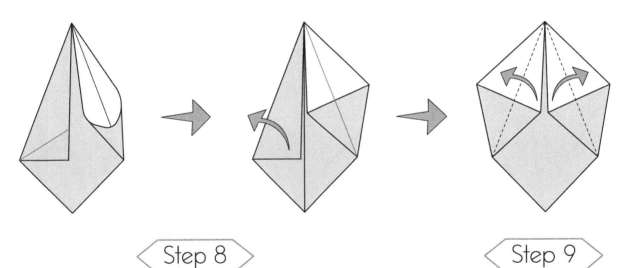

Repeat on the flap on the left side.

Fold the edges sticking out of the sides of the figure backward as shown. Make sure to fold them back on themselves, without going over the bottom layer of the figure.

Star Box

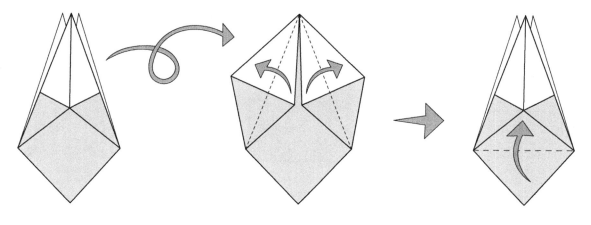

Step 10

Flip the figure over and repeat on the other side.

Step 11

Fold the bottom corner up and unfold.

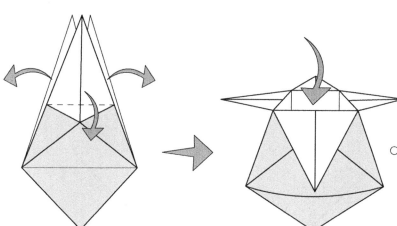

Step 12

Bring all the top corners down as you open the pocket between them and flatten the bottom of the figure.

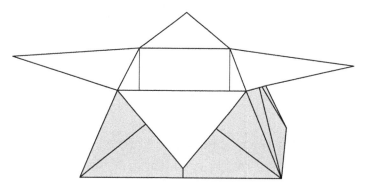

Star Box

Candy Box

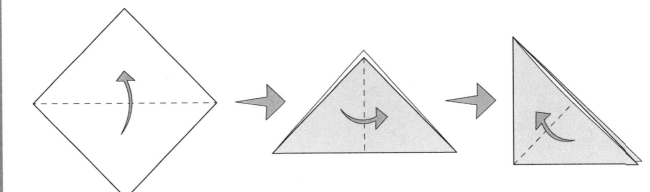

Step 1

Fold the sheet diagonally
up in half.

Step 2

Fold the triangle in
half to the right.

Step 3

Fold the top layer
diagonally up and
unfold it to make a
crease.

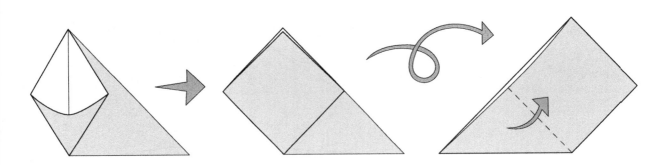

Step 4

Pull this top layer to the left along the crease
you just made and flatten as shown.

Step 5

Flip the figure over and
repeat steps 3 and 4.

272

Candy Box

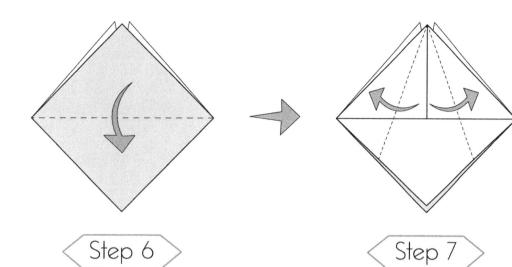

Fold the top layer of the figure down in half.

Fold the side corners backward between both layers of the figure.

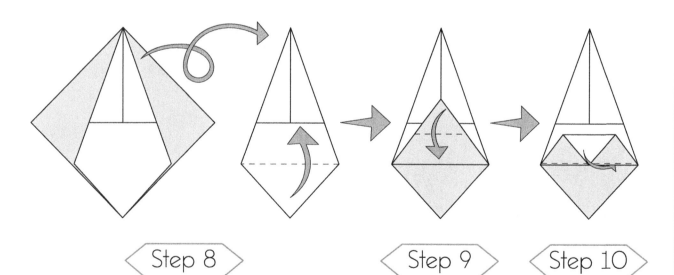

Flip the figure over and repeat on the other side. Then fold the top layer of the bottom corner up.

Fold the same corner down in half.

Now fold the entire flap you just made down and tuck it under the top layer as shown.

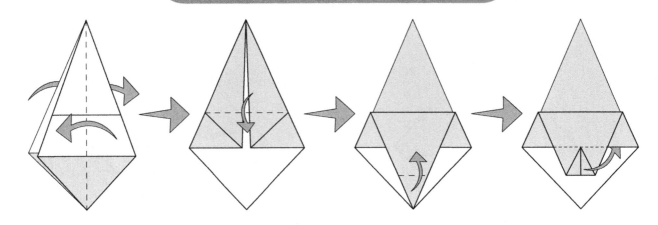

Step 11

Repeat on the other side of the figure, then turn the top layer from the right side to the left as shown.

Step 12

Fold the top layer of the top corner down, and then up again.

Step 13

Now fold it backward and tuck it under the top layer as shown.

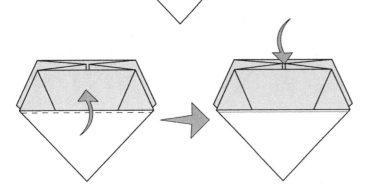

Step 14

Flip the figure over again and repeat on the other side.

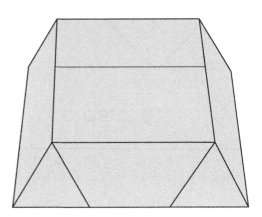

Step 15

Fold the bottom corner up and unfold it to make a crease. Then open the top edge of the figure while flattening the bottom.

Candy Box

Chinese Dish

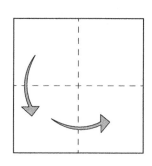 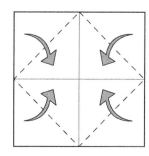 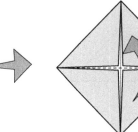

Step 1

Fold the sheet in half lengthwise and crosswise, then unfold.

Step 2

Bring all corners to the center of the sheet, where the two creases from the previous step meet.

Step 3

Fold the bottom half of the figure backward as shown.

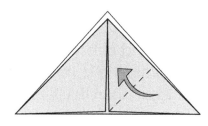 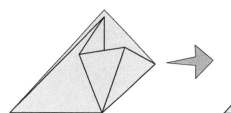

Step 4

Fold the right corner diagonally up and unfold it to make a crease.

Step 5

Pull the crease you just made to the left until the right corner meets the top corner and flatten as shown.

Chinese Dish

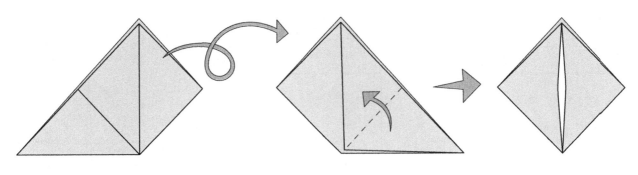

Step 6

Flip the figure over.

Step 7

Repeat steps 4 and 5 on this side of the figure.

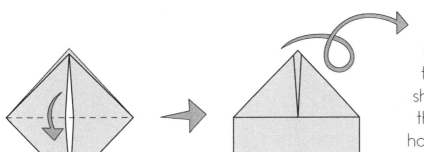

Step 8

Fold the two flaps at the top of the figure down as shown. If you look just below them you will see that they have two inner corners in the middle of the figure, Pull them outward and flatten to get a rectangle in the lower half of the figure, then flip it over.

Step 9

Repeat step 8 on this side. Now bring the top layer of the left half of the figure all the way to the right then do the same on the back side of the figure.

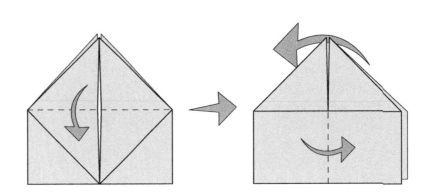

Chinese Dish

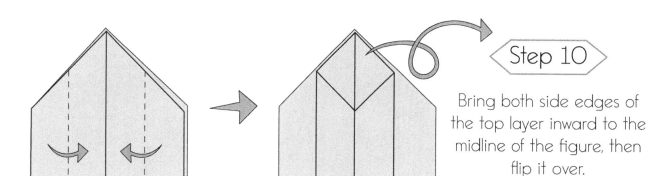

Step 10

Bring both side edges of the top layer inward to the midline of the figure, then flip it over.

Step 11

Fold both side edges inward as well, then fold the top layer forward down in half as shown. Fold the back layer backward down in half as well.

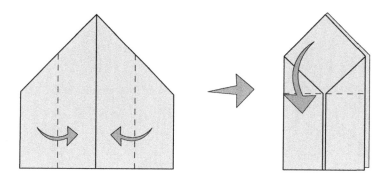

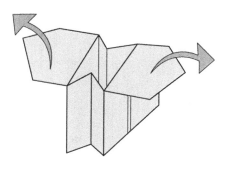

Step 12

Unfold these flaps you just made halfway up and use them to slowly open the whole figure, then flatten the sides.

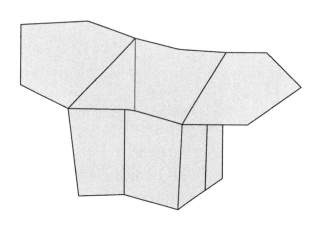

Chinese Dish

Table Box

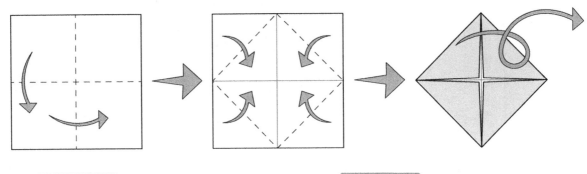

Step 1

Fold the sheet lengthwise and crosswise and unfold it.

Step 2

Bring all corners in to the center of the sheet, then flip the figure over.

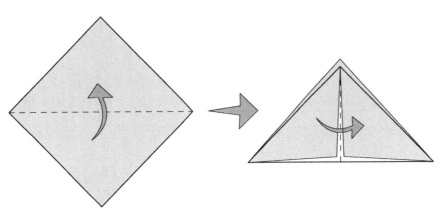

Step 3

Fold the figure up in half to make a triangle, then fold it in half again to the right.

Step 4

Fold the top layer diagonally up and unfold it to make a crease. Then pull this top layer to the left along the crease you just made and flatten as shown.

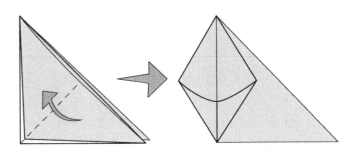

Table Box

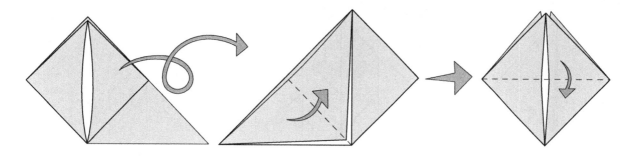

Step 5

Flip the figure over and repeat on the other side.

Step 6

You'll see that there's a pocket right in the center of the figure. Fold the top of the figure down in half as you open that pocket and flatten to get a rectangle in the bottom. Then repeat on the other side.

Step 7

Fold the top layer of the bottom edge up and fatten the sides, then flip the figure over.

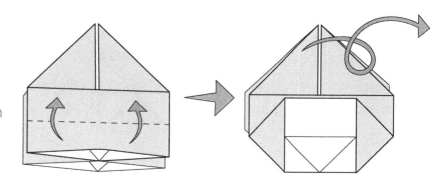

Step 8

Repeat the previous step on the other side, then turn the right half of the figure to the left. Flip he figure over and turn the right half on that side to the left.

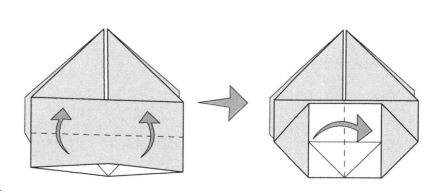

Table Box

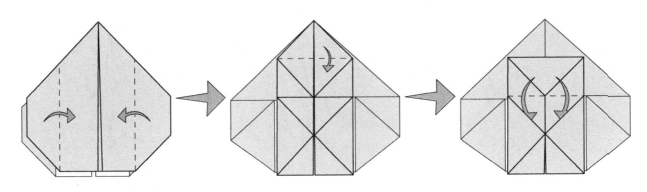

Step 9

Bring both side edges of the top layer to the center of the figure.

Step 10

Fold down the top corner of the top layer as shown.

Step 11

Fold it down again and tuck it under the layer just below.

Step 12

Fold the flaps at the bottom diagonally up and out, and tuck them under the same layer. Flip the figure over and repeat the same on other side of the figure.

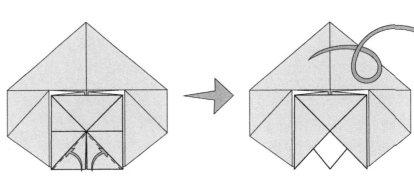

Step 13

Now open the figure from the inside out through the top while flattening the bottom. Make sure the legs of the table stick out from the bottom so you can stand it up.

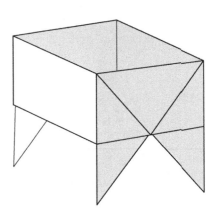

Table Box

Container

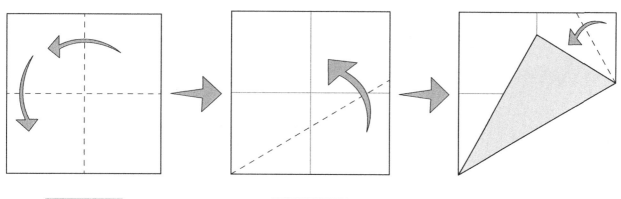

Step 1

Fold the paper sheet in half lengthwise and crosswise. Then unfold it.

Step 2

Bring the bottom right corner up to the vertical midline as shown.

Step 3

Fold the top right corner down to the edge of the flap from the previous step.

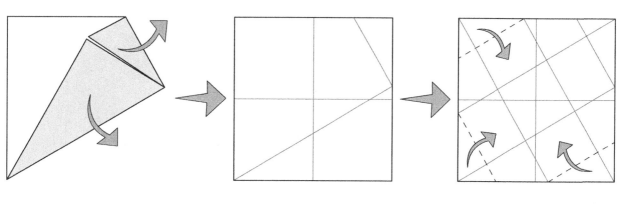

Step 4

Unfold everything to get these creases.

Step 5

Repeat steps 2 to 4 to get the same creases on all corners.

281

Container

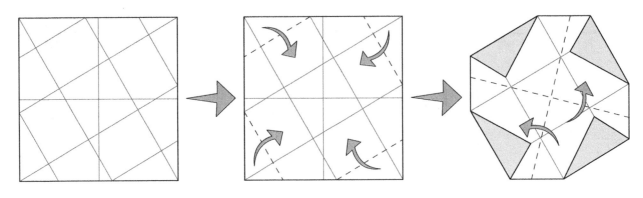

Step 6

Fold all the corners again along the
creases shown in the drawing.

Step 7

At this point you'll see that
the creases you've made form
a square right in the center
of the figure. Fold the entire
figure along both diagonals
of that square, then unfold.

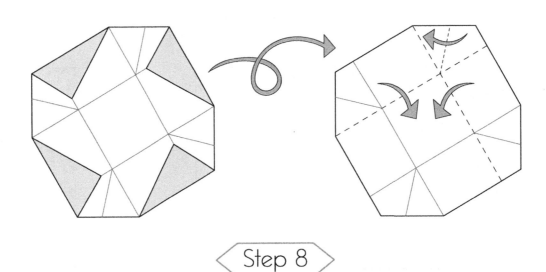

Step 8

Flip the figure over. Fold both top sides halfway up so they end up perpendicular
to each other, while you see the crease you just made to fold in the flap that forms
between these two walls and flatten it.

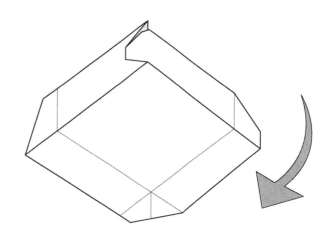

Step 9

Rotate the figure until the outside of that corner ends up facing you.

Step 10

If you slightly open the flap between both walls, you'll see that there's a small pocket on one of the sides. Tuck the corner from the opposite side into that pocket to lock the walls in place. Then repeat in the other corners until all the walls are in place.

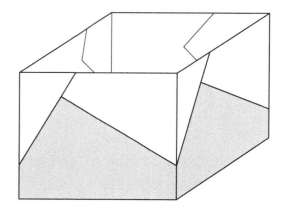

Container

Gift Box

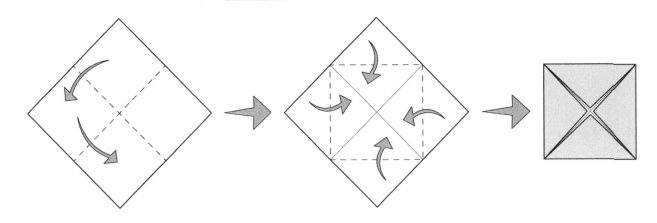

Step 1

Fold the paper sheet in half lengthwise and crosswise. Then unfold it.

Step 2

Bring all corners to the center of the sheet, where the two creases from the previous step meet.

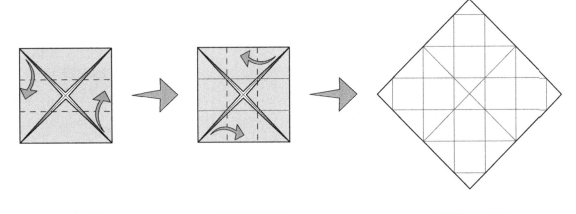

Step 3

Fold the figure crosswise in three equal parts, then unfold.

Step 4

Now fold the figure lengthwise in three equal parts and unfold.

Step 5

Unfold everything else you've done so far.

Gift Box

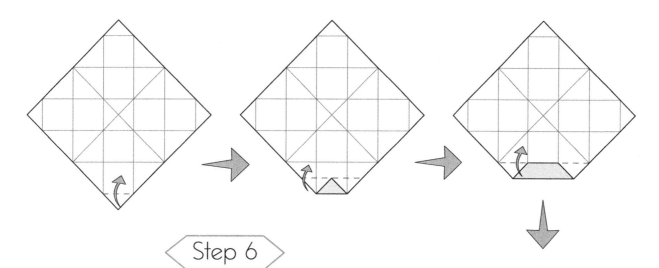

Step 6

Fold the bottom corner up three times in a row as shown: first along the first crease, then at its tip, and then along the second crease you'll find. Repeat this step on all corners.

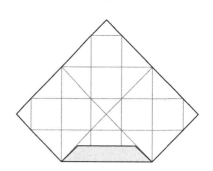

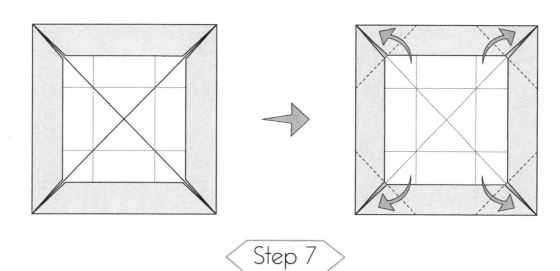

Step 7

Fold all corners diagonally backward as shown.

Gift Box

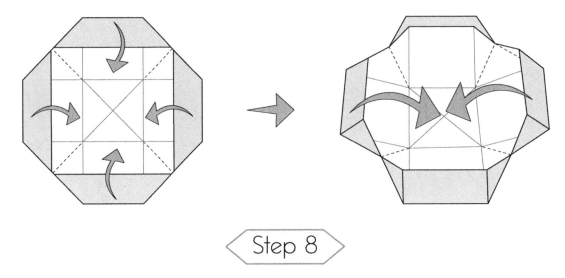

Fold all sides halfway up. To do that, fold the corners inward as shown.

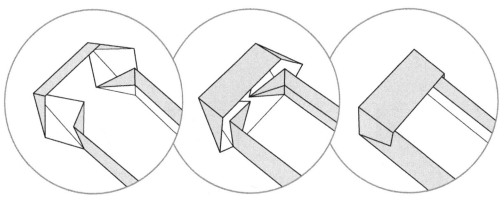

Step 9

Finish folding the walls up, placing both sides above the top and bottom walls. To do this use the flaps you folded back in step 7 to lock everything in place.

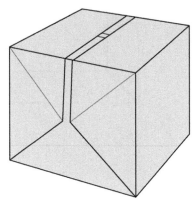

Gift Box

286

Bowl

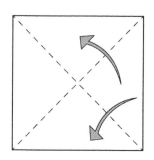 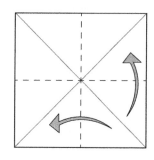

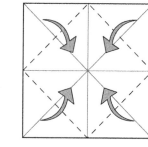

Step 1

Fold the sheet along both diagonals and unfold it.

Step 2

Now fold it lengthwise and crosswise, then unfold.

Step 3

Bring all corners to the center of the sheet and unfold them.

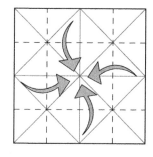 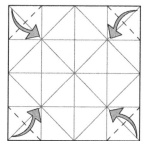  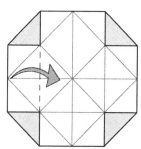

Step 4

Bring the side edges to the vertical midline and unfold. Then bring the top and bottom edges to the horizontal midline and unfold.

Step 5

Fold all corners diagonally in toward the creases from the previous step.

Step 6

Fold the left edge in toward the vertical midline.

Bowl

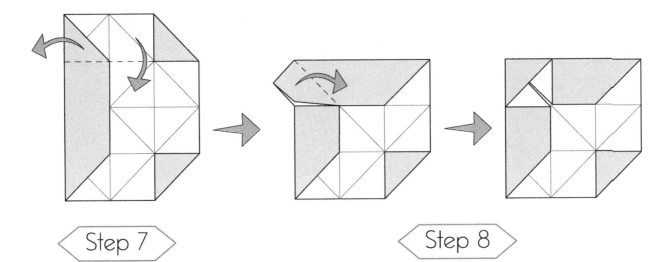

Fold the top edge down to the horizontal midline, while pulling out the top corner of the fold you just made.

Open both layers of that flap and flatten, then repeat for all corners.

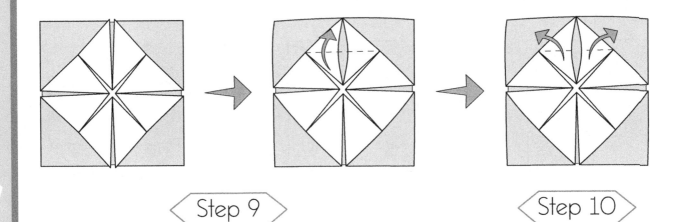

Fold the flap at the top of the figure up in half and unfold it to make a crease.

Now use that crease to open up the layers of that same flap and fold them up to make a rectangle, then repeat on the other corners.

Bowl

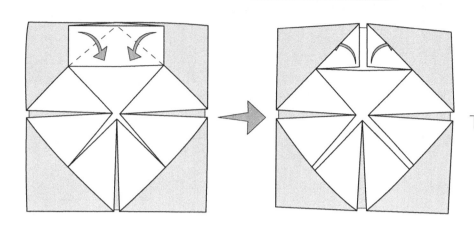

Step 11

Tuck the corners of those rectangles under the corners of the top layer as shown.

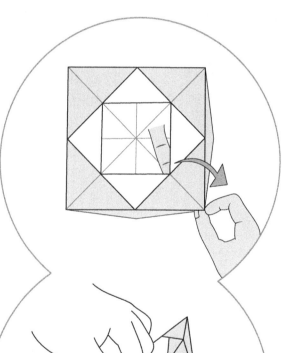

Step 12

Using your finger to hold one corner, Use your other hand to press its sides inward. Then repeat in the other corners.

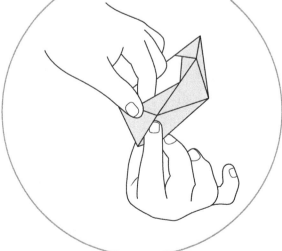

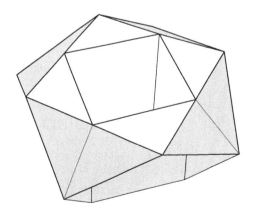

Bowl

Pyramid Box

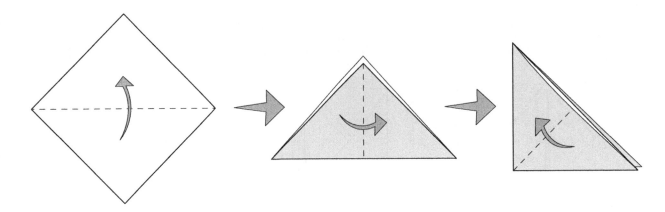

Step 1	Step 2	Step 3

Step 1

Fold the sheet diagonally up in half.

Step 2

Fold the triangle you just made in half.

Step 3

Fold the top layer diagonally up and unfold it to make a crease.

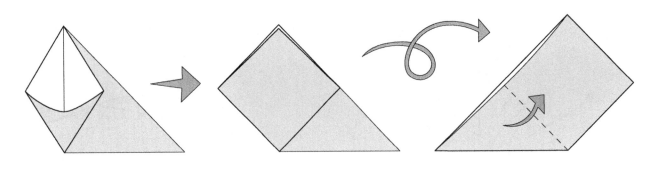

Step 4

Pull this top layer to the left along the crease you just made and flatten as shown.

Step 5

Flip the figure over and repeat steps 3 and 4.

Pyramid Box

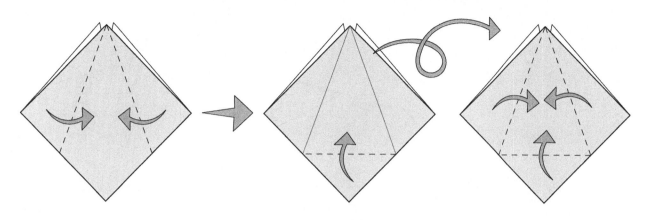

Step 6

Bring the side corners in to the center of the figure and unfold to make a creases.

Step 7

Fold the bottom corner up along the lines that join the creases you just made, then unfold.

Step 8

Flip the figure over and repeat steps 6 and 7 on the other side.

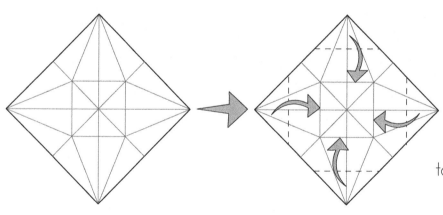

Step 9

Unfold everything and you'll see that there's a square right in the center of the sheet. Bring all corners in to meet that square as shown, then unfold them.

Step 10

Bring all corners in to the creases you made in previous step, then unfold just the side corners.

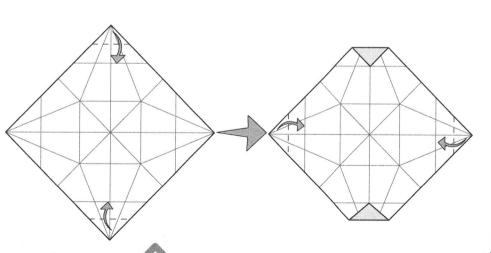

Pyramid Box

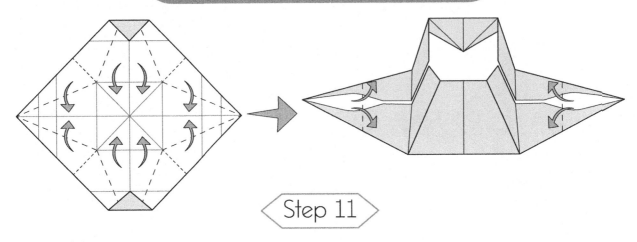

Step 11

Bring the edges of both side corners toward the horizontal midline. As you do that you'll see diagonal mountain folds (see drawing) and valley folds on either side of the top and bottom corners that make them end up an angle to the rest of the figure.

Step 12

Slightly open both sides of the top layer of the side corners, then bring them in to the crease you made in step 9.

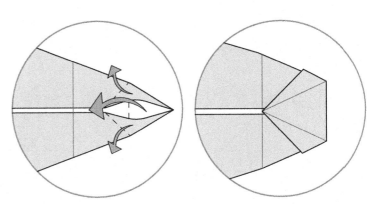

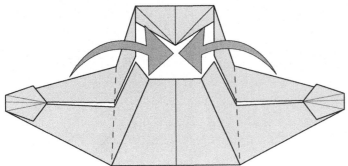

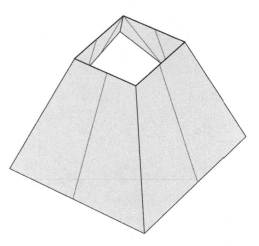

Step 13

Fold both sides up and place the flaps you just made on top of the walls that were already up to lock everything in place.

Pyramid Box

Vase

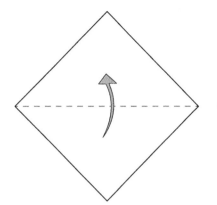

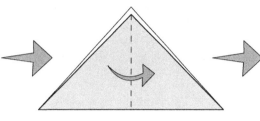

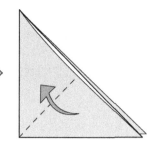

Step 1

Fold the sheet diagonally up in half.

Step 2

Fold the triangle you just made in half.

Step 3

Fold the top layer diagonally up and unfold it to make a crease.

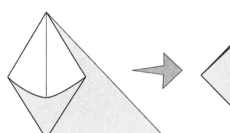

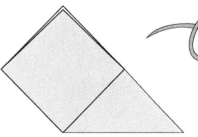

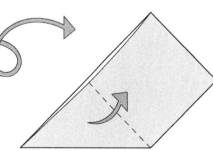

Step 4

Pull this top layer to the left along the crease you just made and flatten as shown.

Step 5

Flip the figure over and repeat steps 3 and 4.

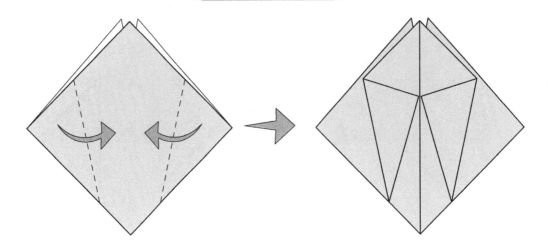

Bring the top layer of the side corners in to the center of the figure, then do the same on the back layer.

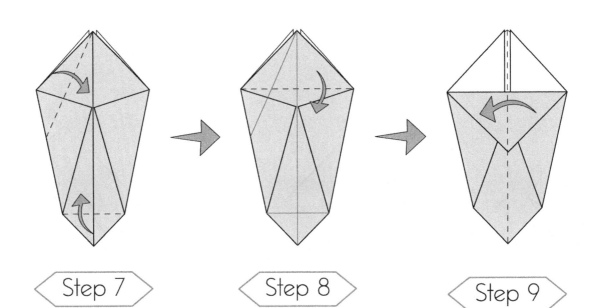

Step 7

Fold the top left corner down to the midline and the bottom corner up as shown, then unfold to make creases.

Step 8

Fold the top layer of the top corner down as shown.

Step 9

Now fold the top layer on the right side over to the left.

Vase

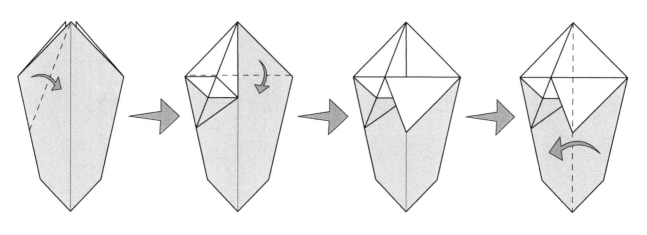

Step 10

Repeat steps through 9 for another side of the figure.

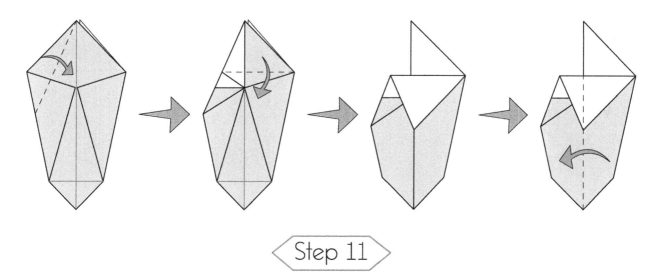

Step 11

Repeat steps 7 to 9 again for the next side of the figure.

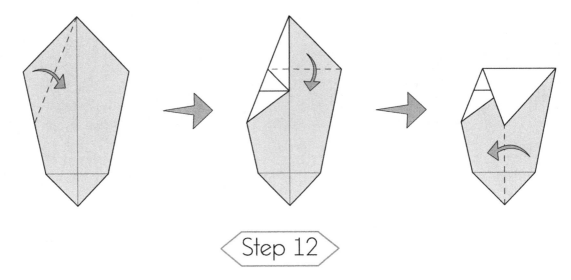

Repeat steps 7 through 9 one more time for the last side of the figure.

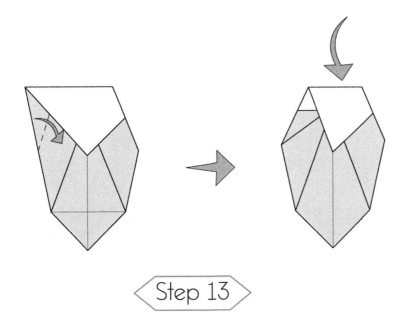

> Step 13 <

At this point you will see that one last corner sticks out. Fold it in as you did with the others and tuck it under the flap at the top of the figure as shown. Then push the bottom of the figure to shape the vase.

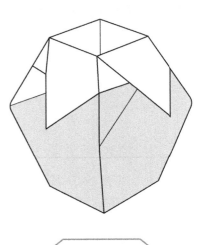

> Vase <

Basket

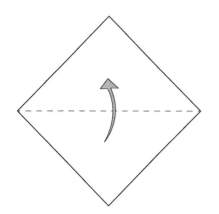

Fold the sheet diagonally up in half.

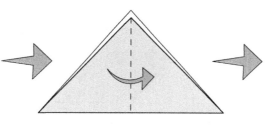

Step 2

Fold the triangle you just made in half.

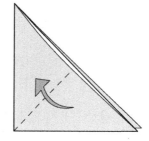

Step 3

Fold the top layer diagonally up and unfold it to make a crease.

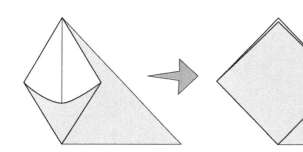

Step 4

Pull this top layer to the left along the crease you just made and flatten as shown.

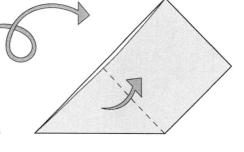

Step 5

Flip the figure over and repeat steps 3 and 4.

297

Basket

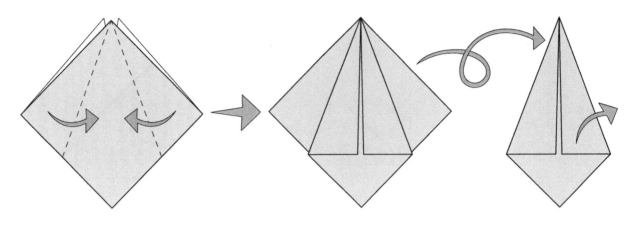

Step 6

Bring the side corners in to the center of the figure.

Step 7

Flip the figure over and repeat the previous step on the other side. Then open both layers of the right flap and flatten.

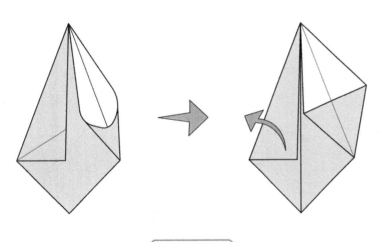
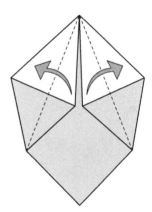

Step 8

Repeat on the flap on the left side.

Step 9

Fold the edges sticking out of the sides of the figure backward as shown. Make sure to fold them back on themselves, without going over the bottom layer of the figure.

Basket

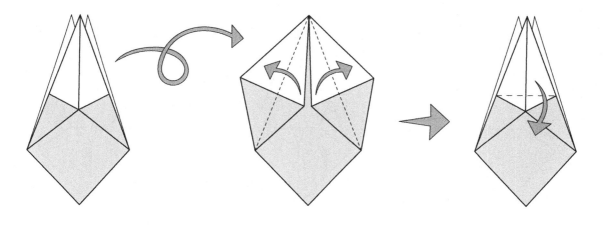

Flip the figure over and repeat on the other side.

Fold the top layer of the top corner down as shown.

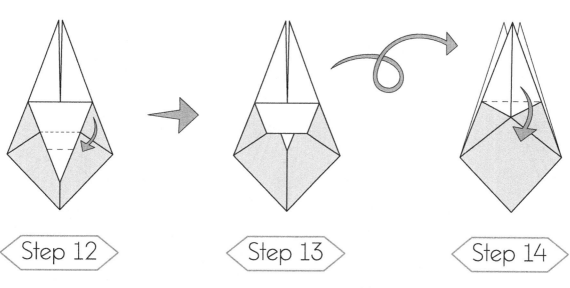

Fold it again backward and tuck it between the flaps just below.

Flip the figure over.

Repeat steps 11 and 12 on the other side.

Basket

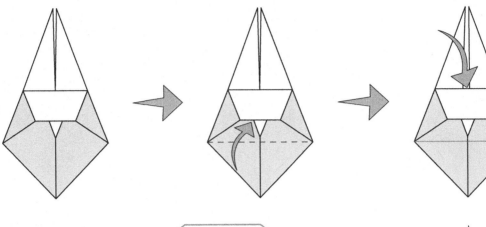

Fold the bottom corner up as shown and unfold it
to make a crease. Now open the top of the figure
from the inside out, while flattening the bottom.

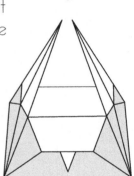

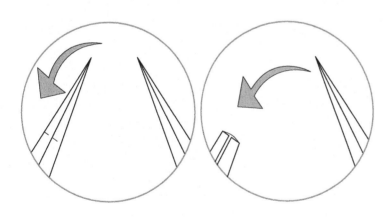

Step 16

Fold down one of the corners sticking out
and tuck the end of the other into that fold.

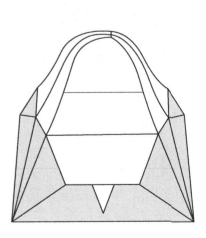

Basket

Diamond Box

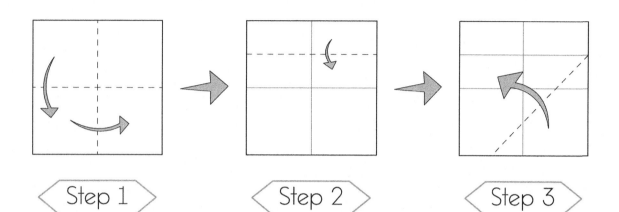

Step 1

Fold the paper sheet
in half lengthwise and
crosswise. Then unfold it.

Step 2

Bring the top edge
down to the horizontal
midline and unfold it
to make a crease.

Step 3

Fold the bottom right
corner diagonally up to
the crease you just made.

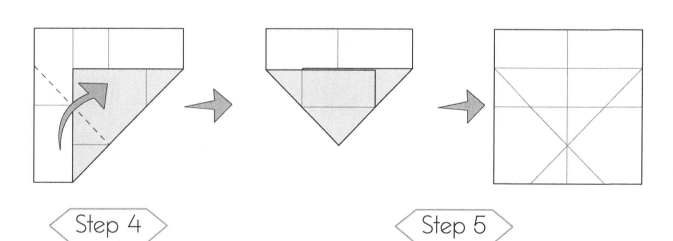

Step 4

Repeat for the left corner
to make a triangle at the
bottom of the figure.

Step 5

Unfold everything, your creases must
match the illustration.

Diamond Box

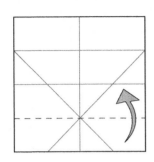 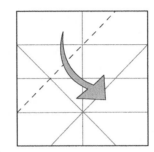 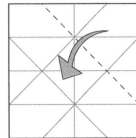

Step 6

Bring the bottom edge
up to the horizontal
midline and unfold
it to make a crease.

Step 7

Fold the upper left corner
diagonally down to the
crease you just made, then
unfold.

Step 8

Repeat for the right
corner and unfold.

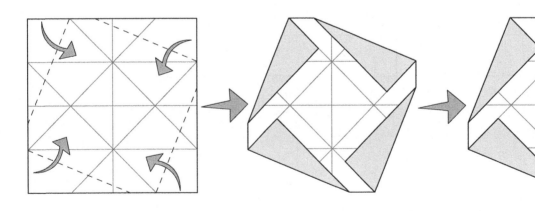

Step 9

Fold all the corners as shown, so that all the flaps end up
being parallel to the diagonal creases you made in the
previous steps with a small gap between them, as you
can see in the illustration.

Step 10

Fold the bottom right
corner in along the
crease shown.

Diamond Box

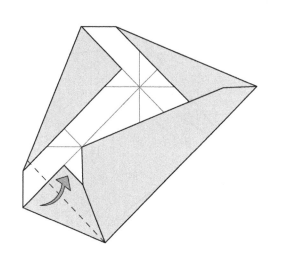

Step 11

Use the crease you just made as a mark
to fold the bottom left corner up.

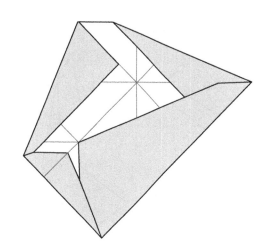

Step 12

Now unfold it to make a crease.

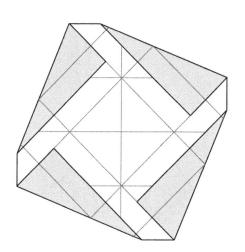

Step 13

Repeat steps 10 – 12 to
make creases at all corners
of the figure.

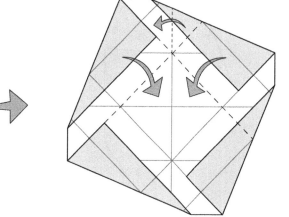

Step 14

Fold both top sides halfway up so they
are perpendicular to each other. At the
same time use the creases you've made
so far to fold in the flap that forms
between these two sides walls and flatten it.

Diamond Box

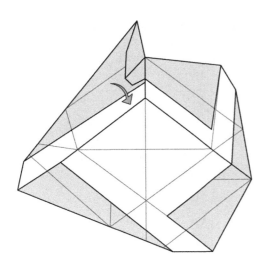

Step 15

Tuck the flap you just made under the
top layer on the left as shown.

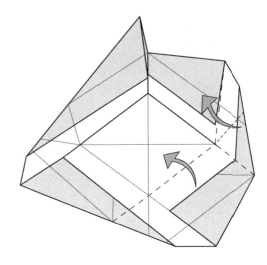

Step 16

Repeat steps 14 and 15 for
all sides of the figure.

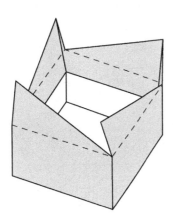

Step 17

At this point you will see a corner
sticking out at the top of each wall.
Fold them halfway down on top of
each other to lock them in place
as shown.

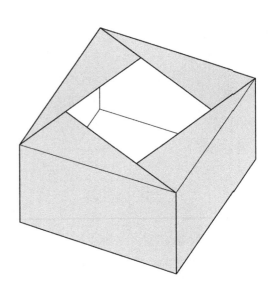

Diamond Box

Hinged Box

Tip

You will need 2 paper sheets for this Hinged Box. One for the box and other for the lid.

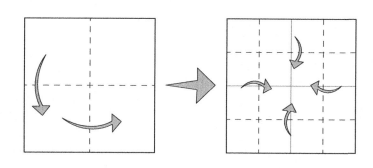

Step 1

Fold the sheet in half lengthwise and crosswise. Unfold it.

Step 2

Bring the side edges to the vertical midline and unfold. Then bring the top and bottom edges to the horizontal midline and unfold.

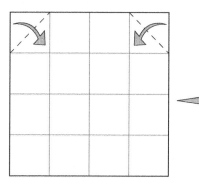

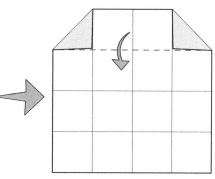

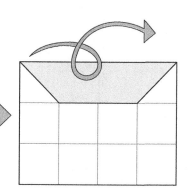

Step 3

Fold both top corners diagonally down.

Step 4

Fold the top edge down to the horizontal midline.

Step 5

Flip the figure over.

Hinged Box

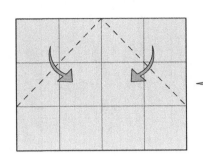

Step 6

Fold both corners diagonally down to the vertical midline.

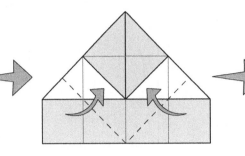

Step 7

Now fold both bottom corners diagonally up to the vertical midline as well.

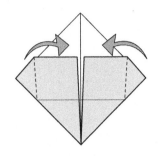

Step 8

Tuck the side corners in between the layers of the figure.

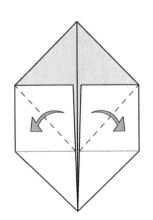

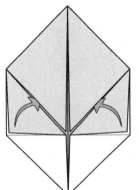

Step 9

Fold both sides of the top layer diagonally down as shown, then tuck them under the bottom layer.

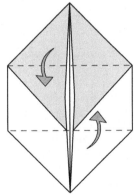

Step 10

Fold the top corner down and unfold, then fold the bottom corner up and unfold.

Hinged Box

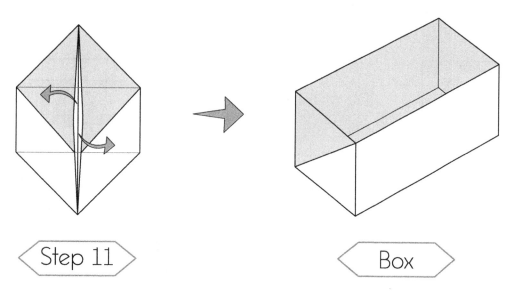

Open the figure from the center to the sides and flatten them.

Box

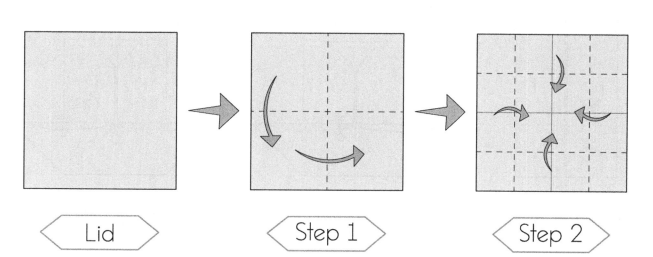

Lid

Take another sheet for the Lid.

Step 1

Fold the sheet in half lengthwise and crosswise. Unfold it.

Step 2

Bring the side edges to the vertical midline and unfold. Then bring the top and bottom edges to the horizontal midline and unfold

Hinged Box

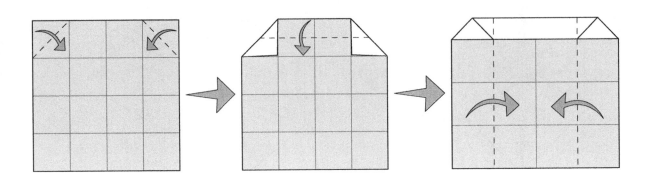

Step 3

Fold both top corners diagonally down.

Step 4

Fold the top edge down to match the crease you made in step 2.

Step 5

Bring the side edges to the vertical midline.

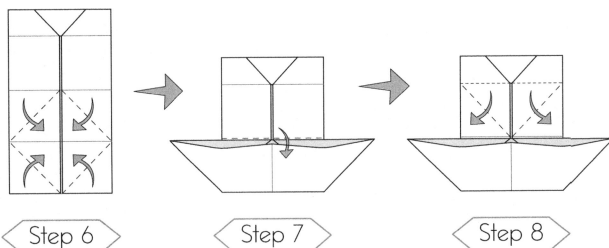

Step 6

Make diagonal folds in the bottom half of the figure to match the drawing.

Step 7

Fold both sides of the top layer outward along the creases you just made. As you do it, you'll see the bottom layer also fold up so flatten it.

Step 8

Fold both side flaps diagonally down and out as shown. As you do that, you'll see that the top and side edges end up being perpendicular to the figure.

Hinged Box

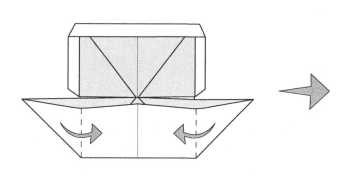

Fold the corners that stick out on both sides halfway forward. Then use them to attach the lid to the box you already made, tucking them into both sides of the box as shown.

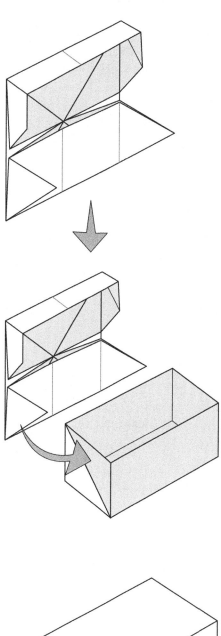

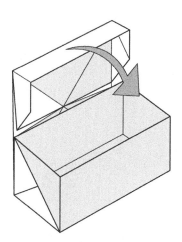

Step 10

Close the lid and your Hinged Box is ready.

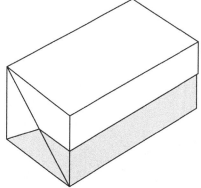

Hinged Box

Rectangular Box

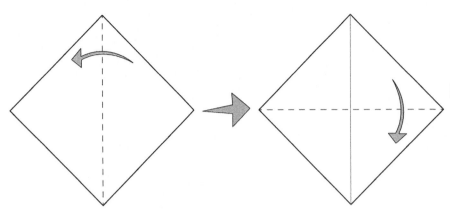

Step 1

Fold the sheet diagonally to the left in half and unfold. Then fold it diagonally down in half to make a triangle.

Step 2

Fold the triangle up in half and unfold it to make a crease. Now fold the top layer of the bottom corner up again to meet that crease.

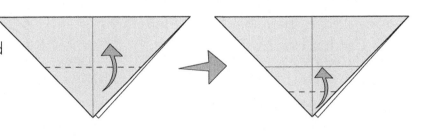

Step 3

Repeat the previous step on the back side of the figure, then unfold the diagonal fold from step 1 as shown.

Rectangular Box

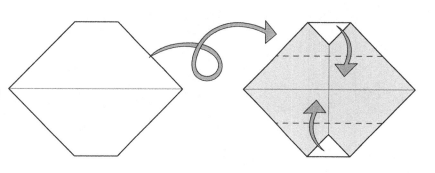

Step 4

Flip the figure over and bring the top and bottom edges to the horizontal midline.

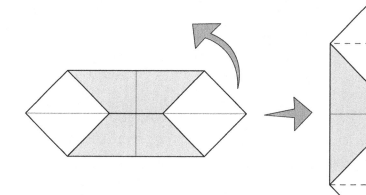

Step 5

Rotate the figure clockwise. Then fold the top and bottom corners inward as shown to make two triangular flaps.

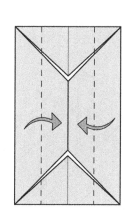

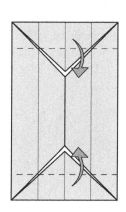

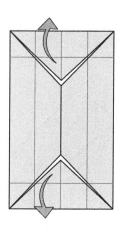

Step 6

Bring both side edges in to the vertical midline and unfold.

Step 7

Bring the top and bottom edges forward, folding the triangular flaps in half and unfold.

Step 8

Unfold the triangular flaps.

Rectangular Box

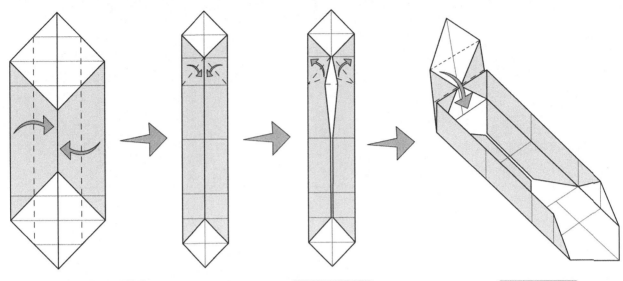

Bring both side edges in to the vertical midline again. Then fold one of the top corners diagonally down, unfold, fold the other diagonally down as well, and unfold as shown. Repeat on the bottom corner.

Step 10

Unfold both side edges halfway up, while using the diagonal creases you just made to fold up the top corner until these three sides are perpendicular to each other.

Step 11

Fold the part of the corner that sticks out down over the folds you just made to lock the sides in place as shown.

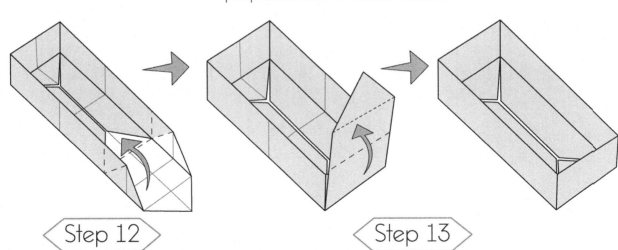

Step 12

Use the diagonal creases you made on the bottom corner to fold it halfway up as well.

Step 13

Fold the part of the corner that sticks out down over the sides to lock them in place as shown. The box is ready!

Rectangular Box

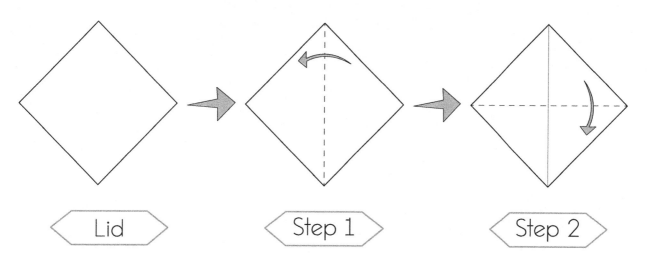

Lid

Use another square sheet for the Lid.

Step 1

Fold the sheet diagonally to the left in half and unfold.

Step 2

Fold it diagonally down in half to make a triangle.

Step 3

Fold the triangle up in half and unfold it to make a crease. Now fold the top layer of the bottom corner up again to meet that crease.

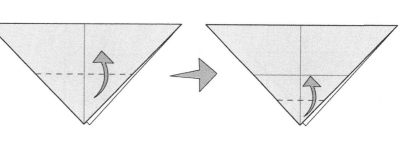

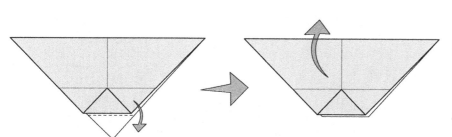

Step 4

Repeat the previous step on the back side of the figure, then unfold the diagonal fold from step 2 as shown.

313

Rectangular Box

Step 5

Flip the figure over and bring the top and bottom edges to the horizontal midline.

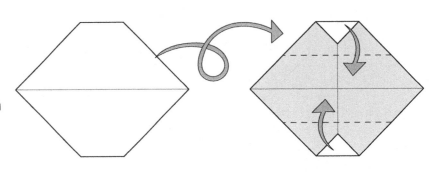

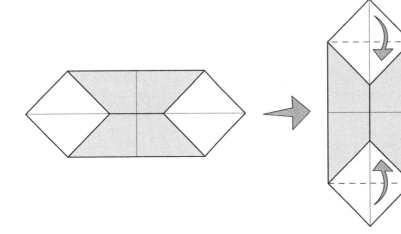

Step 6

Rotate the figure clockwise. Then fold the top and bottom corners inward as shown to make two triangular flaps.

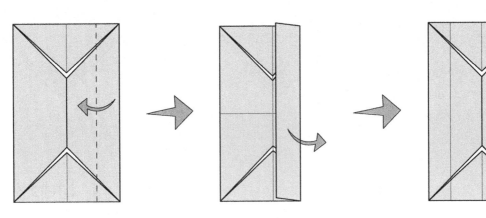

Step 7

Fold the right edge in, not all the way to the vertical midline this time, and unfold.

Step 8

Repeat for the left edge.

Rectangular Box

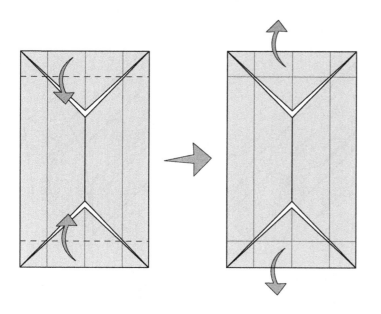

Bring the top and bottom edges forward, folding the triangular flaps in less than half this time, and unfold. Then completely unfold the triangular flaps.

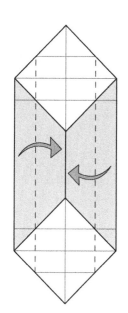 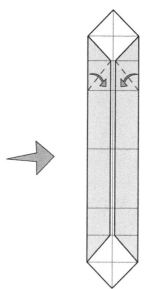 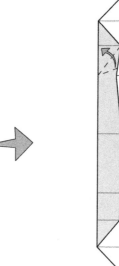

Step 10

Bring both side edges in along the creases from steps 7 and 8.

Step 11

Fold one of the top corners diagonally down, unfold, fold the other diagonally down as well, and unfold as shown. Repeat on the bottom corner.

Step 12

Unfold both side edges halfway up, while using the diagonal creases you just made to fold up the top corner until these three sides are perpendicular to each other.

Rectangular Box

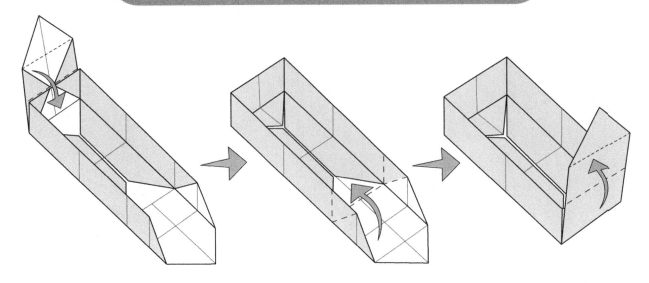

Step 13

Fold the part of the corner that sticks out down over the folds you just made to lock the sides in place as shown.

Step 14

Use the diagonal creases you made on the bottom corner to fold it halfway up as well.

Step 15

Fold the part of the corner that sticks out down over the sides to lock them in place as shown.

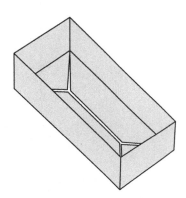

Step 16

The lid is ready and now you can put it on top of the box.

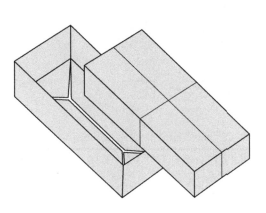

Rectangular Box

Tall Box

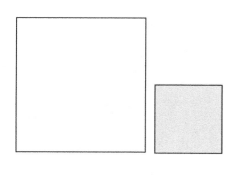

You will need 2 paper sheets for this Tall Box. The 1st sheet should be twice as big as the 2nd.

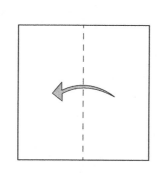

Step 1

Fold the 1st sheet (the largest one) in half lengthwise and unfold it.

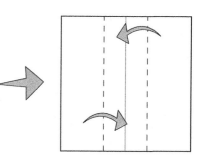

Step 2

Now fold the sheet lengthwise into three equal parts and unfold to make creases.

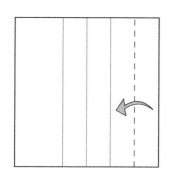

Step 3

Bring the right edge up to the crease you just made on the right side, then unfold.

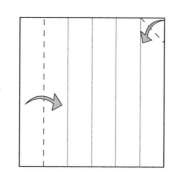

Step 4

Now bring the left edge up to the same crease on the left side. Then fold the top right corner diagonally down as shown and unfold it to make a crease.

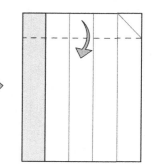

Step 5

Fold the top edge down just below the diagonal crease you just made. Unfold it to make a crease.

Tall Box

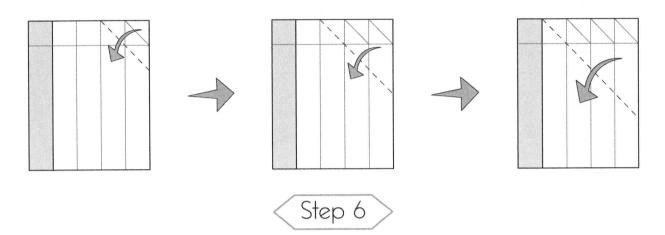

Step 6

Fold the top right corner down to meet the next vertical crease as shown and unfold. Keep repeating this step until the top right corner reaches the left edge and you have diagonal creases all across the top of the figure as shown in the drawing.

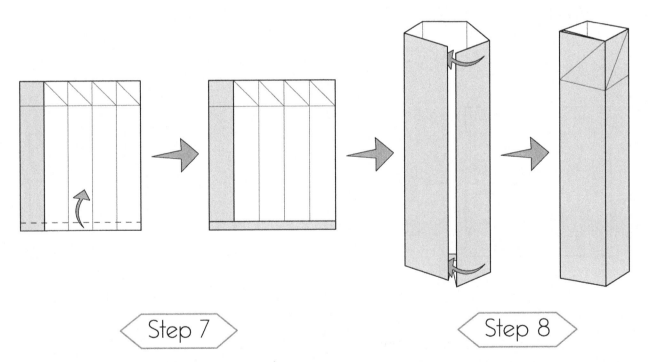

Step 7

Fold the bottom edge upward just a little.

Step 8

Fold the figure on itself until the two ends overlap. Use the small fold from previous step to tuck one end into the other and lock them in place.

Tall Box

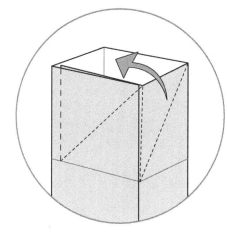

Starting on the side where two walls of the figure overlap, fold the top corner of the inner layer diagonally down. Then fold also diagonally down the top of the next wall, to do this you must make a mountain fold on its diagonal as well as a valley fold on its left edge. You'll see that the first side folds halfway down to end up being perpendicular to the figure.

Step 10

Repeat on the next side so that it overlaps the previous one. Repeat it again.

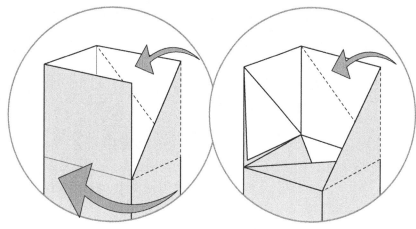

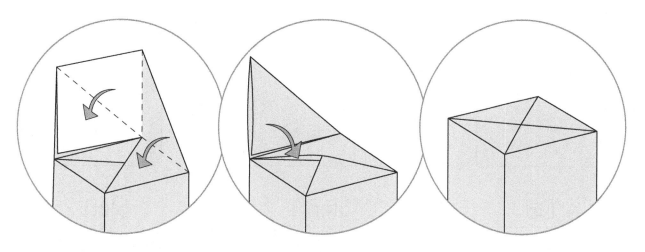

Step 11

Once you've finished folding all the sides, you'll see one last tip sticking out. Carefully tuck it under first fold you made to lock everything in place.

Tall Box

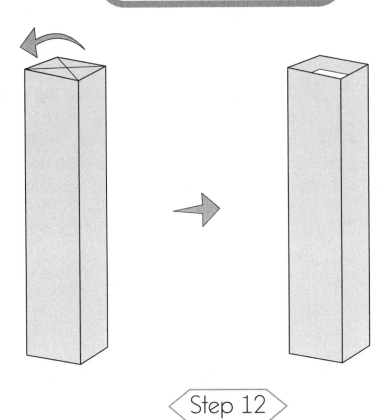

Step 12

Rotate the figure upside down.

Lid

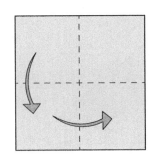

Step 1

Fold the paper sheet
in half lengthwise and
crosswise. Then unfold it.

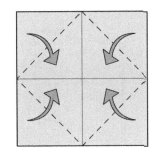

Step 2

Bring all corners in to the
center of the sheet.

Tall Box

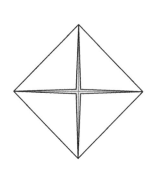 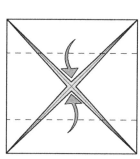 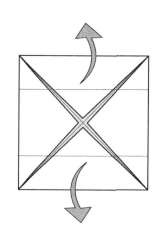

Step 3

Rotate the figure, then bring the top and bottom edges to the center of the sheet and unfold them to make creases.

Step 4

Unfold the top and bottom corners.

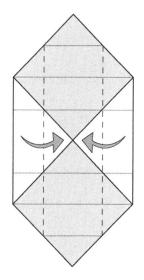 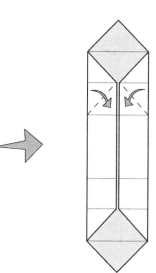 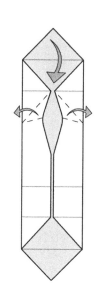

Step 5

Bring both side edges to the center of the sheet.

Step 6

Fold the figure diagonally and unfold it to match the creases in the drawing.

Step 7

Use those creases to open the sides halfway up, while the top corner also folds up.

Tall Box

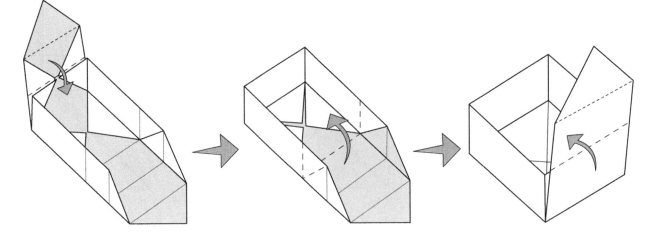

Step 8

Fold that corner back down over the folds from the previous step to lock everything in place.

Step 9

Repeat steps 6 and 7 on the other end of the figure.

Step 10

Fold this corner over the previous folds to lock them in place as well.

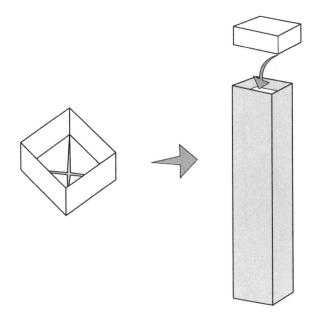

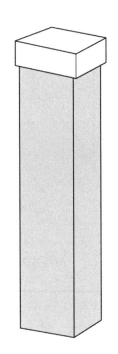

Step 11

This is the lid, so place it on top of the box and your Tall Box is complete!

Tall Box

Dollar Bill Origami

Heart

Step 1

Fold the bill in half
lengthwise and unfold it.

Step 2

Fold both sides in
towards the center
crease you just made.

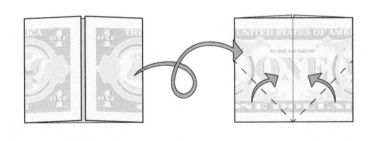

Step 3

Flip the bill over and
fold both bottom corners
up as shown.

Step 4

Fold the top edge of the top
layer of the bill down
and unfold it to make a crease.

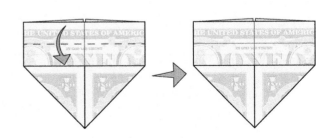

Heart

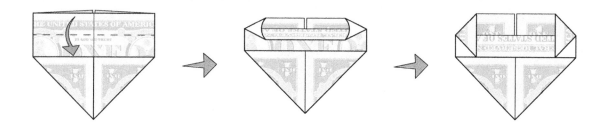

Step 5

Fold the top edge of the top layer of the bill down
and flatten the corners as shown.

Step 6

After step 5, you will see
two corners right in the center
of the bottom layer. Fold them
forwards and down as shown.

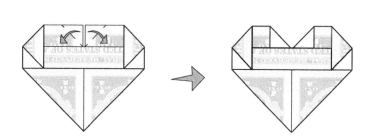

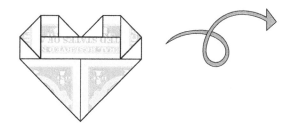

Step 7

Flip the figure over.

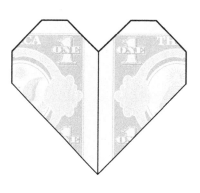

Heart

Swan

Step 1

Fold the bill in half lengthwise and unfold it to make a crease.

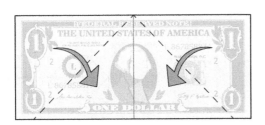

Step 2

Fold both top corners down so that their top edge ends up matching the vertical crease from previous step.

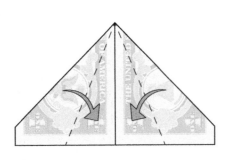

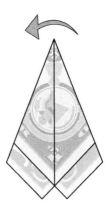

Step 3

Fold both sides again toward the vertical mid line, then rotate the figure so its tip ends up pointing to the left.

Swan

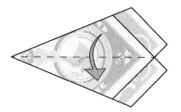 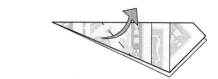

Step 4

Fold the figure in half

Step 5

Fold the left corner up
as shown and unfold to
make a crease.

Step 6

Use the crease from the previous
step to make an outside reverse
fold on the left corner.

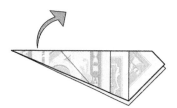

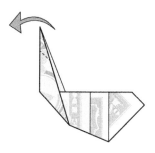

Step 7

Then make another outside
reverse fold on the tip as
shown to make the swan's head.

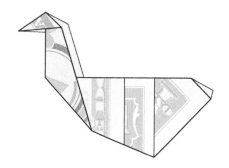

Swan

Pigeon

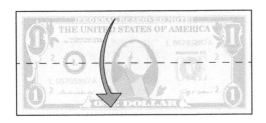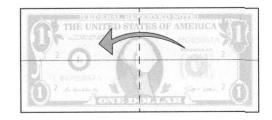

Step 1

Fold the bill in half lengthwise
and crosswise and unfold it
to make a crease.

Step 2

Fold both top corners down
so that their top edge ends
up matching the center
vertical crease from previous
step.

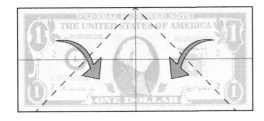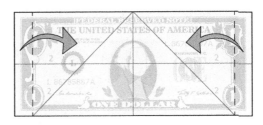

Step 3

Fold the excess part backward and unfold it
to make a crease. Then Fold both edges
inward on the crease you just made.
Fold the bill along those diagonals again
to make a triangle.

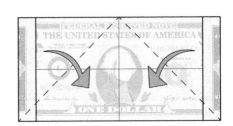

Pigeon

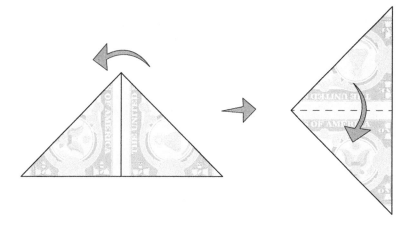

Rotate the figure to the left and fold it down in half.

Fold the top layer back up a shown, then do the same on the other side of the figure.

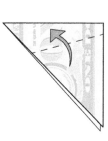

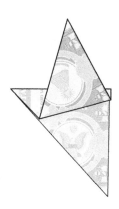

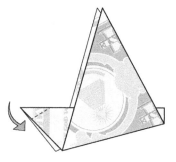

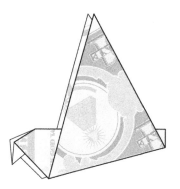

Make an inside reverse fold on the left tip of the bill to make the pigeon's beak.

Pigeon

Rocket

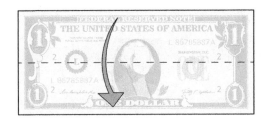 

Step 1

Fold the bill in half crosswise and lengthwise and unfold it make a crease.

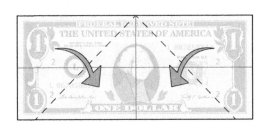 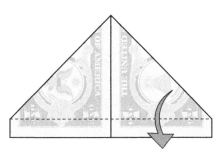

Step 2

Fold both top corners down so that their top edge ends up matching the vertical crease from the previous step.

Step 3

Fold both bottom excess edges backward and unfold it to make a crease.

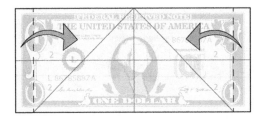

Step 4

Now fold both edges inward on the crease you made in previous step.

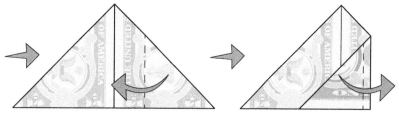

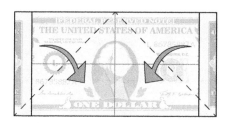

Step 5

Fold the bill along those diagonals again to make a triangle.

Step 6

Fold the right corner inward as shown.

Step 7

Fold it back outward leaving a small gap between the two folds as shown.

Step 8

Fold the right corner again until its tip matches the fold from the previous step. Repeat the same for the other side and match the illustration.

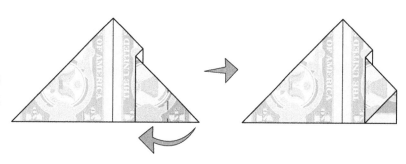

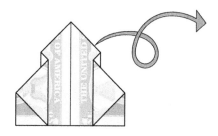

Step 9

Flip the figure over.

Rocket

Car

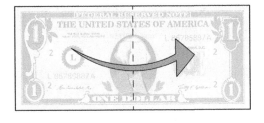 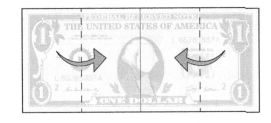

Step 1

Fold the bill lengthwise and unfold. Then fold both sides in towards the center line you just made.

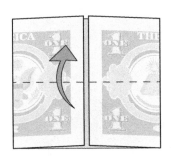 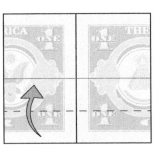 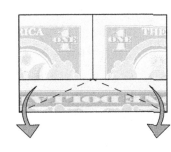

Step 2

Fold the bill in half crosswise and unfold it.

Step 3

Bring the bottom edge forward to that crease.

Step 4

Fold both bottom corners down as shown.

Car

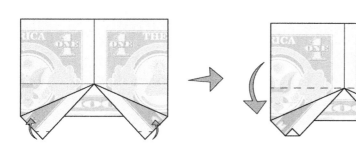

Step 5

Fold the tips of the flaps you just made back up. Then fold the top half of the figure down.

Step 6

Fold the top half back up, but leaving a small gap at the top. Fold both top corners down as shown.

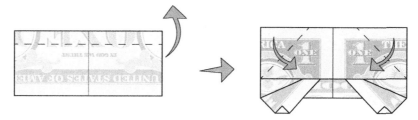

Step 7

Flip the figure over.

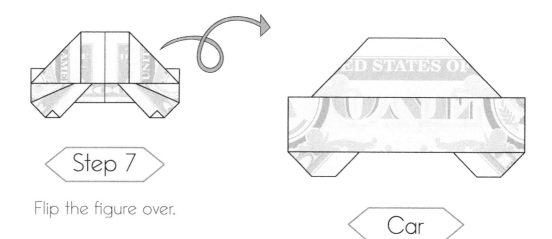

Car

Shirt

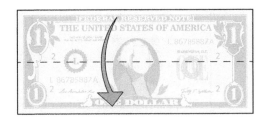

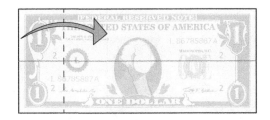

Step 1

Fold the bill in half
crosswise and unfold.

Step 2

Fold the left edge inward.

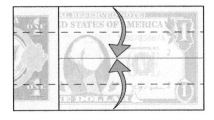

Step 3

Bring the top and bottom edges
forward toward the center crease
from Step 1.

Step 4

Fold the flaps on the left
side out as shown. These
will be sleeves of the shirt.

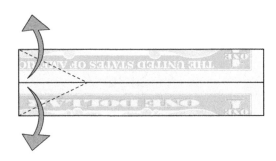

Shirt

 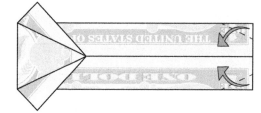

Step 5

Fold the right edge
backward as shown.

Step 6

Fold the tip of the right
corners backward to make
the collar of the shirt.

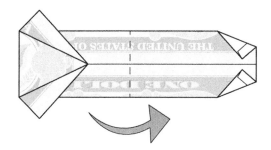

Step 7

Fold the left side of the
figure over the right side.

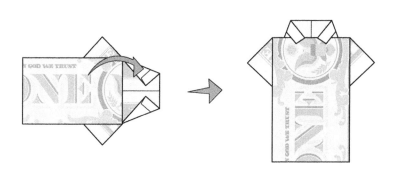 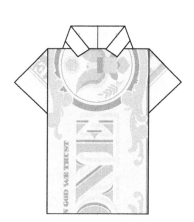

Step 8

Tuck the top layer under it
as shown. Rotate the figure.

Shirt

Pants

Step 1

Fold the bill in half lengthwise
and unfold it to make a crease.

Step 2

Bring the top and bottom
edges forward toward the
center crease you just made.

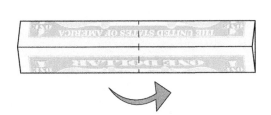 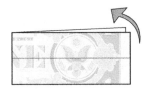 

Step 3

Fold the bill lengthwise
as shown.

Step 4

Rotate the figure until the fold from the
previous step sits at the bottom and
the free edges are at the top.

Pants

Step 5

Fold the bottom left corner up and unfold it, then use that crease to tuck the corner between both layers of the bill. Repeat with th lower right corner.

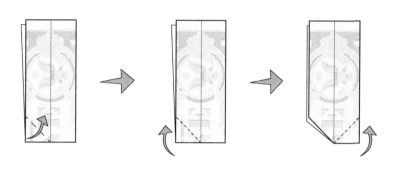

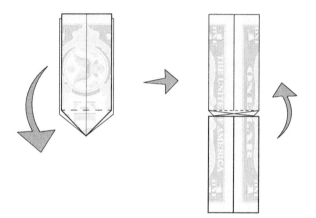

Step 7

Fold the top layer down leaving a triangle under the flap that you are going to make as shown. Flip the shape over and repeat with the other side of the bill.

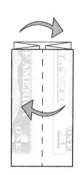

Step 8

Fold the top layer in half, then flip the figure over and do the same with the other side.

Pants

Diamond

Step 1

Fold the bill in half lengthwise and unfold.

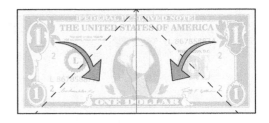

Step 2

Fold both top corners down so that their top edge ends up matching the vertical crease from the previous step.

Step 3

Fold the bottom edge of the left flap inward to match the bottom layer to make a crease and unfold. Now unfold the left flap completely.

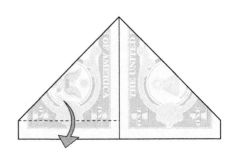

Step 4

Fold the edge back in along the crease you just made.

Step 5

Fold the top left corner back down along the crease from step 2.

Diamond

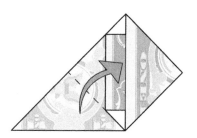

Step 6

Now fold the left side up, slightly overlapping the right side.

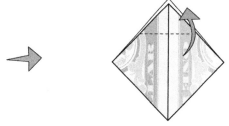

Step 7

Then fold the top tip down and tuck it between both layers of the bill.

Step 8

Fold the right side up in half as shown. Fold both corners of the top layer inward.

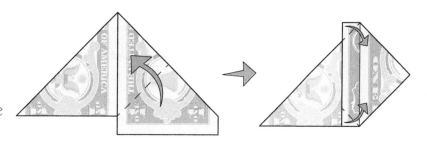

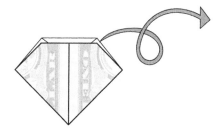

Step 9

Flip the figure over.

Diamond

Fish

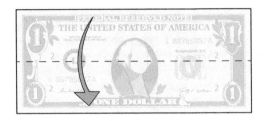

Step 1

Fold the bill in half crosswise
and unfold it to make
a crease.

Step 2

Fold both left corners
forward to that crease.

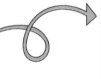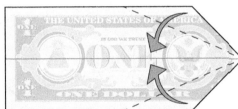

Step 3

Flip the bill over. Now the corners that you folded in the previous step
are on the right side. Fold them forward again to the center crease.

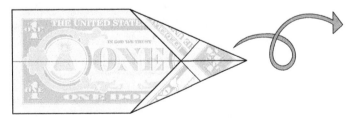

Step 4

Flip the figure over. Unfold the flaps on the tip of the bill as shown.

Fish

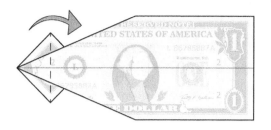 

Step 5

Fold the tip of the bill inward to make a triangle.

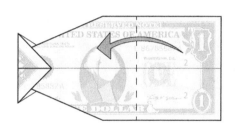 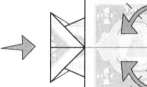

Step 7

Fold both right corners forward to the center crease to make a triangle on the right side of the bill.

Step 6

Fold the right edge inward until it meets the tip of that triangle.

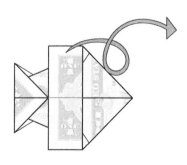 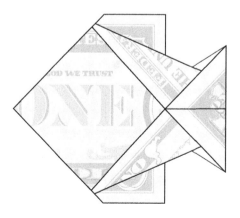

Step 8

Flip the figure over.

Fish

Santa's Hat

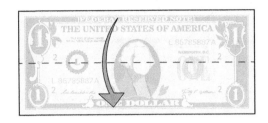 

Step 1

Fold the bill in half lengthwise and crosswise and unfold it to make a crease.

Step 2

Bring the left edge to the vertical mid line.

Step 3

Fold both left corners diagonally to make a triangle on that end of the bill.

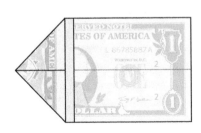 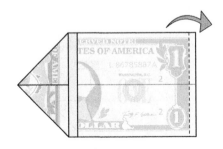

Step 4

Fold just a little bit of the right edge backward.

Santa's Hat

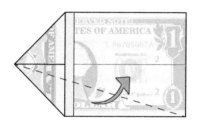 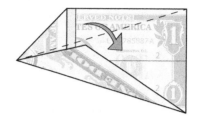

Step 5

Fold the bottom left corner up along the line that joins the tip of the triangle and the bottom right corner.

Step 6

Repeat for the top left corner as shown.

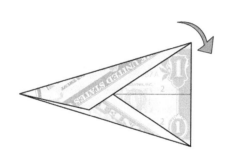 

Step 7

Rotate the figure so that the tip of the triangle ends up pointing up.

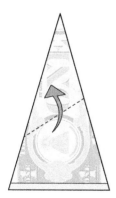

Step 8

Fold the figure back roughly in half with a diagonal fold as shown.

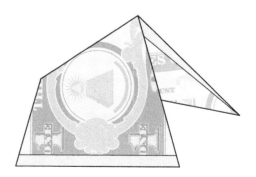

Santa's Hat

Sail Boat

 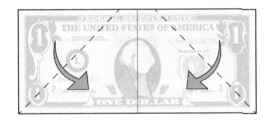

Step 1

Fold the bill in half lengthwise and unfold.

Step 2

Fold both top corners down toward the bottom edge of the bill.

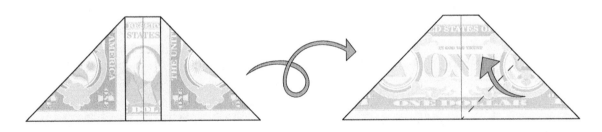

Step 3

Flip the figure over. Fold the right corner up to the vertical mid line.

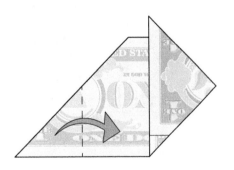 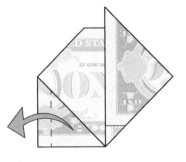

Step 4

Fold the left corner inward until its tip meets the vertical mid line.

Step 5

Fold the left corner back out, leaving a small gap between the two folds.

Sail Boat

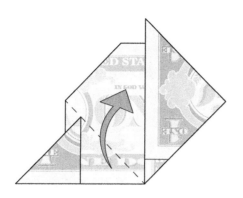

Then fold the same corner up
to the vertical mid line as shown.

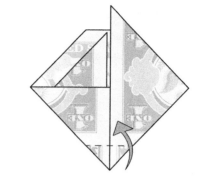

Step 7

Fold the bottom corner
up as shown.

Step 8

Flip the figure over.

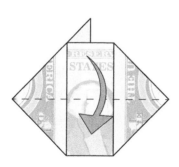

Step 10

Fold the top layer
down in half.

Sail Boat

Bottle

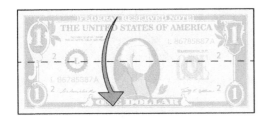

Step 1

Fold the bill in half
lengthwise and unfold.

Step 2

Bring the top and bottom
edges forward toward the
crease you just made.

Step 3

Divide the bill into 3 roughly
equal parts and fold the
left side inward.

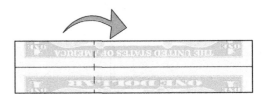

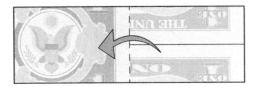

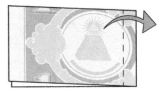

Step 4

Now fold the right side
inward over the left side.

Step 5

Fold the top layer back
out, leaving a small gap
between the two folds.

Bottle

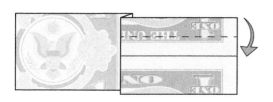 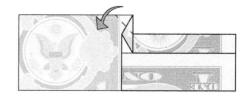

Step 6

Fold the top edge of the top layer down to the mid line. As you do it, you'll see the fold from the previous step open up to make a triangle. Flatten it.

Step 7

Now you can see a corner sticking out. Fold it diagonally down and flatten it.

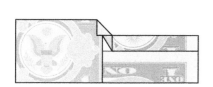 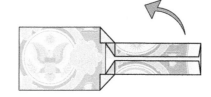

Step 8

Repeat the steps 6 and 7 for the bottom edge, then rotate the figure until these folds end up pointing up.

Step 9

Flip the figure over.

Bottle

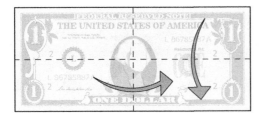

Step 1

Fold the bill lengthwise and
crosswise, then unfold it.

Step 2

Fold the right edge backward
to the vertical center line
as shown.

Step 3

Fold the top and bottom
edges slightly forward and
inward as shown.

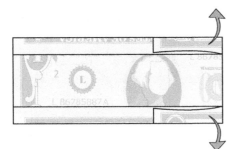

Step 4

Open the flaps on the right
of the top layer and flatten
them.

Step 5

Fold the lower right corner
forward and up as shown.

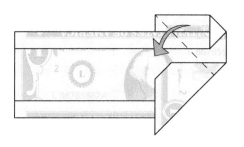

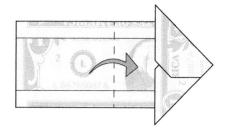

Step 6

Repeat for the upper right corner. Make sure both corners overlap.

Step 7

Fold the left edge on top of the right edge.

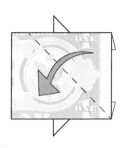

Step 8

Fold the top right corner of the top layer forward an down as shown. Make sure you don't fold the flap you made in step 3 because that will be the chimney. Now rotate the figure as shown.

Step 9

Flip the figure over.

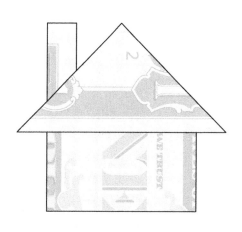

Home

Bell

 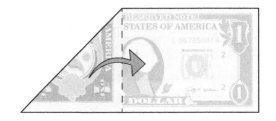

Step 1

Fold the to left corner down to the bottom edge.

Step 2

Fold the right side of the bill inward along the edge of the flap you just made.

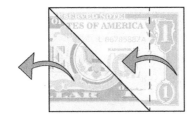 

Step 3

Fold the right edge forward at the tip of the fold from the previous step as shown and unfold it. Then fold the right edge on the crease you just made.

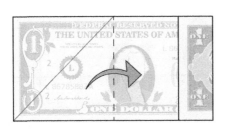 

Step 4

Fold the left edge over the right edge. Rotate the figure until the folded edge sits on the top right side.

Bell

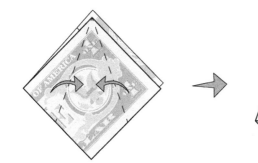 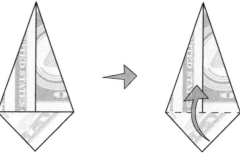

Bring both sides in toward the mid line.

Fold the bottom corner up as shown.

Step 7

Fold the bottom corner down again, leaving a small gap between the two folds, then fold the tip up again. Fold the top corner down and up again, leaving a small gap between the folds as well.

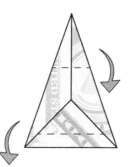 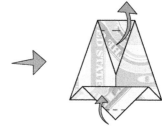

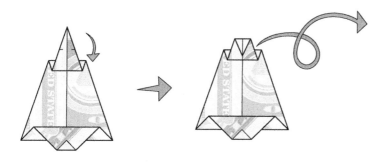 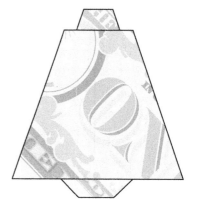

Step 8

Fold the top tip down as shown. Flip the figure over.

Bell

Gown

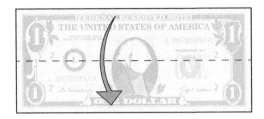

Step 1

Fold the bill in half crosswise and
unfold it to make a crease.

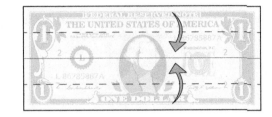

Step 2

Fold the top and bottom edges
forward toward the crease you
just made and unfold it.

Step 3

Now fold the bill in
half lengthwise. Fold
the top left corner
to make a crease
s shown and unfold it.

Step 4

Rotate the figure until the fold from the
previous step sits at the top and the
free edges are at the bottom.

Step 5

Fold the right edge of the
top layer in along the creases
shown and flatten the top.

Gown

   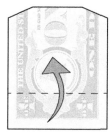

Step 6

Do the same for the left side.
Flip the figure over.

Step 7

Fold up the
bottom edge of
the top layer.

Step 8

Fold the top corners
down as shown. Then fold
their tips down again.

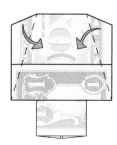 

Step 9

Flip the figure over.

Gown

Bow Tie

Step 1

Fold the bill in half crosswise and unfold. Fold the bill in half lengthwise.

 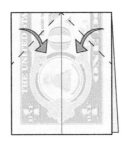

Step 2

Rotate the figure until the fold from the previous step sits at the top and the free edges are at the bottom. Then fold both top corners down and unfold them.

Step 3

Use the right crease to make an inside reverse fold on the right corner. Repeat the same for left corner.

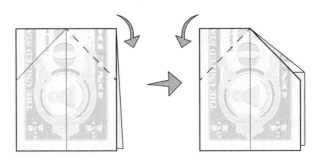

Bow Tie

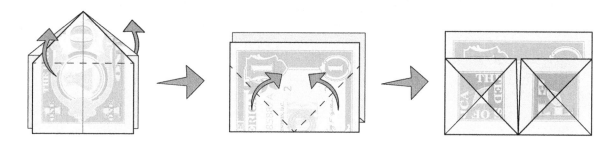

Step 4

Fold up the bottom of
the front layer of the
bill as shown. Repeat
for the back layer.

Step 5

Fold both bottom corners up to form
a triangle on the front layer. Repeat the
same for the other side.

Step 6

Rotate the figure to one of
its sides and pull the sides
edges apart to separate
both layers of the bill.

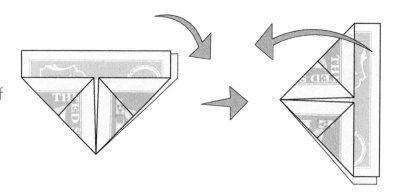

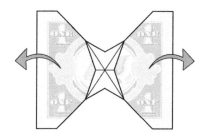

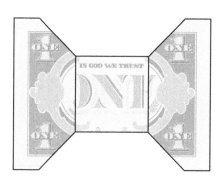

Step 7

While separating both layers,
press the center of the figure
until it's completely flat.

Bow Tie

Tree

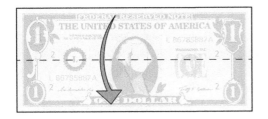 

Step 1

Fold the bill in half
crosswise and unfold.

Step 2

Fold both left corners
diagonally, then unfold them
to make a crease.

Step 3

Fold the top and bottom edges between the creases from the previous step
inward to the center line to make a triangle. Flip the figure over.

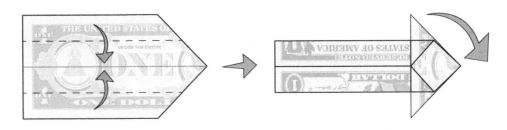

Step 4

Bring the top and bottom edges forward down to the mid line.
Rotate the bill so the triangle ends up pointing down.

Tree

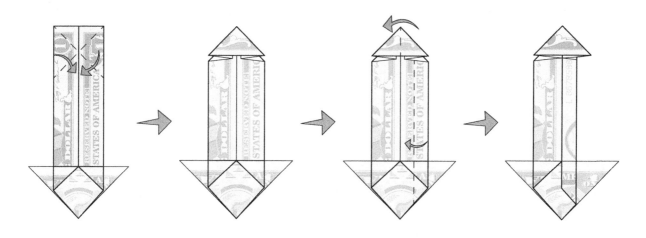

Step 5

Fold both top corners diagonally down,
then unfold them to make two creases.
Repeat the step 3 to make another
triangle on the top edge of the bill.

Step 6

Then bring both side edges up
to the mid line, but make sure to
tuck them under the top layer
of the triangle you just made.

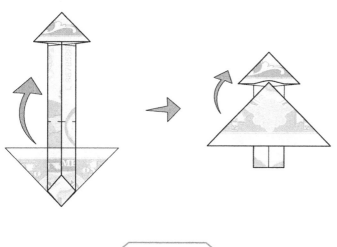

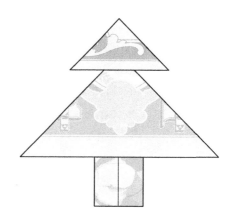

Step 7

Fold the lower triangle up as shown.
Then tuck it under the upper triangle so
that it doesn't move out of place.

Tree

Wallet

Step 1

Fold the bill in half lengthwise and crosswise and unfold it to make a crease.

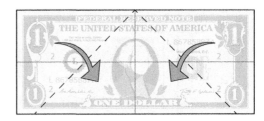

Step 2

Fold both top corners down so that their top edge ends up matching the vertical crease from the previous step. Press and unfold it.

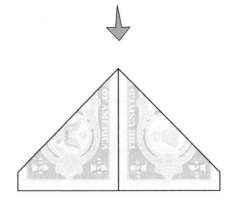

Wallet

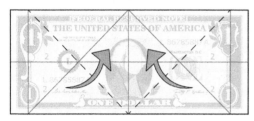

Step 3

Repeat the previous step
for the bottom corners.

Step 4

Fold both side edges inward
along the line that joins the
creases from step 3 and
4 as shown, then unfold it.

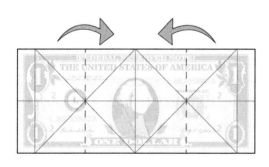

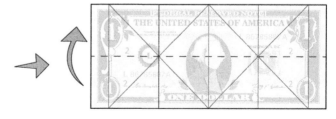

Step 5

Fold both side edges inward again,
this time where the creases from
step 3 and 4 as shown, then unfold it.

Step 6

Fold the bill up in half crosswise.

359

Wallet

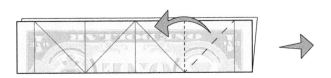
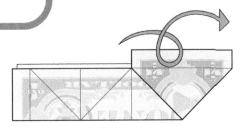

Step 7

Open the right side of the bill by making a vertical valley fold and a diagonal mountain fold at the same time, as shown, to bring the top right corner inward to the vertical mid line. then flatten to make a triangle and flip the figure over.

Step 8

Flip the figure over.

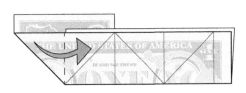

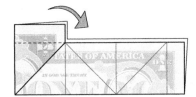

Step 9

Fold the top left corner inward to the mid line as well, and tuck the edge that sticks out at the top between the top layers of the bill.

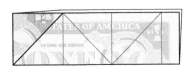
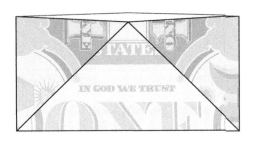

Step 10

Repeat the previous steps for the other end of the bill.

Wallet

Butterfly

Step 1

Fold the bill in half crosswise and unfold. Now fold the bill in lengthwise.

Step 2

Rotate the figure until the fold from the previous step sits at the top and the free edges are at the bottom.

Step 3

Fold both top corners down and unfold them, then use the right crease to make an inside reverse fold on the right corner.

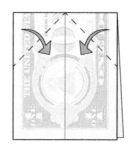 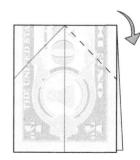

Butterfly

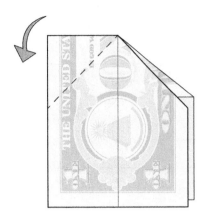

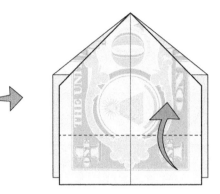

Step 4

Repeat on the left corner
to make a triangle on the top
side of the bill.

Step 5

Then fold the bottom edge of
the top layer backward until it
meets that triangle as shown.

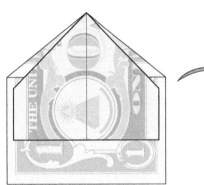

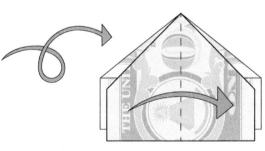

Step 6

Flip the figure over and repeat the process for the other
side of the bill. Then fold the top layer in half,
and fold the other side of the bill in half as well.

362

Butterfly

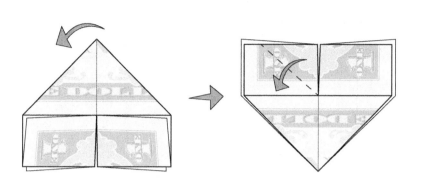

Step 7

You will see that there is a slit in the bottom center of the bill. Turn the figure upside down and fold the left edge of that slit down as shown.

Step 8

Undo the fold and use that crease to open the flap on the left side and bring it down as you can see in the drawing, then flatten it. This will make on of the butterfly's wings.

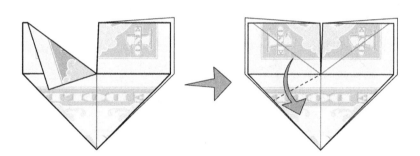

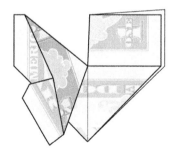

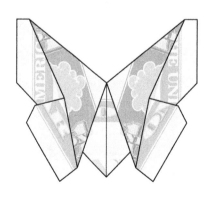

Step 9

Repeat the process on the right side of the figure to make the other wing of the butterfly.

Butterfly

Dog

Step 1

Fold the top left corner down to the bottom edge.

Step 2

Fold the right side of the bill inward along the edge of the flap you just made.

Step 3

Fold the right edge forward at the tip of the fold from the previous step as shown.

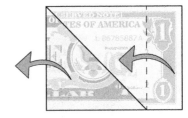

Step 4

Then completely unfold the bill. Fold the right edge on the crease you just made.

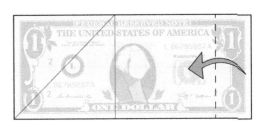

Step 5

Now fold the figure in half as shown.

Step 6

Fold the figure in half lengthwise and crosswise, then unfold.

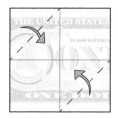 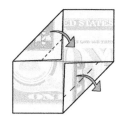 

Step 7

Use those creases to fold the top left and bottom right corners as shown.

Step 8

Fold the tip of the upper left corner that you just folded under itself, and fold the tip of the bottom right corner down again.

Step 9

Fold the figure in half shown.

Dog

 → 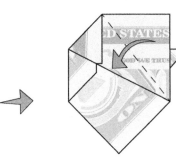 →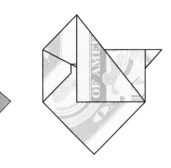

Step 10

Fold the bottom of
the top layer up
as shown.

Step 11

Fold it back down as shown.
Repeat for the other side of the bill.

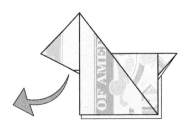

Step 12

Carefully pull the flap between both
layers and flatten as shown.

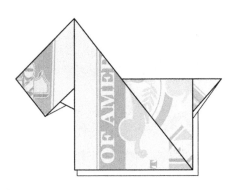

Dog

Conclusion

Congratulations on making it to the end of this enormous book! I'm sure you are now a master of folding paper! After learning how to fold, animals, boxes, dollar bills, flowers, and toys, you can now jump on the adventure of designing and folding your own creatures to share with your friend and family.

I hope this trip has been fun and you've discovered a new hobby!

We would love to see a photo of the Origami world you created with these designs! You can do this by giving us your feedback on Amazon via a review. Let us know your thoughts!

LET'S GROW TOGETHER!

We Would Really Appreciate It If You Could Take A Moment To Leave Us A Review On Amazon!

Made in the USA
Monee, IL
20 October 2022

16260338R00208